RENEGADE

RENEGADE

Defending Democracy and
Liberty in Our Divided Country

Adam Kinzinger

WITH MICHAEL D'ANTONIO

THE OPEN FIELD / PENGUIN LIFE

VIKING
An imprint of Penguin Random House LLC
penguinrandomhouse.com

The Open Field/A Penguin Life Book

THE OPEN FIELD is a registered trademark of MOS Enterprises, Inc.

LIBRARY OF CONGRESS CATALOGING-IN-PUBLICATION DATA
Names: Kinzinger, Adam, author. | D'Antonio, Michael, 1955– author.
Title: Renegade : defending democracy and liberty in our divided country /
Adam Kinzinger with Michael D'Antonio.
Other titles: defending democracy and liberty in our divided country
Description: [New York] : The Open Field/Penguin Life, [2023]
Identifiers: LCCN 2023026389 (print) | LCCN 2023026390 (ebook) |
ISBN 9780593654163 (hardcover) | ISBN 9780593654170 (ebook)
Subjects: LCSH: Kinzinger, Adam. | Legislators—United States—Biography. |
United States. Congress. House. Select Committee to Investigate the
January 6th Attack on the United States Capitol | Capitol Riot,
Washington, D.C., 2021. | United States—Politics and
government—2017–2021. | United States—Politics and government—2021–
Classification: LCC E901.1.K56 A3 (print) | LCC E901.1.K56 (ebook) |
DDC 328.092 [B]—dc23/eng/20230629
LC record available at https://lccn.loc.gov/2023026389
LC ebook record available at https://lccn.loc.gov/2023026390

Printed in the United States of America
3rd Printing

Set in Stempel Garamond LT Pro
Designed by Cassandra Garruzzo Mueller

THE OPEN FIELD

Dear Reader,

Years ago, these words attributed to Rumi found a place in my heart:

> *Out beyond ideas of*
> *wrongdoing and rightdoing,*
> *there is a field. I'll meet you there.*

Ever since, I've cultivated an image of what I call the "Open Field"—a place out beyond fear and shame, beyond judgment, loneliness, and expectation. A place that hosts the reunion of all creation. It's the hope of my soul to find my way there—and whenever I hear an insight or a practice that helps me on the path, I love nothing more than to share it with others.

That's why I've created The Open Field. My hope is to publish books that honor the most unifying truth in human life: We are all seeking the same things. We're all seeking dignity. We're all seeking joy. We're all seeking love and acceptance, seeking to be seen, to be safe. And there is no competition for these things we seek—because they are not material goods; they are spiritual gifts!

We can all give each other these gifts if we share what we know—what has lifted us up and moved us forward. That is our duty to one another—to help each other toward acceptance, toward peace, toward happiness—and my promise to you is that the books published under this imprint will be maps to the Open Field, written by guides who know the path and want to share it.

Each title will offer insights, inspiration, and guidance for moving beyond the fears, the judgments, and the masks we all wear. And when we take off the masks, guess what? We will see that we are the opposite of what we thought—we are each other.

We are all on our way to the Open Field. We are all helping one another along the path. I'll meet you there.

Love,
Maria Shriver

For Sofia and Christian.
I hope I make you proud.

Contents

Introduction

started writing this introduction on January 5, 2023, two days after I was *supposed* to end my time in Congress. Kevin McCarthy, head of the GOP caucus, was expected to become Speaker of the House on January 3. Instead, those who joined the government to tear it down reached the logical end of their effort—utter chaos that paralyzed the legislative branch. McCarthy was being denied a majority by about twenty members who seemed to believe they were engaged not in a political process, but in an inquisition. They had found that he had sinned against their orthodoxy of conspiracy theories, worship of former president Donald Trump, and devotion to the destruction of social norms. He had not atoned by giving every member of the House the singular power to call for his removal and be indulged with a vote. And so he struggled on, losing three votes on day one, three on day two, and another one on day three. All this mattered to me only because although I had resigned months ago, I would not be fully freed from my office—representative for Illinois's 16th Congressional District—until someone became Speaker of the House. Only then would new members be sworn in and the work of the 118th Congress, such as it is, would begin.

I would eventually be replaced by a veteran representative named Darin LaHood, who became eligible for my seat due to redistricting. He had grown up the son of GOP giant Ray LaHood, a figure of great decency who was so respected that Barack Obama ignored party ties and named him to be secretary of transportation in his administration. The elder LaHood's autobiography was titled *Seeking Bipartisanship: My Life in Politics.* In 2016, he said he could not vote for Donald Trump because of the terrible slurs he has uttered about women, Muslims, and prisoners of war.

When Darin first came to Washington, he joined the moderate Main Street Caucus, which focused on using government to help communities and bucked the GOP trend by saying climate change had a human cause. (Republican orthodoxy held, contrary to science, that the link between air pollution and rising temperatures was unproven and climate change could be a natural phenomenon.) The blowback Darin felt from the more reactionary corner of the local party was so intense that he abandoned his moderate positions, quit the Main Streeters, and raced to the unreasonable Right. In 2022, LaHood assessed the state of the party and accepted the campaign aid of the man his father couldn't bring himself to support. A member of Congress who had bragged continually about his commitment to open, honest government had tied himself to the most unethical and least transparent president in history.

My guess is you've never heard of Darin LaHood, even though he holds a high-status position. Like most members, he's essentially unknown outside his constituency. This seems to be by design. In seeking to create a body of officials who were "representatives" of their districts, America's founders ensured that they would be concerned, mainly, with the folks back home. Thus, while Congress as a body wields true power, few individual members ever do. The only truly powerful representative is the Speaker of the House. The Speaker is the one who sets the legislative agenda and bargains with the White House. This individual power explains why you know the names of the two most recent Speakers, Nancy Pelosi and Paul Ryan. Their vision and skill made an unwieldy institution function and, occasionally, achieve something important.

IN EARLY JANUARY 2022, WITH THE NEW GOP MAJORITY IN THE chamber, unlike his predecessors, Representative Kevin McCarthy of California was busily negotiating with a number of GOP extremists in order to win their support for his drive to become the 55th Speaker of the House. McCarthy was, like Darin LaHood, a former moderate who read the relentlessly rightward trend in his party and scrambled to join it. The trouble was that he had criticized Trump after his loyalists attacked and occupied the Capitol. McCarthy tried to make the hard-line Trumpers forget this spasm of moral clarity, but it was too late for twenty members of the nihilist wing of the party, who decided to punish him by blocking his bid to lead the

House. Thanks to them, for the first time in a century, the main candidate for Speaker failed to win the office on the first ballot. McCarthy also lost on the second ballot, and the third. As he lost the seventh ballot, he became the losingest candidate for Speaker since Frederick Gillett needed nine tries in 1923. Still he pressed on, acting as if he were in some kind of war in which surrender was just not a possibility.

Having served in a real war, I have watched with increasing alarm as many politicians speak and behave as if Congress itself were a battlefield, and as if they had been elected not to serve the public and protect the Constitution but to score points for their side, no matter the cost. Ever since my final falling-out with the GOP on the day of the deadly January 6 attack on the Capitol by Donald Trump's followers, I have wanted to tell the inside story of how my party and my faith have been hijacked by extremists who represent a real danger to our democracy. This book is the result, a full telling of my experience—from a pilgrim with genuine values to a conservative who has no home but is determined to play a role in our recovery from a devastating political conflict that became increasingly destructive during my lifetime, until it reached the point of physical combat on January 6.

Ironically, if McCarthy had stood the ground he had seized in the aftermath of the Capitol attack, when he denounced Trump, the party would have had an opportunity to move toward the center. More centrist candidates would have added to the party's 2022 majority, and McCarthy would have become Speaker on the first vote. Instead, he immediately visited the man who had raised the GOP derangement level to eleven and aided his drive to be not an election loser but the martyred victim of a conspiracy. This is why, on the day McCarthy intended to achieve his goal in life, he was forced to call a meeting of the entire GOP caucus. He said that he was being blocked by grandstanding wackos. The head, a high school dropout from Colorado who embraces the bizarre conspiracy theories of the so-called QAnon website, cried, "Bullshit!"

Another scandal of that day—all of which reflected McCarthy's failure to stop the GOP's decline into a cult built on dangerous nonsense—involved the arrival of freshman Republican congressman George Santos of New York. Santos had fabricated his entire identity, lying about working for two major Wall Street firms; attending a prestigious prep school and graduating from both New York University and Baruch College; founding an animal rescue nonprofit; employing four people killed in the Pulse nightclub mass shooting; and grieving a mother who was killed when the World Trade Center was destroyed by the terror attack on 9/11. None of what Santos claimed was true. In May 2023, Santos was indicted on charges of wire fraud, money laundering, stealing public funds, and lying on federal disclosure forms, and McCarthy still did not ask him to resign. And, oh yeah, he was wanted for arrest by the Brazilian government. True to form, Santos issued a press release announcing that he had been sworn in when he had not been, and when reporters confronted him in a hallway, he ran away. No one would sit near him when he was seated in the chamber, where he occasionally yawned without covering his mouth.

Knowing good drama when they see it, cable news channels covered the McCarthy debacle and the arrival of George Santos minute by minute. If the Santos story marked a special low for a GOP candidate for Congress, then McCarthy's pursuit of the speakership offered more serious evidence of how Republican leaders will debase themselves.

McCarthy's hunger for power was so strong that even as he endured a total of fourteen humiliating rejections, he never stopped suggesting compromises to win support from the extremists. One of their number, Marjorie Taylor Greene of Georgia, lent McCarthy early support, which reassured hardcore right-wingers who doubted him. Greene's status as an extremist was undeniable. She had risen to fame with stunts like holding a military-style assault rifle in a campaign photo and supporting ideas promoted by anti-government conspiracy theorists. She has stated, falsely, that there "was never any evidence" that a "so-called plane" commandeered by terrorists crashed into the Pentagon on September 11, causing 187 deaths.

After she helped McCarthy win the Speaker's job, he appointed her to two highly coveted committee assignments: Homeland Security and Oversight and Accountability. Both give members a chance to investigate officials, policies, and programs in the executive branch. Others who had fought McCarthy's campaign to lead the House won a rules change that would force the House to vote on any call for McCarthy to resign, even if it were offered by a single member of the House.

This meant that instead of setting a policy agenda and organizing the GOP caucus to follow him, McCarthy would have to carefully consider what ordinary members wanted before moving forward on anything. In effect, he would be as much a follower as a leader. Those he would have to monitor closely included more than a dozen members who had joined Donald Trump's deranged effort to persuade the country that the 2020 election had been rigged against him. Their loud campaign to somehow overturn Joe Biden's seven-million-vote victory persuaded huge numbers of people to believe that the election, conducted by the most reliable system in the world, had been riven with corruption. And they demonstrated how they could, on a whim, paralyze the legislative branch. A once radical anti-government fantasy had become a reality. As House Democrats chomped popcorn and marveled at the disarray, McCarthy was chewed up by a monster he helped create.

ONE WAY OR ANOTHER, THE HIGH-LEVEL FIGURES—INCLUDING Trump—who planned, organized, and incited the violent attempted coup will be held accountable. In the meantime, it seems as if the radicals in Congress, who inflame partisan hatreds and seek attention through various stunts, are following his example by doubling down on obnoxious behavior. One of the most prominent in this group, who is the political version of a juvenile delinquent, posed such a big threat to party leaders that they agreed to let her into their circle of power. Once she reached this goal, Representative Marjorie Taylor Greene of Georgia returned to her narcissistic nihilism. Weeks after she helped him become Speaker, McCarthy welcomed President Biden to deliver his State of the Union address, and she tried to turn the gathering into a pro-wrestling match. Dressed in an oversize white alpaca coat with a giant white fur collar, she heckled Biden with shouts of "Liar!" and stood to signal thumbs-down, as if she were Caesar at the Colosseum. (By the way, the best research shows the signal for a gladiator's death was a thumbs-up, not thumbs-down.) The coat made it easy for TV viewers to focus on her and guaranteed that her likeness and behavior would get the kind of attention that can be converted into power within the party.

I feel some responsibility for January 6 and the rise of Greene and her ilk, if only because I was a participant in, and witness to, the GOP's gradual descent into a dysfunctional and destructive force in our politics. Intoxicated by my status and addicted to the level of attention, I made compromises to—let's face it—feed my ego and sense of importance. The correction I made as I embraced my inner renegade and voted to impeach a president of my own party came late, but it did arrive.

This book is a memoir, a declaration of principles, and a call to action. It draws on my life experience, beginning with the lessons I learned from family, school, church, and community, and ending with military and government service. You might say that my journey from Illinois kid to Congress marked me as a success. I did reach my goal of higher office, becoming one of just 535 members— counting representatives and senators—in the most important legislative body in the world.

I accept that people across the political spectrum could reject my voice in national affairs. Millions of people in what's left of the Republican Party clearly detest me as a traitor, and many of those outside the party mistrust me. However, I believe this book will explain my journey and clarify my values. It is not an argument against hard-fought politics. I am no innocent. I participated in, and often enjoyed, sharp-elbow campaigns for office. I didn't realize, though, how the most extreme tactics and positions would cripple the institution I fought so hard to join. No one tells you that a campaign based on sowing fears and treating opponents as enemies, not as rivals, eventually infects even your side. Both major parties do this, but I'd have to say we in the GOP have been more aggressive and effective attack dogs. Consider the habits this style ingrains and the kind of observers who say to themselves, "I want to do that!" and it's easy to understand how after thirty years of these tactics Republicans are using them against one another, on live television.

As Kevin McCarthy's humiliation continued, I watched as one of sixty-six members who had resigned or been defeated and were waiting for their successors to be sworn in. This couldn't happen without a new Speaker there to administer the oath of office. I was suspended between my old role and a new, as-yet-undefined one, as founder of a new centrist political organization and as an analyst for CNN. I do know I will continue to argue that no one should ever be exempt from accountability, and I will plead for a return to a politics of good faith.

Where do I get off writing a book like this one? Well, for one thing I have lived through all of the shifts in religion and conservative politics—I long considered myself to be a religiously inspired conservative—that led to the Republican Party backing an authoritarian for president. I know the culture of resentment that Donald Trump has tapped for his core base of support, and I have dealt with the man himself, in the Oval Office. I have also dealt with political violence and threats of personal assault. I have lived with police officers on guard outside my home. I was present on Capitol Hill when the Trump mob attacked.

This is why I felt it was important to write not just about January 6—you likely know all about that day and its aftermath—but to also describe the life path that brought me to the point where I would defy the party I had embraced forty years ago. I had dedicated my working life to becoming a kind of star within the GOP and for a time, that was who I was. Now, to my surprise, all that effort has led me to the point where, instead of acting as a GOP champion, I am required to act as its critic.

We have just survived the most threatening attack on our democracy since the Civil War. This success, and today's demonstration of the dysfunctional reality of a party that has become Donald Trump's cult of personality, prove that we are stronger than many expected. It is not the crisis that matters, but how we respond. I am arguing for us to prepare for the next one, which, without our vigilant opposition, could lead to the breakup of the country.

And by the way, McCarthy finally got what he wanted on the fifteenth ballot. I can find no record of any candidate for Speaker needing that many mortifying ballots to finally win. Thus, he made history, of a sort. He took the Speaker's chair so beholden to the extremists whom he had to court with promises of power that he literally taught them how they could thwart his agenda in the future. It's hard to imagine how he could have made himself weaker.

RENEGADE

CHAPTER 1

What Do You Stand For?

The list of appalling events examined by the House committee investigating the lethal attack on the US Capitol on January 6, 2021, was too long even for me, a member of the panel, to track. The worst was that for weeks President Donald Trump riled his base to support his claims of election fraud, even though aides told him they were false. Knowing it was likely illegal, his lawyers helped construct a failed campaign to send to the Electoral College fake pro-Trump electors who would insist that they represented the true results of voting in key states like Pennsylvania and Michigan. Then, called by Trump to Washington for a day he promised "will be wild," his followers waged a bloody, medieval attack on the Capitol. As the police battled them for 187 minutes, Trump watched the violence on TV and refused to call the attackers off. He watched and waited as his loyalist marauders injured more than a hundred police officers and entered the Capitol waving Confederate flags and chanting, "Hang Mike Pence! Hang Mike Pence!"

America has never experienced anything like January 6, which was what we must call an attempted coup. Now a movement backed by tens of millions, this Trumpism is un-American in the extreme. It seeks to undermine our elections, place controls on the press, sharply restrict immigration, politicize the judiciary, and polarize the people. This is a reality that demands that we all examine our basic beliefs. Do we want a democracy governed by free and fair elections? Can we consider our differences in matters of politics, ethics, and faith in a respectful way? Do we value our pluralism? Our success at managing these issues has made us the envy of the world for centuries. Do we want to discard what the Constitution gave us? What do we, as Americans, stand for?

I stand for the values I learned in my formative years, before Trump and, for that matter, before conservatism and the GOP began its slide away from policies and toward gaining power at any cost. For years I accommodated this trend, hoping it would stop while I enjoyed the time when we, the Republican Party, were in the House majority. I approached a breaking point with Trump's first impeachment but was talked out of voting *for* the Articles of Impeachment that authorized a trial in the Senate. The second time around, when he was impeached for January 6, I crossed the partisan line with nine GOP colleagues and voted "Yea."

A record number of his own party's senators voted to convict Trump, but he prevailed because of the rules. A two-thirds vote is required to convict an impeached official. The 57–43 tally showed that my party was still in a wilderness of its own design.

My vote for the House impeachment article made me a marked man among Republicans, even as it brought me praise from Democrats and independents who make up the overwhelming majority in our country. It also earned me an appointment to the investigating committee. On the committee, I was privy to a huge volume of documents, video evidence, and testimony. I also came face-to-face with the people who developed and executed Trump's scheme to overturn the election, as well as its aftermath. However, no one was affected as directly—not *nearly* as directly—as the vastly outnumbered police officers.

The officers began their defense of the Capitol at 1:00 p.m. as the attackers breached the lightly manned barriers in front of the building. Faced with a mob that included many bearing two-by-fours and toxic sprays and wearing helmets and body armor, the outnumbered police retreated to positions inside the building. More than a thousand attackers came at them in waves, trying to break through windows and doors. At times there were hundreds gathered at a single door, pressing in a grotesque rhythm and shouting, "Heave-ho! Heave-ho!" At times it looked like a child's fantasy of medieval battle. Of course, these were not kids but grown men and women, and they weren't playing. They were determined to stop Congress's certification of Joe Biden's election as president.

• • •

ABOUT SIX MONTHS AFTER THE ATTACK, SOME OF THE OFFICERS WHO had defended the Capitol from the mob on January 6 testified before our committee at its first public hearing. I had met each of them and learned how much they had endured, so it wasn't abstract to me as Harry Dunn recalled the racial slurs hurled at him and Aquilino Gonell decried the "continuous and shocking attempt to ignore or try to destroy the truth of what truly happened." Michael Fanone recounted how he had been dragged to the ground by a group of attackers who threatened to kill him with his own gun. They did manage to grab his police Taser and shoot him with it, causing a heart attack. Knowing the world had seen video showing him lose a struggle must have pained Fanone, who in appearance and demeanor seems like one tough dude. At the hearing, he didn't dwell on how he suffered but rather focused on the main events of the day and the aftermath. "I feel like I went to hell and back" to protect members of Congress. "But too many are now telling me that hell doesn't exist, or that hell wasn't actually that bad."

Nothing in what the officers said made me think they felt defeated, but in certain moments their shoulders slumped and sadness crossed their faces, and it was clear their trauma persisted. As they spoke, I felt a lump rise in my throat. They reminded me of soldiers who became like family, bonded by war, and who would forever have my admiration and sympathy. When I got a chance to speak, I said, "You guys may individually feel a little broken. You guys all talk about the effects you have to deal with, and you talk about the impact of that day." It was at this moment that I felt overwhelmed, and my voice trembled a little as I said, "But you guys won. You held." I recovered a bit, but still struggled as I said, "Democracies are not defined by our bad days. We are defined by how we come back from bad days. How we take accountability for that." I then swept away the overheated rhetoric surrounding our committee and said, "Our mission is simple. It's to find the truth and ensure accountability."

Fanone and I embraced after the officers finished their testimony. I was taken aback by the weight he put on my shoulder. Of course, I knew how the mob had screamed for his execution and that many of those in Congress, whom he had helped to save, now denied the seriousness of the attack so they could stay in Donald Trump's good graces. Their attitudes were all the more cowardly given that they had experienced the attack and knew the damage it had done to individuals like Fanone, the institution that is Congress, and the country. I felt honored to have him lean on me a little because the weight he carries—the sounds, the sights, the smell of tear gas, and the sense that he was about to die at the hands of a political mob—is incalculable. He will feel it long after post–January 6 generations are born and grow to adulthood and talk of that day fades.

Those who do consider January 6 will likely focus on President Trump's obvious crimes and the many efforts, including ours, to bring him to account. After more than a year of committee work, in which members and staff interviewed more than a thousand people and received more than one hundred forty thousand documents, I know that sometimes it's hard to recognize anyone but Trump in this event. But then, in a fraction of a second, my mind brings up the sight of those officers as they testified and the feeling of hugging one of them, and that day stands out for the hope it provided in a very dark time.

AFTER THE HEARING I DID WHAT I OFTEN DO WHEN FINISHED WITH work for the week. I drove out to a private airfield in Maryland where I keep the single-engine airplane I use to travel between Washington and Illinois. This little airport is the closest one that allows you to move around the Washington area without being guided all the way by air traffic control. The main thing you need to do is announce the corridor you'll be using to get out of the area—I don't know why but the one I use is called the FLUKY Gate—and you're good to go. In the busy metropolitan area I stay low, beneath the altitude of the big planes, and climb only after I'm well clear of them.

Most people hear you have a plane and they think it's something fancy, or that you must be rich to have one. It *is* expensive, but a middle-aged plane, like the simple Mooney Bravo I fly, was within reach when I was single and is still financially manageable—and safe—now that I have a family. Besides, flying has been in my blood since I was a kid going up with my father, who flew, and once you figure the price of commercial flights and the time involved in traveling that way, a small plane makes sense costwise too. Yes, a commercial jet will make it from DC to Chicago O'Hare almost an hour faster. But add airport hassles and expenses on both ends, plus the hour-long drive to my home in rural Illinois, and there's no question that the Mooney is the better option.

The flight also gives me a chance to decompress. As I cross the Appalachian Mountains and the farmlands of Ohio come into view, I see a different America from the dominant political and economic centers on the coasts. This is the country that raised me, and while I don't harbor the resentments of those who feel they are dismissed as rubes from "flyover country," I do know that they are metastasizing in a threatening way. This is happening, in part, because too many in Hollywood, the press, Wall Street, and Washington *do* look down on small-town people across the country. But we who live in these places know ourselves to be decent, moral, intelligent, hardworking, and committed to our country. We may not write much code, but we make and grow much of what the country needs. Our children make up most of the soldiers and sailors who see combat in our military. This alone should guarantee respect.

As the place where Abraham Lincoln began public service, my home state of Illinois gave America the president who saved the country in its darkest hour. He remains, without peer, the greatest president in American history. I think every schoolkid in the state goes on a class trip to the capital, Springfield, where the sights include the Lincoln Museum, which is filled with documents and artifacts. In 2007, the museum acquired Lincoln's stovepipe hat, to go with his glasses and the bloodstained gloves he was wearing the night he was assassinated. As it turned out, the hat, which a private group bought for millions and gave to the museum, was the wrong size. Although some backed up the board member who bought the hat with "nobody's perfect" arguments, she did lose her job.

Lincoln's hat hadn't been there when my public grade school class visited the museum, but we didn't need to see it to feel inspired and even a little bit proud of where we were from. The man's philosophy was true to the values most of us had learned in our families, schools, and churches. His faith led him to say, "my greatest concern is to be on God's side." His life of service was guided by his belief that "you cannot escape the responsibility of tomorrow by evading it today."

IN OUR PRECISE PLACE, BLOOMINGTON, ILLINOIS, OUR FAMILY HAD the kind of stable and secure life everyone wants. My parents, Rus and Betty Jo Kinzinger, raised me and my brother and sister, Nathan and Chelise, mostly by their example, to be the kind of people Lincoln would have liked. As a third-grade public schoolteacher, my mother was devoted to the kids she taught and used every bit of her intelligence and creativity to help the increasingly diverse population she served to both learn in the moment and develop a lifelong love of learning. She taught a unit on immigration every year that culminated in a party in which the kids dressed in their forebears' dress. They would then do a reenactment of an Atlantic crossing in shadowy steerage, which included a scuttling "rat" that was actually a well-tossed stuffed animal.

My father worked in business, the state welfare department, the American Heart Association, and then as an executive officer with a faith-based organization that provided a range of help for the homeless. He put this private agency on a more solid footing financially and then came up with a creative idea to raise more revenue while boosting the feeling of self-sufficiency in people who had been coming to the organization for clothing. Instead of giving everything away, the agency opened shops, which looked like ordinary retail shops and were staffed by actual workers, not volunteers, who did everything to make these outlets look and feel like regular retail stores. Customers paid small amounts for the clothes they selected, and those who couldn't pay could still get things. Over the years this strategy helped countless people feel more dignified and raised money for more services.

The stores were typical of how my dad found ways to solve problems with a combination of intelligence, business savvy, and faith. Faith was a big part of our lives. The Bible was our guide and inspiration, and we attended church, on average, twice a week. Wherever we lived we looked for churches led by pastors who focused on Christian values and beliefs that they held as ideals.

What I recall from childhood experience is a mosaic of play and school and family that gave me the kind of secure and happy life that represents a midwestern ideal. In summers, a small gang of kids my age played the usual sports, but also epic summer games of hide-and-seek that lasted into the dark of the evening. I missed a game whenever I was hit by a nagging health issue—susceptibility to bronchitis and asthma—that would knock me out of action every now and then. Sometime after my first birthday I became extremely sick when I developed pneumonia, which might have killed me but for expert care. This time the treatment included many days inside a plastic bubble, which protected me from germs. It's possible my experiences with illness made me more understanding of social needs. Compared with today's archconservatives, I have always been more open to the idea that some people get a raw deal and deserve some assistance.

In our subdivision, no one worried about being safe in the neighborhood because we really were safe. Similarly, no one I knew was afraid of a neighbor's political or religious ideals. I'm sure our family friends all held different points of view, but since politics and religion had yet to become grounds for measuring others, I never knew anything about those parts of their lives. I recall very clearly a pair of brothers named Steven and Craig whose house became a sort of mecca because it seemed like they had all the toys and sports equipment in the world, and when home computers and computer games became a thing, they had them first. In our house gifts were generally exchanged on Christmas Eve day, and birthdays were celebrated, but modestly. Christmas and Thanksgiving were shared with our relatives, and there were a lot of them. Overall, we lived in a time and place before large numbers of conservative Christians embraced a radical and rageful politics.

My parents' memories of me include, naturally, some quirky things. They say that I had a well-developed conscience from a young age, but also an independent streak that meant I didn't just accept what others said. For a few years I had a habit of dealing with things I didn't understand by taking walks around the brick border of our driveway, thinking as I made laps until I thought I had settled the issue in my mind. They called it "walking the bricks," and while it was a bit odd, they knew I'd grow out of it, which I did. They also recall me as a child who, when faced with a tough choice, sought their advice and then almost always chose my own path. I might have taken in their point of view, but in general I was more independent than dependent, and since they had raised me to think for myself, I did. Maybe those walks helped me develop this ability to think for myself, and their love made me feel it was safe to act only on what I concluded on my own.

I stopped brick-walking by primary school and wouldn't wrestle with too many challenging mysteries until I reached adolescence and started questioning some of the basic assumptions of the faith I had been taught at our church. Committed to the Independent Fundamental Baptist (IFB) tradition, the church demanded lockstep adherence to its doctrines and rules. The pressure turned many of my peers into trembling zombies. I understood their perspective because I knew that most of their families followed a rule that connected their home, school, and church together. Thus, a sin committed anywhere would be answered with discipline meted out by at least three adults.

It was quite easy to commit an IFB sin because so much of what others consider ordinary life is, in their view, an offense against the Lord. To understand how they compare with other churches, imagine a scale of 1 to 10, where the liberal Episcopalians, who have gay clergy, might rate a 1. On the other end—at about 11 or 12—are

Jehovah's Witnesses. They live so far apart from regular society that they won't vote or join the military. On this scale, IFBs might rate about an eight. They describe their congregations as "called out assemblies," a term that stresses the community aspect of faith. Although each church stands alone, IFBs generally impose the same serious standards. They were, and remain, one of the few "no smoking, no drinking, no dancing" churches around. The list of other "nos" includes: listening to secular music; attending most secular movies; dress codes for everyday living. IFB wives shouldn't work and should always be submissive to their husbands. Sex is confined to heterosexual marriages. Everyone else should follow very conservative sexual mores. Children are to obey every adult in the church community. Obedience to authority figures, especially pastors, whom many believe are anointed by God, is key. Individual churches can adopt stricter rules, but I've never heard of one going the other way. And all the rules are backed by the threat of an endless afterlife in hell. No wonder my friends from church were afraid to risk doing or saying anything the least bit rebellious.

Fortunately, my parents did not take all the IFB rules as, well, gospel. Christian faith was central to how they looked at life. They were and remain firmly against abortion, and when they face a dilemma may think about what Jesus might do in a similar situation. However, they never insisted that people of faith in other churches were lesser Christians or that pastors were incapable of being just plain wrong. Did they agree that my mother shouldn't work or that kids should simply go along with whatever an adult says? No. But they didn't join the IFB church in Bloomington because they agreed with everything that was said there. They joined because they had been looking for a church where their faith would be supported, and they felt welcomed and comfortable. They found these things in a strong, cohesive community where people seemed to genuinely care about one another.

Community is the most powerful benefit of IFB life. It grows out of the constant interactions among members who spend a great deal of time with one another inside and outside the church. With this shared isolation, supported by spiritual encouragement, comes many friendships. If you have a crisis like a death in the family or a happy event like the birth of a child, the church will be with you, both spiritually and physically. And most who stick with the church eventually prefer to live by rules that free them from the burden of decision-making. Few people leave such churches unless it's to join an even stricter movement where they can find an even greater sense of superiority. The stricter the church, the more resilient it is, at least in the short run. On the negative side of IFB cohesion, you find a lack of critical or creative thinking and a tendency for people to view those who differ, and can't be moved, as evil.

Our family's moderate view of IFB rules led, inevitably, to what you could call "incidents." In one case, I signed up for a midsummer bus outing to the giant Six Flags Great America amusement park north of Chicago, which had one of the tallest and fastest roller coasters in the world. The temperature was 95 degrees when I got ready to go, and of course I put on shorts. As I boarded a bus in the church parking lot, I noticed all the other boys were wearing long pants and the girls were all covered up so no one would lust for their knees. How did the youth leader handle it? He told the driver to take us to my house, where I was sent inside to change. This was not something that sat well with my mother and father, but I still had fun at Six Flags. And I heard some of the people there ask one another, "Are those kids Amish?"

Another memorable "scandal" happened when the church youth group, called Singspiration, piled into a bus to go to people's homes and sing Christian songs, as Christian music from certain accepted performers was the only music we were allowed to sing. During this one outing, I used the milquetoast epithet "Son of a biscuit!" which a younger kid found pretty hilarious. When he began repeating it loudly, a teacher, who also happened to be his mom, came on the bus, whacked him, and said, "Jesus knows what you're saying!"

Kids raised under the kind of scrutiny, religious fear, and swift punishment seen in our church community often adapt by hiding their true feelings and becoming secretive about their actions. The stress of this might explain why in my crowd the ones more likely to develop mental health or drug problems were the church schoolkids who never escaped the all-knowing eyes of the church. Adults who are under similar pressure, if not more, become liars and hypocrites who pose as serenely sinless while carrying on affairs or indulging in the occasional beer. This is why people who speak up at a prayer meeting or Bible study will only say something bland like, "I'm struggling," as they ask for support. They are afraid that if they admit breaking a rule someone is going to call the Jesus ambulance, which will take them to the pastor for excruciating "counseling."

In addition to protecting individual souls, the rules and pressure to conform were supposed to protect the church and its community from ungodly outside influences. For generations, a few passages in the Bible—"Be ye not unequally yoked together with unbelievers" was one—had led Baptists to avoid entertainment, the press, politics, much of higher education, and other parts of secular society. In the past century, however, many Baptists dropped separatism and dove into secular activities. This change had been the prime force behind the creation of the IFB movement: While other Baptists started voting and going to movies and dancing, the independent Fundamentalists doubled down on strictures. Although they claimed sole possession of the true faith, the IFBs recently endured their own trouble with breakaway believers who thought the IFBs were too liberal and created the New Independent Fundamentalist Baptist movement.

In fact, the New IFB folks may have a point. Like other very conservative churches, IFB began to flirt with outsiders, especially in the political realm, during the 1980s. This was when Baptist televangelist Jerry Falwell built his Moral Majority organization and used it to back Republicans. I wasn't aware of this movement, but I had become enthralled by political campaigns in the way that a kid might be enthralled by an all-action TV show. My interest was sparked when, during the few years my family lived in Jacksonville, Florida (my father worked in the shipyard), I became fascinated by the mayoral candidacy of a Democrat named John Lewis. Young and energetic, Lewis looked like George W. Bush and was a rising star whose mainstream views made him a very effective state legislator. He attended our church, and I was very impressed by his hot-pink yard signs. Lewis lost his primary. His defeat hit me hard. I responded by trying to learn more about how politics worked. I began looking for newspaper articles I could understand, absorbing bits and pieces about what each party stood for. And of course, like so many kids born in the late 1970s, I looked upon Ronald Reagan as my model of a successful officeholder.

Reagan had been brilliant in working with Christian Right leaders while not sacrificing the traditional Republicanism that appealed to the majority of GOP voters. Reagan's clever approach meant that though Falwell had rallied voters for Reagan and others, he failed to achieve his supporters' main goals, which included a return to prayer in public school, a ban on all abortion, outright dismantling of the US Department of Education, and substantial rollbacks in environmental protection laws. As it became clear that Reagan had given Falwell little and gotten much for himself, the Lynchburg, Virginia, preacher lost his political momentum. The first Christian Right movement had failed. But in the tradition of very conservative churches, a new movement had begun. Falwell's rival Pat Robertson created a more disciplined and "worldly" political organization. He named it the Christian Coalition. I was there, in 1992, when it went big time.

THANKS TO THE SHORT PANTS (AVERT YOUR EYES!) AND "SON OF A biscuit" (cover your ears!) incidents, I had already begun to see the discrepancy between what too many Christians say and what they do. No one is perfect. I knew that. But the more you insist on your own perfection, the more hypocritical you look when you are revealed to be less than. Nowhere was this more obvious than in the doctrine of separation. Groups who declare themselves better than others and try to separate from the outside world tend to resemble cults, and cults almost always break down.

Never committed to a holier-than-thou view of life, my parents, especially my father, were always interested in politics despite its outside-world status. Of course, his political values were influenced by his faith, which made him quite interested when he heard friends John Parrott and Lee Newcom talk about the Christian Coalition. Leaders of our local county Republican Party, they were also in charge of the state branch of the Christian Coalition. They were ahead of their time.

When I was fourteen, my father took me to the coalition's national conference in Virginia Beach. It was 1992, and unlike Falwell's Moral Majority, Robertson's coalition didn't want to help the Republican Party. It wanted to take it over before the next presidential election. With plenty of money and the media reach of Robertson's Christian Broadcasting Network, they succeeded in winning seats for the GOP national convention. This success and potential power had brought President George H. W. Bush to the gathering, which from its "Road to Victory" theme to its patriotic decorations looked very much like a political rally.

In 1988, Bush had ignored the Christian Right's most dramatic demands, like the restoration of prayer in public schools. He was the dog, and he wasn't going to let them become the tail that took over. But in 1992 he realized he needed conservative Christians to defeat a challenger, Bill Clinton, who was far more competent and pleasing to swing voters than Michael Dukakis had been. Bush was still unlikely to pay more than lip service to the Christian Coalition, but he couldn't refuse the invitation to do so.

At the 1992 convention Bush declared common cause with the coalition but wavered in telltale ways. He said he supported American families but did not want to "go back to the days of Ozzie and Harriet," when, in fact, most of the people there wanted the life portrayed on that fifties TV show. He talked of tying America more closely with the rest of the world, which was something the people in the crowd found suspect. They also knew he was a lifelong Episcopalian, which made him a liberal Christian.

I did not understand the finer points of difference between the Christian Coalition and the president at the time. I was more interested in the atmosphere, in the way different speakers made their presentations, and in the reporters and TV crews that worked the edges of the crowd of roughly a thousand. Somehow my father and I had snagged front-row seats, and one of the crews came to the front of the room and focused directly on us. We wound up on the CNN broadcast, which, in those times, was far and away the dominant 24–7 news channel.

It's doubtful that anyone in the convention hall was concerned about the potential danger of a religious movement determined to take over one of the country's two major political parties. First, these were folks who believed that America was a Christian nation, ordained by God to be the salvation of the world. Politics would be a way to loosen Satan's evil grip on their countrymen and become a spiritual beacon to the world. They also believed that the concept of church-state separation was erroneous. Conservative Christians once prized this idea because they feared the state influence over churches. Now they oppose it because they want to exert their influence on the state. Finally, there was the widely felt sense that due to looming demographic change—immigration and the decline in church membership—they were losing social and political status and were running out of time to do something about it.

Urgency has always been a key element of conservative Christianity, which explains the frequent references preachers make to end-of-the-world prophecy and the incredible popularity of so-called End Times books. The most popular of these books, the Left Behind series by Rev. Tim LaHaye and Jerry B. Jenkins, outsold most of the secular books that made it on to the bestseller list of *The New York Times*. After centuries of hearing that "the end is coming," this warning had lost much of its power to create excitement and urgency. So instead, the Christian Coalition said that godless liberals are coming to ruin your marriage, your family, your church, and your country. Just after the convention, Robertson said that feminists want women to "leave their husbands, kill their children, practice witchcraft, destroy capitalism, and become lesbians." If this wouldn't stir conservative Christians to action, nothing would.

In the end, the coalition's plan for 1992 failed, as did its effort to immediately take over the GOP. However, with his trip to Virginia Beach, President Bush had made the first overt connection between traditional and even blueblood Republicans and the conservative Christian activists. A deeper bond would be made with his son, President George W. Bush, who was a genuine born-again Christian. Bush was gentle in his personal faith but allowed his political team to exploit some of the Christian Right's greatest fears by encouraging state referenda on gay marriage to drive turnout that would benefit their man.

Although I wouldn't recognize it for many years, the language of the power-seeking political conservatives began to meld with the religiously conservative perspective to describe the opposition as dangerous, anti-American, anti-Christian, perverted, and, ultimately, evil. For an early example of this aggressive spiritual language, we can look to Pat Buchanan's speech to the Republican National Convention, which also took place in 1992. A Christian Right stalwart who tried to replace Bush as the GOP presidential nominee, he spoke of a war "for the soul of America" waged against "radical feminism" and "homosexual rights" and "discrimination against religious schools." Buchanan was widely criticized as being too extreme, but on the fringes lurked a more radical element of this entwined religious and political movement: the conspiracy believers. These were the forerunners of what would become the QAnon movement.

If you find it hard to accept Christian conspiracists as related to today's plague of paranoia, consider that way back in 1991, before the Christian Coalition convention I attended, Pat Robertson publicly promoted the bizarre notion that a long-dead secret society called the Illuminati was scheming with "atheists and Satanists" to control governments around the world. They could do this through influential organizations like the Council on Foreign Relations and take advantage of their connections to the financial world, which had been forged by Jewish bankers. Their inroads in the United States, he said, could be seen in symbols on the dollar bill, mainstream media's function as Illuminati "propaganda" machines, and Bush's references to a "new world order." Under advice from his liaison to the Christian Right, Bush stopped using this term because many religious conservatives believed it referred to Satan's plan to take over the world.

With the old-school GOP aligning itself with the movement Robertson began, Republican rhetoric became toxic. Extremist characters became leaders of the alliance of the faithful and the political. And their tactics overwhelmed policy considerations outside of their culture war. This occurred in a way that was so gradual that hardly anyone, including me, truly appreciated what was happening. Instead, we played along where we could, ignored the rest, and failed to appreciate how our values were being replaced.

CHAPTER 2

Politics in a Bygone Age

C onsider this for a newspaper headline: CORDIALITY MARKS
DEBATE.

Real or fake?

It's real, and it describes the first political debate of my life, which
had been presented by the local League of Women Voters. Published
in my hometown paper *The Pantagraph* (right beside a supermar-
ket's ad for "Meat Mania"), the headline was followed by an account
of my challenge to McLean County Board incumbent Allen Ware's
attendance record. He had replied by noting the time he spent with
his family and the demands of his job. Yes, he had missed some
meetings, said Ware. But like a kid who misses a day of school, he
had been able to catch up on what had occurred. And, he argued, his
experience in office made him familiar with every issue.

The date was October 22, 1998. The location was Bloomington's
Old Courthouse Museum, where the largest courtroom was used as

an auditorium. The courthouse had been built in 1903, after much of downtown had been consumed by a fire that began in a laundry. It was a time when Midwest communities competed over civic architecture, and the Bloomington courthouse was so beautiful it was eventually placed on the National Register of Historic Places. This setting was a great reminder that we were engaged in a timeless exercise in American democracy.

I was twenty years old and still in college. Despite my inexperience, *The Pantagraph*—the name comes from an ancient device that made a copy of a handwritten document—endorsed me the next day. The newspaper's support did much to ease my insecurity about running. Eleven days later I won the election, 1,725–1,580. It was a squeaker, but a win is a win.

The county board job was not the kind of high-level position that got a lot of day-by-day attention. However, as of 1999, national news had not yet come to dominate the media, and people in McLean County were intensely concerned about local affairs. The editors of *The Pantagraph* understood this, which explained why every week they published a column titled "New Names," in which all the children born in its circulation area were welcomed to the world. At the other end of childhood, those who graduated from high school got the same treatment, as the paper printed the names of everyone in their circulation area who received a diploma. Once common, this kind of thing had been abandoned by most other small dailies in the 1970s. But not ours.

On the day after the election, *The Pantagraph* treated me as though I had won the governor's race, sending a reporter to interview me for a front-page story. They were responding not to the importance of my office but to the novelty of someone so young winning *any* election. Of course, I responded to the questions as if my victory was a big deal, because to me it was. I talked about "all the responsibility" I would accept, and said that I was "humbled" by the trust that had been placed in me.

Oddly enough, in the same election, my dad's friend Lee Newcom, who was also a Republican, was swept out of his board seat by another novice, which just shows the unpredictability of politics. However, there was nothing unpredictable in the way Allen Ware and I had conducted ourselves. Although we called it being neighborly, cordiality and decency were a way of life in our country, and had been born in the farmers' tradition of depending on one another for harvests. Because of this, local office candidates didn't sling mud or conduct opposition research so they could discover irrelevant foibles and incidents to fling at one another. Thank God.

I say thank God because I had lived so little that any investigation of my past would have led quickly to, say, age twelve, when I created a little seventh-grade scandal. We were studying America's first war in Iraq, which had been forced by Saddam Hussein's invasion of our ally Kuwait. Having developed a keen interest in the girls in our class, I noticed they were moved by hearing of neighbors who were deployed, and the fear and uncertainty felt by their families. Eager to impress them, I told them that my brother, Nathan, was in Iraq. Actually, he was in high school, but no one thought to check. Next thing I knew the school administration had enrolled me in a support group for kids with family members who were in combat. I attended in part because I didn't know how to get out of it, and in part because, well, free donuts.

Seventh-grade deceptions being what they are, I stuck to my story and kept elaborating on it. I talked about my brother being wounded in a skirmish in a remote part of Iraq. Then I reported that he was being treated in a military hospital. How did all this end? Well, it turned out that the paper published every name of a local person who was deployed. (There they went again with their hyperlocal coverage.) My classmates kept checking and wanted to know why my brother's name never showed up. I said I didn't know, but my dad was furious about it. Eventually my teacher figured out the truth and told me she knew what I had done. It was discussed in a way that was most unpleasant for me, but my punishment was my own sense of humiliation. My deception wasn't revealed to my classmates, which means some of them may just be learning of it. Decades later, I apologize for the lie to those I offended.

The lessons of middle school helped me get through my public school education with little additional trouble, except for a few drinking episodes. One ended with my parents' car stuck in the mud in a field. As nondrinkers, they were not pleased, and they let me know it. Fortunately, during my high school years I had no other contact with the legal system.

My first year at Illinois State University in Bloomington I dove headfirst into fraternity life. Was it like the movie *Animal House*? Pretty much. My time there even included streaking through Bloomington, being chased by the police, and getting caught after I lost my footing, fell, and tumbled down a hillside in a park. My freshman grade point average tumbled to 0.8. You have to try to do *that* poorly, but I had a surefire method: ignore my studies. When my grades were tallied, I was asked to leave the university.

In my exile, I got a job as the furniture "manager" at Kay's Merchandise, which was a struggling regional retailer sliding toward bankruptcy. Kay's operated showrooms where you could buy anything from a diamond ring to a toaster oven. As furniture manager, I spent my time moving sofas, tables, and chairs around. The best thing about the job was the store manager's daughter, but he made sure that she had nothing to do with me.

I applied for readmission to the university and was accepted under the condition that my grades improve immediately and dramatically. They did, and they remained high until I got my degree. In the meantime, I won the county board seat and began to live out the politics and policy concepts I had studied in political science classes. Nothing could have been better preparation for a life in politics.

The county board was a great place to learn how daily life works for most people who pay little attention to politics. The board dealt with ground-level concerns, from law enforcement and courts to the maintenance of roads. Every driver cares about highway upkeep, but this is doubly true in a place like McLean County, which sprawls across 1,183 square miles, an area bigger than the state of Rhode Island. With a population of just 150,000 scattered people, we needed a network of more than 1,000 miles of roads. These arteries allow farmers to reach the shipping hubs where their harvests begin to travel across the country and around the world. Nothing is more important to the county's economy, which was annually ranked as one of the nation's top five producers of corn and soybeans. Add the farms that specialized in other crops, livestock, and eggs, and you get to $1 billion in sales as of 2020.

It wasn't terribly long ago when much of America generally looked and felt like McLean County. In the 1960s, roughly one third of Americans still lived in rural areas. This number declined as Big Ag consolidated farmlands, but many of the farm families moved, not to big cities, but to smaller communities like Bloomington and the neighboring town of Normal. All this information comes from reliable data, as does the fact that today's rural communities are, in many ways, socially distinct. About 64 percent of people in rural areas identify as evangelical Christians, compared with the national average of 25 percent. Compared to non-rural communities, rural communities have higher rates of gun ownership, far fewer people from minority groups, and many fewer incidents of violent crime. Fear of crime, however, is higher.

Although resentment of "Big Government" and welfare has always been a hallmark of rural America, federal spending is welcome in the form of farm subsidy programs created to keep the food supply stable. Critics call it a form of welfare, but it's more like a national security program. Nothing is more important to a country's stability and strength than a functioning food supply system that can survive wild price swings. More controversial is the subsidy for corn and ethanol fuel, which was supposed to help this industry compete. Forty years later it's still paying for nonfood production. On a national basis the various programs paid a record $23 billion to commodity farmers in the year I joined the McLean County Board.

The money flowing to our farmers made them so important to the local economy that the board often considered them in its work, and they in turn wielded influence over politics at all levels.

FARM SUBSIDIES WERE WAY ABOVE MY PAY GRADE AT THE COUNTY board, but that didn't mean the issues were simple. Lee Newcom had advised me to keep my mouth shut and my head down for the first year of my term so that I could learn the job and show I wasn't a young know-it-all. I followed his recommendation. Then I started offering modest proposals. One of the first called for shifting out meeting times from 9:00 a.m. to 6:00 p.m. so more members of the public could attend. This went down 13–5. I'm not sure why, but it did occur to me that board members found 9:00 a.m. convenient for themselves. Also, they had always done things this way. And maybe they didn't really want too many people to attend because they could be disruptive, demanding, and misinterpret what was going on. I didn't think of this third explanation at the time, but from where I stand today, I see it as a real possibility.

I put my neck out a second time in mid-January 2000 when I signed up to be a delegate for Arizona senator John McCain in the 2000 Republican presidential primary. With no incumbent GOP president, no one had a lock on the nomination, and during 1999 more than a dozen Republicans had said they were giving serious thought to running. They ranged from the fire-breathing culture warrior Pat Buchanan, who was so unelectable he had no chance, to a mild-as-milk former undersecretary of education whose name recognition score was roughly zero. (It was Gary Bauer. Don't know who he is? Look him up.) By mid-February, with five or six weeks to go before the Illinois primary, just two were waging serious campaigns: McCain and Texas governor George W. Bush.

Bush had begun the year with an enormous advantage in the major public opinion polls. On the day I declared myself for McCain, Bush enjoyed 42 percent and McCain was second with just 8 percent. Obviously I wasn't attaching myself to the favorite. Instead, I chose McCain because of his service background—he had been a Navy pilot and prisoner of war in Vietnam—and because he was independent minded and so blunt that the campaign bus he had been riding on since September was called the Straight Talk Express.

McCain was a guy who when a voter called him "misinformed" shot back, "No, you're misinformed." When asked why health care hadn't been tackled by Congress, he said it was because "the Democrats are controlled by the trial lawyers, and the Republicans are controlled by the big money of the insurance companies." When another voter said the United States should cancel trade deals because his industry needed protection, he said, "I would do anything to help your company compete," and then added, "I cannot tell you I would protect your company . . . I am a free trader." All the above happened in less than twenty-four hours, during a visit to New Hampshire, where the first and often most important primary takes place.

Traditionally, New Hampshire Republicans were known to be

open-minded, and many were moderates. Their admiration for Mc-Cain's straight talk earned him a big win there and gave him the momentum to gain a 92–61 advantage in delegates by the end of week three of the primary season. However, Bush's helpers in South Carolina, where his campaign intended to create a "firewall," had reached into the gutter for a line of attack. With fliers and phone calls they alleged that McCain had fathered a child with a black prostitute during a visit to New York City. The proof, they said, was McCain's nine-year-old daughter, Bridget, who had been born in India.

In exploiting a child and bringing together a trifecta of prejudice—race, sex, and a big, bad northern city—these Bush backers created enough doubt to help their man win by nearly 12 points. Although Bush aides said their national campaign had nothing to do with the fliers and calls and disavowed them, McCain's momentum was lost, and he withdrew on March 9. With the mountains of Sedona behind him, and his wife, Cindy, beside him, he said his party should do more to attract moderate independent voters and embrace his main issues. Those had included campaign finance reforms to dramatically reduce the involvement of big corporations and unions, and banning most activities by outside groups like the ones that spread the rumors in South Carolina. The only policy he noted specifically in Sedona was changing the tax code "that benefits the powerful few at the expense of many." With many in the press reporting that Mc-Cain remained angered by how his daughter had been exploited in South Carolina, he acknowledged that Bush was likely to be the

GOP nominee but refrained from endorsing him or pledging to work for him. "I wish him well" was as far as he would go. I didn't blame him.

In Illinois I had told the local paper that I expected McCain to drop out on the day before he made the announcement. As a bona fide politics nerd, I had been tracking the delegate count, eyeing the states remaining—most were Bush strongholds—and comparing the 2000 race to previous ones. I'd studied election results since I was ten years old (like other boys tracked baseball box scores), so McCain's prospects seemed obvious to me. I knew he might pick off a state here or there, but he wasn't going to win. I said I would support Bush but remained proud of my original choice. When the crisis over the Florida recount occurred, I was all for my side and glad Bush won. However, I didn't know all the details about things like the so-called Brooks Brothers riot, which I would learn had been organized by the notorious Roger Stone. And I was concerned that for the first time in 112 years, the Electoral College count gave the victory to the candidate who had lost the popular vote.

ALTHOUGH THOMAS P. "TIP" O'NEILL GETS THE CREDIT, THE phrase "All politics is local" was coined in 1932 by the Chicago pol Finley Peter Dunne. No matter who said it first, the point I learned on the county board and would keep in mind was that local issues mattered. Dunne was also famous for a second bit of timeless wisdom: "Politics ain't beanbag." This meant that it's a rough game—

just how rough depended on the players and the era—and not for the faint of heart. Having won my first and only race—a mild-mannered competition—I had not yet felt the pressure of intense scrutiny, nor had I felt the sting of Election Day defeat. Thus I felt perfectly comfortable encouraging my father to say yes when friends, state leaders of the Christian Coalition, and some major players in the local GOP told him he would make a good candidate.

State senate seats in states like California, Texas, New York, and Illinois are a big deal. In our state, just fifty-nine serve in the senate, which meant they each represented about two hundred thousand people. In 2000, this was more than the population of cities such as Richmond, Virginia; Des Moines, Iowa; and Spokane, Washington. The state senate dealt with billions of dollars in resources and set policies that affected twelve million citizens. Sure, the state spent more than it received in revenues, and the pension debt was accelerating quickly. But as much as voters complained about Springfield in general, they were reliably respectful and deferential to their local senator because he or she was the highest-ranking official they might ever meet. And he or she could often resolve citizens' problems.

Our region's state senate seat had become open when the incumbent, John Maitland, announced he would resign due to illness. Maitland was a Republican, and due to the GOP's greater numbers, it was quite certain that whoever won the party's nomination in March 2002 would prevail in November. Trouble was, my dad was a rookie with a team filled with rookies, going against a pro named Bill Brady, who had been elected four times as a state representative.

He was familiar, compared with my father, and had $75,000 in campaign funds to our $20,000.

We might have overcome Brady's advantages if we had made an effort in the first four months of the race. This time was wasted because I turned down my father's request to be his campaign manager, choosing to be a helper instead of a leader. (I thought this would be better for my relationship with my dad.) His next choice was a retired FBI agent with scant political experience but whose Christian faith was off the charts. So it was that when he came aboard at the end of September, we put our faith in him to get things done day by day and report back when serious problems arose.

Well, the fact is that despite all the confidence they may show, people in politics are no more or less competent than people in any other walk of life. Sure, they may perform well in front of TV cameras and mingle easily with complete strangers, but many are either bad at their jobs or just going through the motions.

In the early stages of my dad's campaign, we assumed we had a committed team determined to put in the necessary effort. When we asked our campaign manager what he was planning or expecting to accomplish soon, his answer was, "I'm praying on it." It was already December when we finally got the truth. Despite his reassurances, it turned out that praying was about all our campaign manager had done. He had made less than the minimum effort on things like fund-raising and chasing key people for their endorsements. In that moment it was decided I would take over, and I immediately began dialing for dollars and for public shows of support. The answer was almost always: "I'm sorry, Adam. You should have asked sooner."

Regardless, from mid-January to early March, we held events all over the district and advertised as much as our small budget allowed. The candidates were in agreement on most issues—they were both pro-life, fiscally conservative, and in favor of small government—so the distinctions that could be drawn were based mainly on character and personality. Having grown up on a farm and worked in the government, business, and charitable sectors, my dad had a much greater breadth of experience than Brady, who was a real estate developer and politician. This made my dad more appealing to voters in the district's farm country and small towns. When he announced he would never accept campaign donations from liquor and gambling interests, he noted that in his job with the Home Sweet Home programs for the homeless, he had worked with many people addicted to gambling and/or alcohol, and his position was a moral matter. When we noted that Brady had taken donations from both liquor and gambling groups, he cried foul but didn't argue with the facts. To this day I still chuckle that we actually made this a thing.

As primary day approached, supporters for both sides published letters in the local papers and talked up their candidates with friends and neighbors. This was long before social media or even email lists mattered. Letters to the editor were one of the best ways to communicate with a wider audience, and people followed them closely. Reporting and commentaries in the Bloomington paper also attracted more interest, and here again, Brady had an advantage. He had been interacting with the local press for years, and journalists had come to regard him as a reliable source. It was hard not to see Brady's hand in a *Pantagraph* pundit's column titled NO-SHOW KINZINGER

LOST OUT ON OPPORTUNITY. The piece was all about how my father had failed to attend the Sangamon County GOP's Lincoln Day luncheon.

Most Americans know that Lincoln Day celebrations are a Republican tradition across Illinois, even if they can't recognize Sangamon County. It's the county that included the state capital, and so the luncheon attracted a who's who of the party's leaders. Brady did attend, and like everyone else, he circulated to impress, well, other Republican leaders. If hobnobbing with a crowd that included perhaps a handful of voters from his district was an opportunity to gain votes, then so was every checkout line at a convenience store. Of course a reporter who dwelled inside the bubble of state politics would think the luncheon was very important.

The same pundit went after us on an issue we had raised, because apparently we hadn't been tough enough. Our attack had focused on a long-standing program that let state senators hand out scholarships to state colleges and universities without any oversight or rules for who might qualify. The columnist gave us a hard time because we hadn't made something out of the fact that Brady had once given four hundred dollars to a political friend's child. But the point my father made was about how he would reject a privilege that everyone else was willing to accept. There was no need to make a big deal out of the four hundred dollars given to some kid.

The most pointed criticism we launched against Brady related to the life he had made for himself outside politics, as a real estate developer. "The choice is someone who farmed," said my father, who grew up on a family farm, "or someone who chose a profession of putting asphalt over farmland."

By the time my father threw that rather soft punch, we knew that a state university poll had put us way behind Brady. No one could tell if it landed, but we did know that we scored with the *Chicago Tribune*'s editorial endorsement. It said, "Rus Kinzinger had neither the money nor the legislative experience of Brady but his understanding of state issues and his creative ideas for cutting waste suggest he wouldn't need much time to get up to speed." It was exciting to see one of the biggest and most influential papers in the country get behind my father. But then the voters went to the polls.

On primary night, Brady won 9,422–4,721. It may seem like a tiny turnout for such an important race, but the fact is that party primaries generally draw only the voters most committed to the GOP. The total vote was similar in other counties, except where the party had a barnburner of a contest. Democrats saw the same dynamic in their races. When ours was over, my father called Brady to congratulate him and told the press that as a complete newcomer he was glad to have won the support he had received. "We're disappointed but we aren't devastated," he added. "The people speak, and we go on with life as it is."

I believe my father was a little devastated, and on election night he began to think that the game wasn't for him. He was especially turned off by fund-raising, which was evidenced by the final tally of campaign revenues. Thanks to support from big groups like the teachers' unions and many individuals who contributed thousands of dollars apiece, Brady had raised about $175,000 compared with our total of about $50,000. No one gave us more than $500. Scan the timeline of our revenues and you can see we started way behind Brady, as during one reporting period when our manager's prayers went unanswered, Brady took in more than $75,000 compared with our $4,000. In an era when money matters in elections, this was the surest path to losing. This happened in large part because my father was unable to stomach asking friends, neighbors, and politically engaged strangers alike for cash.

As it happened, events were leading me to also consider my interest in elected office. I would run for county board one more time, but events were leading me to step back from electoral politics too. It would be one of the few life-changing decisions I would ever make.

CHAPTER 3

Life Gets Serious

The sky was a cloudless blue expanse. The temperature was an ideal 68 degrees. From the west came a light breeze of about five miles per hour. It was, in other words, a perfect morning for flying, and since I had just purchased an old, slow Cessna 150, I felt the itch to get airborne. Instead, I was driving my red '92 Ford Escort from my parents' house to my job at a small technology company located, coincidentally, across the street from the Bloomington airport.

The car radio was tuned to the puerile, profane, but also funny *Howard Stern Show* because, well, I was twenty-three years old. Stern, who was in the worst phase of his drug addiction, was talking about the nude model Pamela Anderson when he suddenly paused and said, "I don't mean to interrupt the fun, but this is a breaking news story, a serious news story. A plane has crashed into the World Trade Center. The World Trade Center is on fire."

When they were completed in 1971, the North and South towers of New York's World Trade Center were the tallest buildings in the world, snatching the record from the Empire State Building, which was a subway ride away. The Towers had been internationally recognized icons of America's financial power for thirty years. Given its symbolic importance, Stern had been right to break the news of an airplane crashing in Manhattan, striking the North Tower, and for a moment the story held the cast's attention. One recalled the 1945 incident when an Air Force pilot, flying in zero visibility, crashed into the Empire State Building. (This was the last time an aircraft had crashed in Manhattan.) Someone else wondered aloud if the crash had been a terrorist attack.

I had the same thought as suddenly my generally mind-numbing commute, with its silly entertainment, was overwhelmed with portents of tragedy, and the talk of Pamela Anderson suddenly seemed extra juvenile and extremely profane.

Since the show was supposed to be defiantly edgy, Stern's confused sidekicks momentarily changed the subject when out of character. Stern is a smart guy, and he returned to the subject of the plane strike. Then a second jet plane hit the WTC's South Tower. A news crew on the scene broadcast the crash as it happened. "So, it *is* a terrorist attack," said Stern. "It's gotta be."

Stern spoke in a way that reflected how millions of Americans felt as every TV network began live coverage that would last for more than a week. Many would have agreed when he said, "It's war." No foreign country would have risked such an act of war against the United States. This left one suspect with the organization and motivation to conduct the attacks: Osama bin Laden. Leader of the violent Islamic network called Al Qaeda, bin Laden had declared war on the United States in 1996. It was unlikely that most Americans would have been familiar with him or with Al Qaeda, but the idea that the attack was linked to terrorism based in the Middle East sprang to many minds. Stern expressed this directly, saying: "We gotta bomb the hell out of them."

WHEN I REACHED THE OFFICE, I FOUND EMPTY SILENCE. I KNEW EVeryone would be downstairs in the office gym, watching the one TV in the building. As I joined them it became clear that we all understood nothing would be the same again for a long time, if ever. Our country was under attack and every citizen had to assume that this immediate crisis would continue until we understood precisely what had happened and the magnitude of our losses.

As we watched the news delivered as it happened by journalists who had raced to cover the attacks in New York, others reported that officials believed there were other targets, including Washington, DC, and that fighter jets were airborne and searching the skies. At 9:37 a.m. a Boeing 757 slammed into the Pentagon. Eight minutes later, at 9:45, the United States and Canada closed North American air space for the first time in history. The last of the four hijacked jets then slammed into a field in Shanksville, Pennsylvania.

At 9:59 the South Tower suddenly collapsed, with one floor pancaking onto the next as the 500,000-ton structure disintegrated in a cloud of dust and debris that rushed down narrow streets and covered everything with what looked like volcanic ash. In less than half an hour the North Tower came down in a similar fashion. There was no doubt that we were suffering the worst surprise attack on America since the Japanese bombed Pearl Harbor on December 7, 1941.

Anger and a desire for retribution replaced the shock and horror I had initially experienced. We were the most powerful nation on earth—militarily, economically, politically, morally. If this attack had been directed by any country, no matter how powerful, our response would be immensely forceful and, no doubt, supported by much of the world. If instead the hijackings and crashes were the work of a terrorist organization, striking back would be far more difficult, because these groups were scattered in small cells and trained in secrecy, often moving inside ungoverned territories of countries like Afghanistan, Somalia, and Yemen. But we had no choice but to try. And keep trying until we succeeded.

SEPTEMBER 11 CHANGED MY LIFE, BUT NOT IN THE WAY YOU MIGHT imagine. It did not compel me to enlist in the military, because, coincidentally, I had begun that process nine months earlier. But it did lead me to war, and to a far deeper appreciation of the US military, of our country's role in the world, and of how each of us can play a part in important events.

As the implications of 9/11 eventually sank in, most of my assumptions about the future of my country shifted. The United States had seemed beyond the reach of enemy nations and terrorists who would carry out mass casualty attacks. Now our vulnerabilities had been exposed, and I was fighting mad. It felt to me like 9/11 was a call to men and women of my generation. I said as much to a reporter named Karen Hansen, who published an article about the immediate aftermath of the attacks in *The Pantagraph*. "We're a generation that everything's been spoon-fed to us," I said. "We've had everything." I then told her that I thought we faced a challenge to our values that could be reduced to a single question: "Is it important to get ahead, or is it important to do what is right?"

I can't remember a time when I wasn't interested in becoming a military pilot. But as a kid, whenever I asked about how someone qualified, I was told you had to have a notable aptitude for math and science and be so disciplined that you could turn those talents into top grades. And it would really help if you graduated from the Air Force Academy. Back then—and occasionally ever since—I was affected by the same self-doubts that affect everyone who isn't a narcissist. So hearing that pilots had to be great at two subjects that weren't my best had discouraged me. I didn't even try for the academy.

Eventually I did some research and learned that my college degree made me eligible to take the two special tests required to apply for training to fly for the Air Force or the Air National Guard: one to determine my intelligence and another to test my flying aptitude. I aced both and began the wait for an opening in Officer Training School.

After 9/11, I was still waiting when the press reported that Americans were flooding recruiters with calls. Unfortunately, this fervor died as President Bush told the public to return to normal life. He said the terrorists would win if people "don't want to go shopping for their families . . . don't want to go about their ordinary daily routines." I know he was thinking about protecting the economy and may have felt the government would respond quickly and decisively, but it was a mistake. He gave a country willing to rally behind a cause no real chance to do so, and by 2005 the Army, to use just one example, had added just seventy-five hundred to its ranks.

As I finally received a report date for the Air Force Officer Training School, I got word that someone had dropped out of a Wisconsin Air National Guard spot. (The Air National Guard and the regular Air Force train together. I could apply to the Air Guard 128th Refueling Wing at Mitchell Field near Milwaukee and, if accepted, fly for a unit that had the same training and mission as the Air Force, *and* some advantages known mostly to insiders.)

Although you may think of the Guard as somehow less proficient than the regular Air Force, this is not true. Guard pilots perform the same duties and fly the same aircraft as their Air Force counterparts and whenever tested—like in mock dogfights—tend to come out on top. This is thanks to the tendency for Guard pilots to be older and more experienced, and to get more flying time. Guard pilots also live in their hometowns and can hold regular jobs and develop careers while they serve. Many fly commercial jets for a living, which keeps them in peak flying condition. Air Force pilots aren't allowed to have regular outside jobs, and they get transferred every two or three years. Even people who love seeing the world get tired of the transfers.

Since I had inquired about the Wisconsin opening on the day of the deadline, I had only a few hours to put together and submit an extensive application package that included many forms and supporting documents. This was the age of faxes, and it was a chore to make the deadline, but I did and soon learned I had snagged the spot. I would train to become an officer and then a pilot who could handle the refueling jets—nicknamed "flying gas stations"—that fill up other aircraft so they can stay in the air longer for a combat mission or a long-distance flight. This is how the US Air Force can reach any place in the world in twenty-four hours or less.

Later, in one of the many phases of pilot training, an instructor asked a classroom of candidates, "Who here is headed for a Guard unit?" Only two of us raised a hand. "Take a good look at them," said the instructor. "They made the right decision."

OFFICER TRAINING SCHOOL GETS THE COLLEGE GRADS WHO ARE accepted for the pilot program and imparts some lessons in military society, command, and leadership. Everyone who graduates from the school is given the rank of second lieutenant. Nearly all those who stay in for twenty years will retire as lieutenant colonels. But while rank comes with privileges, prestige, and responsibility, it doesn't affect the most basic elements of the military experience, which opened my eyes to what is, truly, a culture every American should understand and appreciate. The camaraderie, ethical standards, and education combine to create a cohesive and extremely competent fighting force.

After a few weeks of classroom and simulator training, we were ready to fly in the little twin-engine jets called T-37s—nicknamed Tweets—which looked a bit like the planes on a carnival kiddie ride and were retired in 2007 after fifty-three years of service. They weighed less than many sport utility vehicles and were so small you could fit two on a basketball court. The cockpit, encased in a dome of plexiglass, had room for a trainee and an instructor, who could take control at any moment. The forward wall, painted black and filled with dials and switches, was framed in metal painted Air Force gray.

As small as it was, the T-37 was built like a tank. As the first jet flown by a huge number of military pilots, the ugly little thing was beloved by most of them, from the ear-piercing whine at start-up to a landing that felt like riding a skateboard going 100 miles per hour. In between, the plane had the fastest g-force onset rate in the Air Force—so fast you had to fight not to black out from the gravitational force. Cruising speed could reach 425 miles per hour, and maximum altitude was 35,000 feet. Not bad for a ride used to train people with no more than twenty or thirty hours in a single-engine prop plane.

The first time you stand next to the T-37s at start-up, the sound of the engines and the smell of jet fuel create an irresistible adrenaline rush. With engines described by aviation writer Budd Davisson as a "kerosene-burning siren," the noise made when a dozen fire up builds until you feel like the sound waves might tear you to pieces.

The extreme heat of the exhaust superheats the air, causing the molecules to rise and then fall as they cool, which creates a wavy, mirage effect. For me, the sight and the sound provoked feelings of dread—the risk of vomiting was high, and we expected sauna conditions in the cockpit—but also excitement. No one who signs up for this kind of training isn't eager to strap on a parachute (in case ejection is required) and a helmet and get airborne.

I came close but never puked, and otherwise took well to the jets. Given that the maximum speed for my single-propeller Cessna 150 was 125 miles per hour, and it was easier to land than anything flying, my experience with the T-37 was a confidence booster. It made me feel more mature, less self-doubting, like I had both a natural ability and an acquired skill that meant I could do something meaningful in response to the attack on my country.

However, I was not perfect. I made mistakes that were corrected by instructors, and on a solo flight I made an error that was nearly fatal. Remember what I said about g-forces? On that flight I made a split S, which involves going inverted and pulling toward the ground until you emerge right side up, 180 degrees opposite the heading. Naturally, as you point to the ground, you gain airspeed, so you want to start slow, say 150 miles per hour. I started 100 miles per hour too fast. The g-force pressure pinched the vessels that send blood to the brain. I began seeing stars and then experiencing what's called brownout. Somehow, I remembered that I had been taught to take shallow breaths and tense every muscle from my toes to my chest to send blood back up to the heart. I followed the protocol, came out of it, and got control before the plane became a dagger hammered into the earth. No one on the ground knew what happened because they weren't tracking my flight that closely. And though I told a few buddies, no one in authority heard about my close call.

THE MILITARY SPIRIT OF UNITY IS A POWERFUL BINDING AGENT. IT explains why combat personnel often say they fight for one another, and no mission is taken more seriously than the rescue of a missing soldier, airman, or sailor. It fails only with truly hard cases or when people are under the influence of drugs and/or alcohol. This happened to me in a down-on-its-luck place called Altus, Oklahoma, where pilots learn to handle the KC-135 refueling plane. This was where I first flew a big aircraft with impressive capabilities. The tanker is 136 feet long and has a wingspan of about 131 feet. The pilot's seat is about 35 feet off the ground, which is a perspective that takes some getting used to.

Any weekend flier would find the KC-135's performance mindboggling. Its four engines provide so much power, generating a maximum airspeed of 500 miles per hour, that it can climb faster than many jet fighters. Its range on one fill-up is more than 11,000 miles. Its ceiling is 50,000 feet above sea level, where the sight of the earth's curvature is breathtaking. Although the KC-135 can carry cargo and personnel, I'd estimate that 90 percent of the plane's missions involve gassing up other aircraft. The plane's tanks hold 100 tons of fuel for this purpose.

Refueling involves a kind of ballet performed by $100 million worth of aircraft cruising six miles above the earth. The tail boom that delivers the gas is less than fifty feet long, which tells you how close the planes get while flying at precisely the same speed at exactly the same compass points.

Mishaps are rare, though the KC-135 can survive a little bumping and shoving. In 1970, for example, an SR-71 spy plane pitched up, hit a tanker in the belly, and crashed after its pilots bailed out. The refueler landed safely.

At Altus, it took me a few weeks to get comfortable controlling such a big beast—think of the riders who fly the dragons in *Game of Thrones*—but eventually I felt as comfortable as I did in the driver's seat in a car. You'd be surprised how even in a big aircraft a pilot can sense small changes in performance. You respond naturally, check the data on the instruments, and make adjustments. The experience of acquiring this sixth sense and gaining confidence with the KC-135 was yet one more way that the military helped me grow up. Add the trust that came with handing me responsibility for the plane and the lives of my crew, and flight school made me feel competent in a way I had never felt before.

This compensated for the lifestyle at the base and its community. With no offense intended to the city or the people at the base, I have to say that when I was not flying, Altus Air Force Base was the most boring posting I saw in almost twenty years of service. I'm not the only one who thinks so. In surveys done by the military press, it consistently ranks among the worst in the minds of airmen, right alongside places like Minot Air Force Base, where, for three months a year, the average *high* temperature is 23 degrees.

Part of the problem of life in Altus, in addition to the 98-degree average high temperature in July, is the landscape. Some might find the Western prairie starkly beautiful. I saw endless dust-blown acres as flat as the top of your kitchen table, broken only by cotton plants that formed rows of spindly skeletons that seem to stretch forever. The town itself offers little entertainment for the thousand or so young men and women stationed there. Drinking was their most popular off-duty activity, and all the bars except for one were rough-neck places where the local cops knew the frequent brawlers by name. At the exception, fights were a little less frequent, at least inside the establishment.

On the only memorable night I spent in downtown, five of us pilot trainees left the "good" bar, ready to stumble back. In the parking lot we couldn't help but notice a couple having sex in the bed of a pickup truck. One of my buddies made a joke about it. In a flash, the guy in the truck jumped up and onto the ground and demanded to fight us.

After we refused to fight, the guy started screaming, and we concluded he must be on meth. Like every community, the Air Force has its share of drug use. It was a serious problem in the local town, where hopelessness, stress, and boredom seemed to drive many to use. After standing nose-to-nose with each of us demanding we hit him, the enraged man finally grabbed the hand of one of the other pilots and used it to hit himself. This started a lot of grappling. As two of the trainees ran, three of us stayed and subdued the whacked-out man until he was calm enough for us to let go. As we walked away, he said, "I'm a crew chief, you assholes. I'm gonna break your plane so you crash."

CRASHES, THOUGH EXCEEDINGLY RARE, DO HAPPEN, AND US WAR planes do get shot down during combat missions. Fighter pilots, who fly at lower altitudes and are thus exposed to common shoulder-fired surface-to-air weapons, are especially vulnerable. Tankers, which operate as high as thirty-five thousand feet, fly far above the range of ordinary missiles, including most ground-launched ones. Indeed, high fliers can be reached only by the most powerful ground-launched missiles, which are possessed only by the largest state actors. The most famous case of a high-altitude shootdown involved a US spy plane that flew at the edge of space and was hit by a Soviet surface-to-air missile. (The plane was one of the famous U2s, which entered service in 1957 and still operate today. The pilot of the one that was shot down, Gary Francis Powers, survived and was returned to the US in exchange for a Soviet spy held by the American government. He died seventeen years later when a helicopter he flew for a TV station in Los Angeles crashed.)

The U2 incident illustrates that the chances of surviving a missile strike or a disabling mechanical problem are better than you might think, thanks to ejection seats and parachutes and to the way aircraft are built. But if you do survive and come down in a war zone, it's up to you to locate some sort of cover, find food and water, and

evade or fight would-be captors. This is why everyone who flies un-
dergoes basic survival training that familiarizes you with the equipment carried on every combat mission and with methods for taking
care of yourself before help arrives.

The equipment brought on every combat flight includes a pistol,
night-vision goggles, a flare, some kind of blanket, small lights, some
rations, bandages, a radio, a knife, and something for starting fires.

I would receive far more thorough (even harrowing) training
when I was assigned to a riskier mission flying in Iraq. This course
took place at the Survival, Evasion, Resistance, and Escape—SERE—
school, which is at Fairchild Air Force Base in Spokane.

During a week of classroom instruction, we learned everything
from how to get out of handcuffs to how to communicate with others
should you get captured and imprisoned by the enemy.

The point of the training is not to teach trainees to avoid breaking. As men like John McCain discovered while imprisoned in Vietnam, everyone breaks, even if it's just a little. For those who believed
it was possible to avoid it, the guilt that follows can last a lifetime
and be more debilitating than any physical injury. Since Vietnam,
the military has taught that everyone divulges something during interrogation. The best a captive can do is delay, limit their own injuries, and when they do start talking, try to minimize the value of
what is said.

I learned a great deal in the classroom even though I was anx-
iously anticipating the truly intimidating prospect of the wilderness
simulation. When the time came, I joined a group of a dozen or so
officers who boarded buses that left Fairchild in a hurry and sped

over the suburbs, small towns, and farms to reach a mountainous wilderness. The group spent two days with an instructor who took us beyond the classroom lessons to show us survival techniques. He split the group into three-person units. Each unit was given a map marked with a different spot where we would meet up with our rescuers. Before he helicoptered off, the instructor said, "The enemy will be out there looking for you. Don't get caught."

Since everyone gets caught, this training is more about practicing what we had been taught and mastering our fears and revulsions than about staying out there in the wilderness for some indeterminate time. For example, I have always had a deep-seated fear of spiders but discovered after a while that I could tolerate them crawling all over me. I also overcame my tenderheartedness when I was tasked with killing a rabbit to eat, which was a job every little group was required to do. (Don't try this at home. Rabbits tend to scream before they die.)

Days after our arrival in the wilderness, and already several pounds lighter, I was captured, hooded, and bused along mountain roads to a rustic camp where we were interrogated by men who appeared to be fighters for a fictional enemy nation. They were, in fact, expert civilian contractors and military personnel who posed as either sadistic bad guys or manipulative nice guys.

The camp "commandant" was a sixtyish man with a big white beard whom we immediately began calling Santa Claus, but only among ourselves. We were subjected to repeated interrogations tailored to train us in scenarios we should expect if captured in real life. I got a minimum of shouting and threats. Instead, they tried to talk about my political interests, my bright future, and how I could save myself from some serious psychological trauma if I just talked to them. Having been taught how to manage these interrogations, I responded to the questions in a general, deflecting way that included offering "information" that had no real value.

Although I can't go into great detail, SERE was not enjoyable. Humiliation was a big part of it. We were, for example, accompanied to every bathroom visit and watched as we did what we had to do. And whenever an officer approached, we were required to bend over, grab our ankles, and say, loud enough to be heard, "I hope you're having a great day, sir."

I was placed in various stress positions and confined in spaces that would break anyone with any level of claustrophobia. At many prisoner of war camps, interrogators, and for that matter torturers, practice their dark arts where everyone can hear what's happening. This tactic is supposed to heighten feelings of anxiety, which, I can tell you, it does. Even though I knew it was all make-believe, I was also affected by hearing others undergo intense confrontations.

Sometimes the interrogators bombarded us with blasting sounds intended to disorient us. Imagine hearing the sound of a baby crying, played backward, over and over. Another recording that was particularly disturbing was an over-the-top reading of a Rudyard Kipling poem called "Boots." Recorded on a 78 in 1915—and available today on YouTube—by an American actor named Taylor Holmes, the reedy audio is full of static, and Holmes's delivery is disturbingly monotonous. It communicates, eerily, Kipling's view of a warrior's experience. You can't understand it without knowing at least some of the words.

We're foot—slog—slog—slog—sloggin' over Africa—
Foot—foot—foot—foot—sloggin' over Africa—
(Boots—boots—boots—boots—movin' up and down again!)

There's no discharge in the war!

Seven—six—eleven—five—nine-an'-twenty mile to-day—
Four—eleven—seventeen—thirty-two the day before—

(Boots—boots—boots—boots—movin' up and down again!)

There's no discharge in the war!

Don't—don't—don't—don't—look at what's in front of you.

(Boots—boots—boots—boots—movin' up an' down again);

Men—men—men—men—men go mad with watchin' em,
An' there's no discharge in the war!

The recording was played so many times, and so loudly, that I could imagine it as one element of a program designed to drive someone mad. But eventually it stopped, and so too the prison training ended. I got a hint that we were about to finish on the last day, when Santa Claus passed me at a distance of about fifteen feet. I immediately assumed the position and shouted, through my legs, "I hope you're having a great day, sir." Santa stopped, came over to where I was still bent over, and said, "Son, you don't have to be so eager to do that."

Although we had been there for just a week, the simulation had been so effective that most of us were swept with a feeling of relief when it was finally over. I for one struggled to hold back tears. We were congratulated on completing SERE, and Santa shook each of our hands. I gripped his hand tightly, in a no-hard-feelings way, but there was a part of me that felt like beating the crap out of him.

Some in our group didn't make it to the little ceremony where we were dismissed from the camp. These few had dropped out and would not be permitted to fly. Some others, who hung in there even as they went a little nuts, didn't quit but were pulled out of the program by trainers who saw they were struggling too much. They were told they would get a chance to try SERE again. I would bet that they all did, because they wanted to finish what they started. This is the essence of the training that our military personnel receive. A commitment to serve is matched by a commitment to provide the very best support possible. Whatever your specialty, you get the best training on earth, and you will have a method for dealing with whatever comes your way.

My training paid off about a year later when, during some active-duty time in Milwaukee, I was walking with some buddies during a night out. All of a sudden, a woman ran out of a bar with blood streaming out of a gash in her neck, followed, step by step, by a man with a knife. She stood in the middle of the street screaming, "He cut my throat, he cut my throat." By this time, we were close enough that I was able to confront him, grab the wrist of the hand that held the knife, and twist him down to the pavement. I put my knee on his arm and managed to avoid getting knifed myself before the police, who had been called by a witness, arrived with their patrol car lights flashing.

After the police got control of the situation I got to my feet and felt the effects of the adrenaline—pounding heart, rapid breathing, heightened senses—that had surged through my body as I fought. I was also a little surprised by my own actions. I was not the fighting type. In fact, I had never been in a fight where I was in danger of suffering the kind of wounds that could have been inflicted by the enraged, knife-wielding man. The important result was that the woman he had slashed escaped and survived and her attacker wasn't able to go after anyone else.

The police took my statement and snapped my picture, then they bid me a simple farewell. I got in my car and drove back to my apartment building wearing a shirt covered with blood. I was in a little shock, but since there are no debriefings for citizens who intervene to stop a violent crime, I would have to deal with things on my own. I rode numbly up to the fifteenth floor, got inside the apartment, and peeled off the shirt. For some reason, I left it in a corner of my bedroom for about a month before I threw it away.

This was a big moment in my life. I proved to myself that I had the skills and the instinct to fight, even when someone posed a serious threat. I probably told the story best to reporter Michael Warren of the *Washington Examiner*:

I hear this commotion and screaming and this girl is running at me across the street, and she's just holding her throat, with blood pouring out, I don't know if you've been in a situation where you've separated from your body almost, because it's just unreal, and that was one of those.

The victim of the slashing was being chased by the guy who had done it. With the knife still in his hand and a look on his face that I could only describe as "psycho," I knew that if he caught her he would likely kill her. The only option was to run at him, block him, and somehow subdue him.

I had no previous experience fighting someone with the means and intent to kill me. The techniques I had been taught in survival school had been defensive. But something I had learned in the Air Force had helped me stay calm. With the trainers' help, I had developed a mindset that allowed me to recognize danger and respond without hesitation. This is the way pilots save themselves and their crews in an emergency. It is also, apparently, good training for dealing with a deranged guy waving a knife.

The police report, spotted by a reporter, made the confrontation an item in the local press. This was followed by a surprise "hero" award from the Wisconsin Red Cross. Then I won the National Guard Valley Forge Cross for Heroism and the Airman's Medal from the Air Force, which is awarded to service members who risk their lives for others outside of armed combat. It's rarely given and is ranked higher than the Bronze Star, which is given for battlefield heroism. The award is approved by the president, signed by the secretary of the Air Force. I received it in a ceremony in my unit.

It's a strange thing to be recognized for something I did without much thought. Setting aside my own gratitude, which is substantial,

I do understand that this kind of award draws attention to the value we place on acting out of concern for one another. Yes, the attention moved me as a recipient, but I hoped that through the media reports others would be inspired and, if confronted by a similar emergency, let themselves take action.

CHAPTER 4

Defend Your Country, See the World

had become a military pilot to join the War on Terror. By the time I was qualified, America had invaded Afghanistan, driven Al Qaeda from its camps, and all but destroyed its operational ability. The terrorists' sponsors, the Taliban, had been defeated and a democratically elected government had been established in Kabul. In Pakistan, the CIA and local security agents had captured the mastermind of 9/11, Khalid Sheikh Mohammed. In Iraq, our forces had deposed Saddam Hussein and cleared the way for a new constitution and government. Saddam had been captured and faced trial for mass murder.

Eager as I was to contribute to the effort, the National Guard wasn't just going to send me into combat as soon as I got my wings. If I was going to be effective in war, I needed to learn what it was like to work in unfamiliar settings.

I considered my postings to be opportunities, observing what

I could about local culture and history and resisting the usual life-style led by military personnel on overseas deployment. At every post and base, almost everyone basically commutes between their workplaces and the bars that sprout beside every American military installation. Of course, I made those trips sometimes. However, I also took pains to spend time with locals, on and off the base, and if there were historic sites I tried to get to all the significant ones.

As I would appreciate even more later, America's global engagements—in trade, diplomacy, and defense—mean that people everywhere have preconceived ideas about us. Some of these notions are based on influences ranging from movie fantasies—*Rambo* any-one?—to news about mass shootings or real-life encounters with Americans. You'd be surprised by how many local people assume you are either CIA or a fabulously rich investor. These factors deter-mine the spirit of an adversary, civilian morale, and military com-mand style. Just look at how the Ukrainians responded to Russia's invasion. You can't learn how to do this overnight. But even short postings overseas can remind you that your life may depend on knowing your enemy.

My operational training involved refueling many of the aircraft I might encounter in a variety of conditions. No matter how many missions you fly, the start of the refueling process always brings a pulse-raising feeling about how we're performing this work so many miles above the earth. The big transports glide up like battleships, stately and overpowering in their size. Fighters often buzz around in groups, with left and right wingmates positioned slightly behind and to the side of the leader. As one latches on and drinks up fuel at a rate of six hundred gallons per minute, the others wait to drop back when it's their turn.

The training we do is so effective that after a few refuelings, in whatever type of plane they fly, pilots never seem to show they are nervous as they pull up to the pump. In fact, over time they also develop some mad skills. You can see what I mean if you search online for photos of a camera crew standing in the open bay of a C-130 cargo plane to photograph a British Typhoon fighter. When they asked the pilot to come as close as possible, he almost put the nose of the Typhoon into the bay. You might call this the high altitude version of a fighter performing a stunt at an air show. Definitely cool. But definitely against the rules.

Those of us flying what is, essentially, a giant, airborne fuel bomb have our own talents and extremely reliable technology, especially for an airplane that first entered service in 1958. Boeing, the manufacturer, based it on its first jetliner, the 707, which captured the airline market with superb engineering and manufacturing. The KC-135s have been upgraded, but some still fly with the original equipment in the cockpit, which makes settling into the driver's seat like taking a step back in time. However, you can also feel the solid build. It is a safe and reliable machine, which helps explain why only five KC-135s have been lost in airborne accidents in sixty-five years.

The only time I ever found myself in serious trouble while refueling a jet occurred with a pilot attempting his first gas-up in a B-2 bomber, a stealth jet that is basically a tailless wing, which makes it very difficult to fly. It also costs a billion dollars per copy, which is why the United States operates just twenty of them. This one created a bow wave, which is a force that causes major instability. When I heard our boom guy key the mic and say, "Oh shit!" I said, "Break away! Break away!" and we climbed out of the danger zone.

My first overseas deployments took me to Latin America, Guam, and Turkey. In these places I would get experience that approximated war-zone operations. Every foreign assignment, especially those close to an adversary's border, brings the possibility of an international incident, and this added pressure to every flight. While there, we got some on-the-ground exposure to history and geopolitics, which was fascinating to a policy nerd like me.

In Guam we flew out of Andersen Air Force Base, which is one of fourteen full-scale bases the United States operates on the Pacific Rim. A tropical paradise, the island is six thousand miles from the US mainland and considered the most isolated speck of US territory in the world. It is also a living museum. Archaeology buffs come to see the three- to five-thousand-year-old pictographs that have been found inside a limestone cave made by a population of farmers and fishers who had come, originally, from coastal China. They called themselves Chamorros and lived in a class-based society run by women.

The Chamorros' first experience with true outsiders came with the arrival of Ferdinand Magellan and his men, who landed at a small bay on the southwest edge of the island. They were intent on finding an alternative westward route for trade between Europe and Asia. Their landing in Guam is recalled with a seaside obelisk and plaque that make no mention of the Native people. "Ferdinand Magellan landed near this place on March 6, 1521" is all it says. Believing that the Spice Islands (modern Indonesia) were a three days' sail from where he departed at the tip of South America, Magellan had in fact journeyed for three months. He arrived with a sick and weakened crew that had survived on about a week's worth of rations and seen dozens of their number starve to death. The Chamorros saved the survivors with food and water and then, assuming they were trading, took items like knives from the ships. Magellan considered this stealing, and after they recovered their health, he had his men kill a handful of Chamorros and burn their houses. The explorer then named Guam and its archipelago the Islands of Thieves.

The case of Magellan and the Chamorros is one of history's many examples of how people who don't understand one another can fall into tragic conflict. This is a problem that invading countries have encountered time and again. The United States suffered from this dynamic in Vietnam, Somalia, Iraq, and Afghanistan. We're not the only ones. The Soviets failed to learn their lesson in Afghanistan and the Russian Federation repeated it in Ukraine. In Magellan's case, hubris ruled the day on his next stop after Guam, where he tried to intimidate the people of the Philippines with a display of modern cannon fire. They answered with a force of more than a thousand fighters, who killed Magellan and drove his men back to their ships.

In Guam, visitors who are inclined toward military history learn that 150 years after Magellan the Spanish returned to the island to protect—what else?—trade. They built forts at harbors where galleons crossing the Pacific stopped for supplies. (At sea these ships were on their own against pirates.) Madrid held on in Guam until they lost the Spanish-American War and ceded control of the island, as well as Puerto Rico and the Philippines, to the United States. They also gave up their claim to Cuba, site of the war's beginning, leaving it, too, under American rule.

Twenty years passed, and then the American military in Guam engaged in a new war. As World War I raged in Europe, the Pacific became a little-noted theater of war as allies attacked German colonies and outposts along a five-thousand-mile arc from the Marshall Islands to New Guinea and then China. When a German gunboat called the *Cormoran II* arrived in Guam seeking fuel, the military governor refused to provide it and held the crew on land. Then a cable announcing the United States had joined the war prompted the governor to order the ship seized in America's first attack of the war. The *Cormoran II*'s crew scuttled the ship. Seven of the crew died in the fight and are memorialized by a German-language marker in an oceanfront cemetery where the six bodies that were recovered are buried alongside American Marines and civilians.

Although isolated and sparsely populated, Guam's strategic location continued to make it a vital military asset. The 200-square-mile island was attacked and seized by Japan two days after the bombing of Pearl Harbor. American submarines harassed enemy ships near Guam until one entered the harbor and sank the troop carrier *Tokai*

Maru. (It came to rest three yards from the keel of the *Cormoran II*, which lies on its side.) Guam was not liberated until 1944, in a battle that cost the lives of about eighteen hundred Americans and nearly twenty thousand Japanese. For twenty-six years after the war, a Japanese sergeant named Shoichi Yokoi hid in the forest, sleeping in a cave, hunting and gathering at night. Many believe he didn't know the war was over. In truth he had hidden to protect his honor.

All of these places, from Magellan's landing site to the side-by-side graves of the two enemy ships to Shoichi Yokoi's hand-dug cave, are open to visitors. In fact, the sunken warships draw more than a thousand divers annually. How many tourists understand the full military story and the lessons it can teach? Probably very few. Heck, I know most servicemen are far more likely to visit one of the many strip clubs within a minute's drive from both Andersen and Naval Base Guam. However, those of us who rolled down the runway to take off over the five-hundred-foot-high Anao Cliffs were hit smack in the face with a sober sign of America at war. Just past the beach, and visible from the air, a submerged B-52 lies in the clear water.

Assigned to a Vietnam War initiative called Operation Arc Light, which targeted the North's so-called Ho Chi Minh Trail, the plane developed mechanical problems as it cleared the runway and crashed. The entire crew was killed. Thirteen others were lost due to pilot error or mechanical failure. In one case, two B-52s collided in the air as they circled in the sky, awaiting a KC-135 sent to refuel them. Additionally, the North's Soviet-supplied anti-aircraft batteries would take down eighteen B-52s. No wonder veterans talk of how many pilots feared the missions to Vietnam, and how many more questioned the decisions made in Washington to fight the war in this way.

When we got to Guam in 2005, Andersen was a bit frayed around its edges. A drive down Arc Light Boulevard—how many young airmen knew why it had this name?—revealed a landscape overgrown with tall grass and weeds. Birds built nests near the runways and migrating ones swooped down to feed on seeds. In 2016, a B-52 pilot sighted a flock of birds as he rolled down the runway for takeoff. As he tried to abort, the drag shoot that would help stop the huge plane failed to deploy. The aircraft went off the runway and caught fire. The crew escaped harm, but the $112 million plane was destroyed.

Our job would be to support bombers and surveillance planes that patrolled the coastlines of North Korea and China. Both countries were no doubt irritated by our flights, and they tracked us with their radar. This response came with a price, because it allowed us to pinpoint their air defense systems. From time to time the Chinese would scramble fighter jets to shadow American patrols, just as the Russians do. However, they cut way back on these challenges and stopped menacing our aircraft with dangerous maneuvers after a mishap that occurred in the air over the South China Sea in 2001.

In that incident, two Chinese fighter jets flew out to meet a Navy EP-3 surveillance plane. Powered by four propellers, with a cruising speed of 200 miles per hour, these aircraft are packed with technology that intercepts and records signals. On this flight, an aircrew of three sat up front while twenty-one specially trained people—among them cryptologists, linguists, and technicians—monitored the machines. One of the Chinese fighters made a couple of passes, coming within feet of the EP-3. On his third approach the pilot realized he was about to collide with the slow-moving American plane. He failed to correct in time. As the fighter hit the outer propeller on the left wing of the EP-3, the blade cut the fuselage in half, sending the cockpit cartwheeling higher. The pilot ejected and plummeted down toward the South China Sea, as the cockpit broke into pieces. The damaged EP-3 rolled onto its back and made a steep dive from eighteen thousand feet to about four thousand feet. Somehow the pilot got it righted and flying level. With the crew announcing an emergency, they were allowed to land at a Chinese base on the island of Hainan.

Although the Americans were able to destroy some data while in the air, they were forced out of the plane soon after it came to a stop. The Chinese obtained a trove that included cryptographic codes, surveillance manuals, secrets related to our technological capabilities, the names of US agents, and significant amounts of data gathered from our adversaries around the world. The Americans were released after ten days, but the Chinese held on to the airplane for months. This loss of secrets and specialized technology was one of the worst in history.

Tales of what can go wrong on military missions are more than dramatic bits of history that spice up a barstool conversation or, for that matter, a book. They stand as constant reminders that both human lives and national interests are on the line in every flight, whether it's a training exercise in the States or electronic eavesdropping on a geopolitical rival. On our surveillance missions we kept our focus on our job, knowing that the possibility of an emergency was always a moment away.

In Turkey we operated from the NATO base at Incirlik, which is about twenty-five miles from the Mediterranean. This was another place that had begun to decay but was coming back to life to support the wars in Iraq and Afghanistan. On nights off we sometimes went out to explore empty facilities, including a base housing area that felt a little like a small town circa 1985 that had been hastily abandoned by every townsperson. The buildings were relics of the Cold War, when Turkey served as part of the bulwark that to Moscow's constant consternation contained the Soviet Union. The most famous chapter in the story of US-Turkey relations occurred in 1962, when the Soviets tried to break our defensive line by placing nuclear-tipped missiles in Cuba. President Kennedy threatened war and the United States military was placed on high alert, which kept B-52s continuously armed and manned for takeoff. War was averted when Moscow relented, and Kennedy gave the USSR the face-saving gift of removing fifteen obsolete nuclear missiles—"those friggin' missiles," Kennedy called them—from Turkey. The Turks, who opposed this move, would soon get better nuclear protection from bombers based there, but this was done quietly. It also received foreign aid separate from military spending.

Forty-four years later, Turkey's role in joint anti-terrorism efforts

began after 9/11, when it was one of the first countries to offer con-
dolences and volunteer to join the American-led War on Terror.
Turkey's help included the allies' use of the base at Incirlik, which
was vital for transporting supplies, armament, and personnel to both
Iraq and Afghanistan, and open passage through their skies for any
aircraft headed to war zones. The Turkish government also shared,
secretly, a wealth of intelligence based on its well-developed network
of spies and its ability to intercept and analyze communications.
Planes carrying Al Qaeda fighters who had been captured on the
battlefields in Afghanistan refueled in Turkey, and this level of cooperation occurred despite the way it irritated other countries where
Islam predominates. For the most part, the Turkish people seemed
to support their country's role in the global anti-terrorism campaign,
and this was true of people in most of the countries that had joined
the effort.

Our mission had become routine for KC-135 crews, who were
rotated in and out of Incirlik. We usually took off at night and flew
350 miles across the width of the country to the Black Sea coast,
and then to a designated part of the sky called an "anchor" or "box."
There we flew in set patterns, waiting for one of the big C-5 and
C-17 transports headed to Iraq from Europe to appear out of the
darkness—think of a giant shark suddenly appearing in a shadowy
ocean.

The C-17s are big enough to carry combat vehicles, including
tanks. The larger C-5 is such a beast airmen call it the FRED, for
Fucking Ridiculous Economic Disaster. It's funny, but also wrong.
Capable of operating under extreme conditions, including on dusty

dirt airfields, no other plane can supply a ground force so efficiently. Built at a fraction of the cost of a B-2 or an F-22 Raptor, many C-17s have been flying for more than thirty years. The environmental record is harder to assess, but given that the US military is the single greatest consumer of fuel in the world, the C-5 probably accounts for a very small percentage of the total.

Although US aircraft operated overhead almost every day, most Turkish people never noticed us. Most of my missions were conducted at night, and we were back at Incirlik before people in Turkey got up for the day. On our few daytime assignments, we followed the rules for minimizing the noise we made and got so high in the sky that you would have to know we were up there to spot us.

We felt good to be participating in an anti-terrorism campaign, which, by most measures, was going well. In Afghanistan we had delivered lethal accountability to Al Qaeda and its protectors and had captured other bad guys from around the world. Yes, errors in the assessment that brought us to invade Iraq had created a growing controversy. But that war had become a magnet for terrorists whom we were able to confront there. Also, our success in preventing Islamic terrorism was undeniable. The United States had suffered no more successful attacks. Among our NATO allies, France, Germany, Italy, Denmark, Canada, Belgium, Poland, Turkey, and others also suffered no lethal attacks. Tragically, Spain and Great Britain had each experienced multiple mass-casualty events in a single day. Altogether, 249 people were killed. No one should diminish these devastating attacks. However, in the ensuing decade, just one person, a soldier, would be killed by an Islamic extremist in Great Britain. Spain would suffer no fatalities for an even longer period. It's impossible to say how many plots were thwarted in that time. However, at least thirty major planned attacks were stopped.

Given Turkey's proximity to countries that spawn terrorists— Iraq, Afghanistan, Syria, Iran—its experience was noteworthy. Indeed, as the Cold War gave way to the War on Terror, America continued to play a big role in safeguarding its security. The United States also provided economic aid. Together, defense and dollars gave American presidents decisive leverage with countries spanning the world. Today we backstop security for half the world's population and shoulder the main responsibility for keeping trade routes open for the entire planet. These roles explain why every branch of the armed forces, even the Coast Guard, operates important foreign bases. Indeed, if you count tiny outposts, we have about 750 foreign locations.

My time in Turkey turned out to be a perfect moment to be exposed to the country's political and strategic importance. Bilateral relations were still on the path set immediately after World War II. Turkey's democracy remained a model for the Muslim world. Progress was being made in granting women and ethnic minorities equality, and Islamic extremism had been unable to put down roots. Prime Minister Recep Erdogan, who was, at that time, committed to gaining admission to the European Union, had even begun negotiating with Turkey's large Kurdish population—thirty million or so—which was part of a community of fifty million that considered the region where Turkey, Iran, Iraq, and Syria meet their native land. Wherever they lived they shared an indigenous culture and a passion to correct a wrong done to them at the end of World War I. Back then, the allies promised them a state, only to withdraw the pledge three years later. Ever since, their yearning for freedom has appealed to many in the American foreign policy establishment. They became even more deserving, in their eyes, when, after 9/11, they became our allies.

Given my consuming interest in foreign affairs and military policy, I soaked up both the history and current state of Turkish-American affairs. Although I quietly harbored dreams of getting involved in the American side of international issues, I couldn't have known I would eventually become one of those in the US government who supported the Kurds out of respect for the blood they shed with us in Iraq and for their inextinguishable desire for self-determination. It would become clear to me that in our relationship with Turkey we should use the usual carrots and sticks to encourage Erdogan to give the Kurds more autonomy. We would owe the Kurds even more after they fought and died with us in the successful campaign—from 2014 to 2017—that brought down the medieval "caliphate" established in Syria and Iraq by a vicious terror organization called ISIS.

Any other American president would have rewarded the Kurds by doubling down on our efforts to advance their cause. Donald Trump would not. In an episode I will cover in greater detail later, Trump retreated from a commitment to protect Kurds who had fled Turkish forces and taken refuge in neighboring Syria. He removed

American troops who had been protecting the Kurds. Then Erdogan, whom Trump had once called his "favorite dictator," invaded Syria. As Kurdish civilians were killed by Turkish troops, Trump declared that the United States had no interest in events in a place he called "a lot of sand." More than two hundred Kurdish civilians would be killed by Erdogan's troops.

What did Trump do after Erdogan defied him? Just before he left office in 2020, he *increased* Turkey's foreign aid to more than $200 million in domestic aid, more than triple the amount given during the previous decade. Why did Trump do this? It might have had something to do with his stated affection for strongmen—Erdogan, Kim Jong Un, Xi Jinping, Mohammed bin Salman, Abdel Fattah al-Sisi—or with his business in Turkey, where he had earned $13 million for lending his name to a real estate project. His daughter Ivanka had lobbied for the development's approval by the Turkish government. She might want to do it again.

IN MY THIRD DEPLOYMENT OUTSIDE COMBAT ZONES IN COLOMBIA, we refueled planes that searched for illegal coca farms and processing facilities as well as elements of a rebel army that had begun—I kid you not—in 1964. This army, called the Fuerzas Armadas Revolucionarias de Colombia (FARC), funded itself through hostage taking and ransom demands and taxing the coca farmers and processors in the regions they controlled. The FARC was not some ragtag band of freedom-seeking idealists. They were hardcore Marxists who terrorized civilians. When I arrived, they had recently committed mass murders and been condemned for these acts by the United Nations.

When they weren't killing Colombian soldiers and local citizens, the FARC was kidnapping them and demanding ransoms. Thousands of people were abducted and detained. Most were held for short periods of time in relatively decent conditions and released when the FARC received ransoms of a few thousand dollars per person. However, the guerillas demanded as much as $1 million for high-profile captives. When they didn't get the money, the hostages were subjected to horrific treatment. Routinely deprived of food, shelter, medical care, and clothes, some were chained to trees while others grew ill from malnutrition. All were forced to participate in frequent long marches through the jungle so they would not be found by searchers.

Three Americans—Thomas Howes, Keith Stansell, and Marc Gonsalves—had been captured by the FARC in 2003 after their airplane crashed into a tropical forest the size of California during a joint surveillance operation with the Colombian military. About a tenth of the region had been abandoned by the Colombian government and was being run by the guerillas as a kind of country within a country. In this area, vehicles could navigate just two two-lane roads. Elsewhere people traveled along footpaths or in small boats that plied muddy rivers. FARC soldiers, who had lived all their lives in the region, were far more familiar with the geography and landscape than the military. This meant the army had to hope for a stroke of luck or a FARC mistake to find a camp location, which almost never happened. Meanwhile, the information received by families of prisoners was generally restricted to photos of a loved one holding up a recent newspaper as proof of life.

The more brutal tactics were likely a desperate response to a sweeping Colombian-American security and social program offensive called Plan Colombia. Begun in 2000, during the Clinton administration, which committed $10 billion to it, Plan Colombia was not just about spending money to fight the FARC and feed the poor. The antidrug element of the program stepped up efforts to eradicate the coca crop while helping farmers raise legal cash crops and get them to market. At America's insistence, $20 million per year was invested in reforming civil institutions like courts and law enforcement agencies. The corruption in Colombia's government, at every level, was both undeniable and a key factor in support of the FARC in rural areas.

Plan Colombia continued under President George W. Bush, and an attack on a new heroin trade—some farmers had switched from coca to poppies—was added. Contrary to what many political critics assumed, the initiative worked well, driving down the acreage farmers devoted to growing drug crops and destroying more and more processing facilities per year. The amount of coca seized by authorities had risen sharply, and within a year the estimated production of cocaine fell off a cliff. Progress would be less dramatic in ensuing years, and for short periods the bad guys made their own gains. However, the trends remained positive overall well past 2010.

The civil society reforms saw a two-thirds reduction in homicides and an even greater reduction in kidnappings.

The success of the program affirmed that the United States was still what many called the "indispensable nation" when it came to addressing serious international issues. With the end of the Cold War and the collapse of communism (even China and Cuba were reforming), people everywhere were seeking freedom, peace, and stability like ours. So many countries turned to us for advice and aid that it seemed, at the time, like we might lead an international push toward democracy. However, one of the other dynamics of foreign policy, which becomes clear when you spend time in Latin America, is that we also tend to favor authoritarians if it suits our interests. People there remember that we backed this kind of leader in Panama, El Salvador, and Nicaragua. This makes our pro-democracy endeavors much more difficult.

Unfortunately, a certain segment of American citizens has always been isolationist or anti-interventionist, imagining we could safely ignore the world. This idea appealed to some even *after* 9/11, when polls suggested that as many as half of Americans gave some credence to conspiracy theories about the attacks. These 9/11 "truthers" were led by characters like radio host Alex Jones, who said the events of that day were orchestrated by a powerful cabal intent on establishing a "new world order" that would replace sovereign nations with a single regime. Joining others in a global anti-terror effort would only advance the plot.

Conspiracy theories are an extreme end point for an argument that begins with complaints about spending money overseas instead of at home—though since we reap strategic and economic benefits from military and development aid, this is a false argument. When it came to the illicit drug trade, the dark fantasies included: President Nixon began the War on Drugs to lock up Black voters; the CIA had sparked a wave of addiction by sending cocaine to urban centers; harsh sentencing laws for drug crimes were intended to fill prisons with Black men.

Debunking conspiracy claims is extremely difficult, especially when they reference national security or high levels of government. (Consider that more than fifty years later, millions of Americans still think the first moon landing—Apollo 11—was faked.) When you consider the sources of the conspiracy theories, they seem less convincing. They include overzealous journalists and activists who felt they had legitimate claims to make and former officials who may have had questionable motivations. For example, Nixon's counsel who went to prison following the Watergate scandal, John Ehrlichman, might have wanted to hurt Nixon by accusing him of pursuing a racist policy. In fact, there's no concrete evidence that Nixon wanted to reduce the Black vote via drug arrests. Similarly, only flimsy circumstantial evidence supports the charge that the CIA created a drug crisis in inner cities. And though harsh sentencing laws did hurt minority communities most, this was an unexpected by-product of the laws, not an intended outcome.

My attitude toward drug policy was very conservative, and I was certain that aside from occasional political grandstanding, most government leaders had been genuinely concerned about the effects of illegal drugs. In the late 1980s, media coverage of drug abuse—a crack cocaine "epidemic" hyped beyond reality—was so intense that in 1989 pollsters found that 64 percent of Americans considered drugs the top problem in the country. No issue had ever scored so high. Lawmakers responded to the voters with policies they believed would help. But as the press cooled off and drug abuse ceased to be a leading public issue, official concern remained. So did the laws that led to a truly incredible spike of incarceration—from less than four per one thousand men in 1985 to nearly ten when I went to Colombia.

I had been taught from the first grade on that drugs posed a terrible threat and that our efforts were necessary. In the beginning, I heard First Lady Nancy Reagan's "Just say no" message. Then, in sixth grade, daytime TV began running spots featuring an egg being fried in a cast-iron pan and a narrator announcing, "This is your brain on drugs." Like just about every kid, I had attended D.A.R.E.—Drug Abuse Resistance Education—classes in school. And then there were alarms about drugs sounded at church, and of course all the messages I received from my family. (I trusted these authority figures even though, in a twist of great irony, the D.A.R.E. officer who visited my sixth-grade classroom would be arrested and criminally charged with—yep—drug possession.)

Between my concern about America's drug issues, and interest in an alliance that made Colombia part of America's world, I welcomed the chance to participate in Plan Colombia. It was yet another example of how our contact and cooperation with other countries improves our standing in the world. Add our military's response to natural disasters, and people in need everywhere consider our engineers, aviators, search-and-rescue personnel, and ordinary troops who move lifesaving supplies to be heroes. Learning about our impact on the world and comparing it with the attitudes of people back home would prove invaluable to my future life in politics. But at the time I just filed away what I saw and heard and anticipated future deployments where I might fulfill the mission that motivated me to enlist. To be blunt about it: After leaving home and family and waiting for years, I wanted in on the fight.

CHAPTER 5

Lessons of War

At thirty thousand feet, the landscape of war can look like the landscape of peace. When I began flying tanker missions in Iraq in 2005, what lay below us was a land where sparsely traveled two-lane roads sliced across vast swaths of tan- and rust-colored desert. Green farms flanked the Tigris and Euphrates rivers. Quiet villages baked in the sun.

From the windows of our plane, it was hard to tell that on the ground people were fighting, and dying. You couldn't sense the fear and hopelessness that were growing among everyday Iraqis and that a growing insurgency, fueled by Islamic fundamentalism, was pulling the US military into a quagmire.

The stalemate of 2005 would have been unimaginable in the early days of the war when the American-led allied force began a now famous four-day bombardment—commanders called it "shock and awe"—and then a "running start" attack by ground forces. Our armored divisions and infantry, which had assembled in neighboring Kuwait, moved forward at a pace that was so rapid that the enemy fell into disarray. Officers lost contact with troops and troops felt so disoriented that many abandoned their positions, choosing to surrender or go home rather than face the onslaught. Baghdad fell in just under three weeks. Three weeks later, President Bush landed on an aircraft carrier at sea to give a rousing speech in front of a banner that declared "Mission Accomplished."

This celebration obscured the growing evidence that the war in Iraq had been authorized on the basis of flawed intelligence. Iraqis didn't aid the 9/11 attackers, as officials first speculated, and, though Saddam Hussein confused the issue, his forces didn't possess weapons of mass destruction. These were the two justifications offered for war by the Bush administration, but by the time he announced the start of the invasion, the president had stopped suggesting a connection between Iraq and 9/11. Instead, he spoke only of liberating the Iraqi people from strongman Saddam Hussein's rule and protecting the world from "an outlaw regime that threatens the peace with weapons of mass murder."

This claim of "Mission Accomplished" would prove premature as a robust insurgency of Islamic extremists and veterans of Saddam's military grew to wage war against the allies. They planted thousands of bombs called improvised explosive devices in the roads, and soldiers were killed or injured when their vehicles drove over them. They also carried out direct attacks that became ever more brazen and ambitious. In 2004, thousands of insurgents fought US forces in two battles over the city of Fallujah. Ten weeks of combat, in total, left 122 Americans dead, and though it was not a defeat, Fallujah made more folks back home realize that the war was not going as well as they assumed.

Americans would have been better informed of the realities of the war if more people had had direct contact with those who served. In fact, only about seven tenths of a percent of Americans were in the military, and everyone else, outside of their friends and families, had taken to heart what President Bush said about going about their lives as if 9/11 had not happened. It was widely accepted that this would prove that the terrorists had failed and, indeed, it had the benefit of averting the economic catastrophe that would have come if people did not continue to work and live as they had before.

This life-as-usual approach reflected a statement a high-ranking Bush official made to a reporter two years into the fighting: "We're an empire now, and when we act, we create our own reality. And while you're studying that reality—judiciously, as you will—we'll act again, creating other new realities, which you can study too, and that's how things will sort out." The same writer who revealed the empire remark reported an on-the-record statement from former Reagan administration official Bruce Bartlett, who predicted that if Bush won reelection in 2004, despite Iraq, "There will be a civil war in the Republican Party." This fight, which did come after Bush won a second term, pit extremely conservative, faith-guided Republicans against traditional policy-oriented Republicans. Bush would lead the religious side. "He truly believes he's on a mission from God," said Bartlett. "Absolute faith like that overwhelms a need for analysis. The whole thing about faith is to believe things for which there is no empirical evidence." Bartlett paused, then added, "But you can't run the world on faith."

I understood the kind of faith that moved Bush and his supporters, and I felt it too. As a conservative Christian and patriot, I supported the war effort and was especially concerned about protecting our troops. But unlike our soldiers and Marines, tanker crews, including mine, were assigned to Al Udeid Air Base just outside Doha, Qatar. Located on a peninsula that juts into the Persian Gulf from southeastern Saudi Arabia, Qatar is a mega-rich petroleum state governed by an authoritarian but pragmatic monarchy that preserves itself by using a light touch when it comes to rights—women are allowed to drive there—and by spreading the wealth. The country's 250,000 native-born citizens constitute the richest population in the world. Nine out of ten work at government-funded jobs. However, no amount of money could buy tiny Qatar the military needed to give it security in a region that is one of the most dangerous in the world. Thus they needed our help and offered, in exchange, a base that could support the fight in Iraq and serve as another outpost for our global military.

For those of us stationed there, Al Udeid was as safe as any base in America. In fact, when a European think tank measured terrorist attacks since 1979, the country didn't even appear in the top fifty. The murder rate was one fifth the rate in the United States, and perhaps because the government imposed the death penalty on people caught dealing, Qataris' use of illegal drugs—everything from marijuana to opioids—was less than 1 percent of the rate in the US. In the meantime, their country was fast becoming a desert wonder.

One shopping mall's interior was built to resemble Venice, complete with canals. At a new air-conditioned "sports city," you could attend events or play yourself. In the cooler evening hours, you could ride a camel or watch a bunch of them race, hang out at a five-star resort, take a desert safari, or go "dune bashing" in a 4x4.

All of the above contributed to the unease I felt about my role in support of the people whose lives were at risk every day as they engaged with the enemy directly. War at a remove can challenge a fighter's identity. Are you really at war, personally, if your role involves flying miles above the range of any enemy weapon just to support others? Is your status diminished, especially in the eyes of others, when you are based in a noncombat region of the theater, where you never hear the alarm and the warning—"incoming, incoming, incoming"—that announces an attack?

I don't mean to say that Al Udeid was a perfect paradise. It could get as hot as a pizza oven, and since it was surrounded by a very warm sea, the humidity was relentless. On the worst days, it felt like you were breathing through a hot, wet towel. Although officers got decent accommodations, the housing for airmen resembled the temporary classrooms you see at some schools. When the aged air conditioners failed or the plumbing stopped working, frustrated inhabitants would sometimes trash their own quarters. Also, morale was eroded by some of the unusual laws in a devoutly Muslim country. Public displays of affection, Bible studies, and public consumption of alcohol were forbidden everywhere except on base. Out of respect for local sentiment, alcohol consumption was limited to a three-drinks-per-day limit.

Worse than the limits set by Qatari officials were the bullshit rules that governed life inside the gates of the base, which got worse as each new commander tried to demonstrate a greater commitment to safety and order. Veterans of Al Udeid will tell you about the ridiculous requirement that everyone wear a reflective belt at all times. Designed to be worn only by people who worked on the tarmac, the belts ensure safe operations around aircraft. Nowhere else was I ever required to wear one as I went about my daily business. But at Al Udeid I did. I also did my workouts with my T-shirt tucked into shorts because . . . well, I can't say why. It was just a rule.

At other bases, officers understood that a little leeway is great for morale, so they let most minor infractions slide. The commander at Al Udeid was different. He maintained a small army of enlisted men and women—the type who would have been hall monitors in junior high—to police the belt requirement, T-shirt standard, and other rules. I once got caught in the chow hall wearing something out of regulation. I demonstrated to the soldier that I was fed up with the rules—or, to be more precise, I reminded this particular guy that I outranked him. He ran and fetched an officer who outranked me, which left me with no choice but to comply. If I could go back in time, with my current rank of lieutenant colonel, I'd fire half those monitors and all the people who crafted the ridiculous regulations.

While the uniform narcs were insufferable, the teams that supported our refueling mission were top-notch. Maintenance crews kept the old planes in top shape and the people who ran things on the ground worked with the perfect combination of efficiency and caution. The main hazard for military fliers who left the bubble of

Al Udeid came on takeoff and landing and involved industrial-caliber lasers, flashed from the ground, that could produce blinding light inside a cockpit. When this harassment began, local officers wondered if these were low-level enemy attacks. However, this theory was dismissed in favor of the belief that it was just a matter of pure jackassery. Idiots all over the world were shining these things at planes. Among those who were caught were some who said they just wanted to see if they could hit a plane with their beams. Others wanted to feel the power of forcing a pilot to react. Fortunately, the chance of a serious incident was low, but even so, at takeoff and landing we were required to wear uncomfortable and ridiculous-looking red goggles as a precaution.

Once we were airborne and over the Persian Gulf we might hear impotent squawks from Iranians talking on an emergency frequency. They would say, "American aircraft at thirty thousand feet tracking one eighty-five, you are entering Iranian airspace. Turn immediately." Their order to "Turn immediately" suggested they would take action if we didn't, but they never sent up any aircraft to challenge us. In fact, the only planes that ever menaced us over the Gulf were our own fighter jets, flown by hotshots who thought it might be fun to bother us a little.

The most taxing aspect of these refueling flights was the time we spent aloft, which could stretch to eight or nine hours straight. During this time, we flew inside our assigned "box" in a certain part of the sky, listening to voices from air traffic control, airborne early warning aircraft, and planes headed our way. Every once in a while a fighter or bomber would pull up behind us. We'd engage in our little refueling dance and, after their tanks were full, they would go back to chasing and firing on the bad guys. For us, the work was no different from exercises over the United States except that we knew that the planes we fueled were being used to take out real enemies and protect our men and women. This was a key moment in the war. American fatalities had roughly doubled between 2003 and 2004 and would stay at a relatively high level of about nine hundred per year for three years. The number of wounded approached the same level monthly. Consider those with life-changing wounds that resulted in amputation or those with post-traumatic stress disorder and you get a sense of how much suffering was taking place on the ground.

I HAD MY CLOSEST ENCOUNTER WITH COMBAT-WOUNDED SOLDIERS when my plane was refitted to ferry the wounded from the war in nearby Afghanistan to medical care in Germany. We could carry more than a dozen soldiers—some in seats, others on secured gurneys— as well as medical staff and supplies and devices including medical-grade oxygen, anesthesia equipment, and surgical kits. The doctors and nurses had everything they needed to provide almost any kind of care, including emergency operations.

Medical evacuation flights were made at night, when the enemy would have the most trouble targeting a blacked-out plane flown in an evasive way. But though we were not fired on, we once had an emergency when we discovered that the landing gear on one side of the airplane had failed to retract after takeoff. In flight, a dropped wheel and its supports create drag, which can add enough to fuel consumption to affect whether we could reach our destination. We had a little success using a manual crank to raise the wheel but after we did all we could, our boom operator peered out some tiny windows in the belly of the fuselage and saw that the gear was still hanging.

Knowing we would be taking a little risk on fuel, we plotted a landing at a midway airfield. The crew favorite was Turkey, for a frivolous reason—we knew we could de-stress with a drink there. The trouble was that the medical team didn't know if the base in Turkey could offer the high level of care they wanted for one soldier whose critical condition had been the main reason for the flight. This meant the best choice would be either a return to the air base at Bagram, Afghanistan, or the risk of making an unplanned, almost emergency, diversion on the way to Germany. Bagram was the obvious choice. This time we operated in daylight, but there was no anti-aircraft fire. The stuck landing gear went down with no problem and was repaired by mechanics so we could depart again about fifteen hours later.

Partway through the second flight I walked back to visit with the injured, who had everything from traumatic brain injuries caused by improvised explosive devices to life-threatening wounds suffered in firefights. The first soldier I spoke to, who was the first freshly wounded combatant I had ever talked to, was in one of the beds. He was practically covered in bandages and his eyes were filled with blood. However, he was able to talk.

"I just want to go back," he said. "I left my, my boys behind."

Many people may enlist out of a love for their country, but they fight hard because of the bonds they form with one another. The higher the risk of their mission, the tighter the connection, until, to a person, they say they are primarily concerned about the soldiers to their right and left.

In general, I found that America's fighters in Afghanistan were motivated and, at least prior to 2010, optimistic. I think that this was because there was no real controversy around their deployment, as there was in Iraq, and the locals, especially women liberated from extreme religious laws, said their lives were better than they had been under the Taliban.

The World Trade Center site was still smoking when, on October 6, 2001, American bombs and cruise missiles rained down on Afghanistan, where the Taliban government had protected Al Qaeda. Twelve days later our first ground troops arrived and, with our allies, took the country in a matter of a few weeks. We were denied complete victory when, in December, we tracked Osama bin Laden to the mountains bordering Pakistan, and he escaped. Nevertheless, the swift and powerful approach was considered such a big success that once the country was more or less stabilized, resources were shifted to Iraq.

THINGS GOT SO HAIRY IN IRAQ THAT BY 2006 THE WHITE HOUSE had decided to send about 25,000 additional troops—it was called a "surge"—to try to reverse a rise in coalition casualties and bring a level of safety to cities and towns. Millions of Iraqis were afraid to go out to work, shop, attend school, or worship at a mosque for fear of getting caught in a battle or forced to pay a bribe to someone who claimed to be an insurgent "tax" collector.

One key to making life safer for regular Iraqis and our troops would be to remove (a euphemism for "kill" or "capture") the ground-level commanders who were directing the enemy's hit-and-run attacks and receiving supplies and even tactical advice from the military in neighboring Iran. (This was the country where people called the United States "the Great Satan" and marched chanting "Death to America.") Especially concerning to us were new Iranian-made mines that could pierce our armored vehicles. The problem was that these guys were hard to find and, if they were located thanks to an extraordinary effort or a lucky break, many moved before a team could be organized and sent to get them. The same was true for the Iranian advisers who were difficult to track as they came in and out of the country.

According to a story I heard, this problem came up at a command center as two generals—one Army, one Air Force—crossed paths in a restroom. The Army general voiced frustration about enemies who escaped because of inadequate surveillance. The Air Force general told the other that he had a solution: a nimble little surveillance plane flown by the Air National Guard. Called the RC-26, it was a two-engine turboprop packed with electronic eavesdropping devices and video cameras. It could fly fast and low, capturing the signals from thousands of cell phones. When one matched a number known to be used by insurgents or their Iranian allies, the technology could pinpoint the location, capture video of the area, and send both to ground troops without delay. With the right coordination, a target could be reached in minutes, not hours.

Eager to be more directly involved in the war, I moved from the KC-135 wing in Milwaukee to the RC-26 group in Madison, Wisconsin. After training, I was sent back to the theater of the war. But this time I was posted in-country, at a joint Army and Air Force base in the city of Balad, which was about fifty miles north of Baghdad. Since no one was supposed to know what we were doing—really it wasn't known that we existed—our unmarked facilities were in buildings set apart from all the others. We were not permitted to take photos or tell anyone what we were up to. The secrecy was aided by the fact that the RC-26, which is a converted Fairchild Metroliner, looks like the kind of plane used to ferry bigwigs.

At Balad we pilots joined ground operators who belonged to Task Force 16 and Task Force 17, which were elite groups within the Special Operations structure. These were the fighters who would race to the spots we identified and kill or capture the enemy. A third element involved people you might call informants. Some monitored insurgents in Iraqi cities from Tikrit to Baghdad. Others were CIA spies who worked in Iran to get us a clearer sense of who was talking to whom. We used this information to track phone connections.

The CIA had been reluctant to use their people in Iran to track key players in the cross-border scheme. The spy bosses said they thought the mission was too risky, but it's also quite possible that they were bothered by the idea that the military would carry out an elaborate, indefinite clandestine operation outside of their control. Unwilling to take no for an answer, our side kept pushing. It took a year, but the CIA eventually signed off. The work, which was sometimes called "man hunting," began.

The target-kill-or-capture work was challenging, but we had been selected for the level of our skills. Our men on the ground were the fiercest and most well trained, well equipped, and motivated on the planet. And thanks to the information coming from our spies in both Iran and Iraq, including a network long operated by our Kurdish allies, we received accurate reports on whom we should look for and where they might be. This didn't mean the teams completed every assignment without problems. Critics said that too often the operators acted with too much aggression and violence. Of course, these critics weren't on the scene, putting their own lives at risk.

In one of the few RC-26 missions made public, a different team tracked a key Iranian official who was flying in to Baghdad. When they cruised over the city they found his cell phone signal emanating from an airport terminal and headed to check the taxi queue. When he emerged from the terminal, the plane's video cameras confirmed his identity. Our guys on the ground moved fast and captured him.

Sent by Iran's Islamic Revolutionary Guard's elite Quds Force, whose paranoia about Israel runs rampant, the captive first assumed our guys were Israelis. (So much for the assumption that only they have the most effective commando teams.) What followed next, unfortunately, showed that we also faced political obstacles that could be more formidable than the operational ones. The captive's diplomatic passport, and fear of reprisal, led the Iraqi government to release him. The local authorities also put Baghdad's Sadr City neighborhood off-limits, for fear of inciting the many residents who were inclined to support the insurgents. This had the effect of providing safe haven inside the capital of Iraq for terrorists determined to defeat the United

States and its allies and take control of the Iraqi government. Ordinary Iraqis themselves were growing impatient and began saying that their lives during Saddam's time in power had been safer and more economically stable. People were employed. The utilities worked. Kids went to functioning schools. These memories led many to switch sides, backing the insurgents over the forces they once welcomed as liberators.

The anti-insurgent missions came with far more risk than refueling flights. (By the way, once I transferred to the RC-26 unit I never went back to the KC-135.) Departing Balad required the fanciest flying I would do in the war. Hostile small arms fire was frequent enough, and if you don't think it poses a danger to warplanes consider that after Russia's recent invasion, a farmer in Ukraine brought down a low-flying enemy fighter with a hunting rifle. The key, as you might guess, is to aim in front of the plane and get off enough shots to improve your odds. That farmer got very lucky.

I evaded gunfire by racing down the runway and skimming along just high enough to get over the fence marking the airbase boundary. I'd then climb fast and at such a steep angle—it's called "standing a plane on its tail"—that small-arms fire couldn't reach us. I wouldn't say it was impossible to hit us with a bullet, but no one could do it deliberately. A freakish lucky shot? Perhaps. A perfectly timed, intentional round? Never.

The only moments when I felt like I was in danger in Balad came when I was taxiing and the runway was shut down because incoming fire had been detected. Apparently someone studied it and determined that a plane is more vulnerable moving under these circumstances than staying still. However, it was excruciating to sit there waiting to see whether a mortar landed nearby or, God forbid, directly on top of us. Over time I would take reassurance from the fact that these alerts were often false alarms—they could be set off by something as mundane as a welder's torch—or that the incoming rounds were destroyed by our own defenses before they landed. The few that got through landed where they did no harm.

With each attack, our side made some effort to chase down whoever might be shooting at us. However, the enemy did have ways to avoid getting caught. For example, they would freeze the mortar barrels and rounds, quickly position them in the field, and then run away. When the tube thawed and expanded, the round would fall down the barrel, hit the plate that compressed the firing pin, and take flight. Mortar tubes were so cheap, it meant nothing to abandon them, and though they never hit anything important, these attacks made us stop what we were doing and take cover.

Like everyone at Balad, I got used to the "incoming" alarms, which went off so often that people called the base Mortaritaville. Although I always took cover, I wasn't worried about a hit on our shelter. Everyone on our team was nonchalant about the whole thing, knowing that after a few minutes of talking shit we'd be returning to work. Unfortunately, this casual attitude led me to give my parents the biggest fright of my deployment. We were talking on the phone when the "Incoming, incoming!" alarm sounded. It was loud enough for them to hear, and I just said something like, "Hey, I gotta go!" Not realizing how all this would sound to them, I was relaxed about calling them back. As a matter of fact, days passed before I did. During that time, they were struggling to control their fear that I had been wounded or killed. I wouldn't do that again.

FROM MY PERSPECTIVE, THE SURGE WORKED BECAUSE IN ADDITION to increasing our fighting force, the Army got much more involved in projects that made things better for the Iraqi people. Street patrols and suppression efforts like ours reduced the violence. Utility repairs restored electricity and water supplies. Schools and other community buildings were repaired and updated. And as people emerged from their homes to discover the streets were safe, normal life returned.

This strategy followed the US Army/Marine Corps Counterinsurgency Field Manual, which suggested a hybrid approach that combined concentrated fighting adapted to wars with no front lines and more peaceful contacts with civilians. The author of the field manual, General David Petraeus, had spent much of his career studying the Vietnam War, which the US lost because so many of the people we promised to save from communism had concluded that we were actually making their lives more miserable. They began to support insurgents who brought the fighting into cities and towns that were supposed to be secure.

Petraeus had concluded that insurgencies grow when communities lose faith in outsiders who promise but fail to bring stability and

when they lose patience with incompetent and corrupt local officials. This frustration can lead to a level of nationalism and civilian
resistance that no amount of firepower can overcome. No matter the
nation, might cannot defeat people who are convinced they are
right.

In Iraq, some commanders didn't think Petraeus's strategy would
work and resisted using it. They represented a wound that had
opened after Vietnam and remained unhealed. The American military's experience after our loss in Vietnam, and the Soviet Union's
experience after its failed ten-year war in Afghanistan, suggest that
these defeats end up dividing the officer corps that fought and confusing the decision-makers who either hesitate to take future action
or don't learn the lessons of the past. As you have likely noted, even
those who were civilians during the war have strong opinions about
the choice to go to war, how it was conducted, and the politics surrounding the conflict. (As the war neared its end, almost no one was
ambivalent. Critics of the whole endeavor said manipulative politicians and deceptive military leaders had blood on their hands. Supporters believed that protesters had made it impossible for Washington
to authorize the proper use of force and that they were the ones who
should be blamed for the casualties.)

In Iraq it became obvious to me that Vietnam still cast a shadow
over the US military. Officers who had fought there fell into two
camps. On one side were those who agreed that soldiers were under-
mined by Washington, but who also said that the reason for going to
war was suspect and that diplomacy, aid, and investment should
have been used instead. On the other side were those who believed

the initial military mission had been justified and the US could have won, if only our fighters hadn't been handcuffed by harebrained policy.

In a paper he wrote soon after he was released from a prisoner of war camp in North Vietnam, future US senator John McCain focused on a US government that he said failed to "explain to its people, young and old, some basic facts of its foreign policy." On his side of the discussion there was wide agreement that the war was lost by the leaders at the very top, not the troops who were unprepared for asymmetrical war and did not receive a consistent message about the goals they were supposed to achieve. Also, Washington's rationale for war—to stop a communist takeover guided by China and the Soviet Union—defied the fighters' experience. They saw that the conflict was a civil war, not a proxy for the global contest between communism and democracy. How else would you explain the commitment and tenacity of forces that had begun fighting in 1956? South Vietnam would lose two hundred thousand military personnel. North Vietnam estimated it lost one million. These losses were suffered by countries with populations of roughly 20 million (North Vietnam) and 17 million (South Vietnam).

Senator John Kerry, who would become McCain's friend in the US Senate, represented the view of anti-war veterans and civilians. After his service as a patrol boat commander, Kerry became a radically outspoken activist. He talked about how, instead of going to war, we should have made a serious commitment to "soft power," which would have meant spending a huge sum on developing infrastructure and economic opportunity projects that improved the lives of the Vietnamese people. Instead, the United States had dropped more than three times the amount of ordnance that the Allies had used in all of World War II on a territory with few industrial targets and even fewer large military bases. If this couldn't win a war in a country the size of New Mexico, then we would never have won with just a military effort.

Kerry, who went way too far in criticizing our troops' conduct, eventually pulled back on his claims. However, his original stance alienated people in the military and those who have strong pro-military feelings. This sentiment did not change even after Kerry agreed with McCain when it came to fixing responsibility on civilian leaders and their enablers in the military. Both men would vote to authorize the wars in Iraq and Afghanistan, which were central to our response to 9/11.

Two of the key decision-makers in the Bush administration had to be considered part of the Vietnam generation. Defense Secretary Donald Rumsfeld had served in Congress during the Vietnam War. He was not an established hawk at the time. In fact, before his first campaign, he had trouble deciding whether he was a liberal or a conservative. But by 2002 he was an outspoken advocate for the use of military power. He was joined in this view by Vice President Dick Cheney. (After 9/11, Rumsfeld argued forcefully for military action against Saddam Hussein.) Together Cheney and Rumsfeld drove the warrior response to the terror attacks, which satisfied many Americans like me who had been enraged by what occurred and wanted action.

Cheney and Rumsfeld both sensed that America lost in Vietnam because of inadequate firepower and resolve, which led to long years of fighting, more than fifty thousand US fatalities, and nationwide protests against the war. This view of the country's traumatic experience also suggested that a larger force, unrestricted by rules designed to appease opponents of the war, would have prevailed. So it was that when Iraq became our target, the two hawks successfully argued for a huge invasion force that would quickly depose Saddam, defeat all of his forces, and hand the country over to the Iraqi people.

What most Americans—including just about every soldier—didn't know was that at the highest level, the military officers who led our forces into Iraq and Afghanistan were personally burdened by the Vietnam legacy because they had either served there or were commissioned soon after the war ended. Among them were General Tommy Franks, General George Casey, General John Campbell, General Michael Moseley, and Admiral William Fallon, who were all officers during that war. Also, from the day of the 9/11 attacks and for the next ten years, every general and admiral who headed the Joint Chiefs of Staff had fought in the Vietnam conflict.

President Bush hadn't fought in Vietnam, but he had been in the military during that time, serving as an undeployed fighter pilot. After 9/11 he seemed to look for a way to both mount a fierce attack on those countries that had enabled the terrorists while encouraging the American people to return to the lives they enjoyed before the attacks. With the draft a part of history and the US military an all-volunteer force, few would feel the sacrifice, and they could be expected to be more patient than Vietnam-era Americans whose sons were drafted into combat. With all the fighting being done by professional soldiers who were rotated between war and recovery periods back home, many Americans all but forgot the fighting being done in their name, half a world away.

WHATEVER YOU THOUGHT ABOUT THE JUSTIFICATION FOR THE IRAQ war, by the time I got there it was obvious that our strategy wasn't working. We had fired just about every supervisor in the Iraqi government, the Army, and the police. In some cases, entire departments were emptied. When local leaders failed to fill the vacuum, our undersized Coalition Provisional Authority proved incapable of running the country. Crime was soaring. Utilities remained damaged, which meant huge numbers of people lived without running water and with only sporadic electricity service. Today some places still lack clean water. More than $1 billion in cash, which had been sent to pay Iraqis who helped us, had just disappeared.

With the situation worsening for everyone except the insurgency, Washington and the allies authorized a so-called surge that increased the total force—American and allied—by about one third, and our forces employed Petraeus's strategy, which he called "clear, hold, and build." The clearing was done by regular soldiers who then held the territory they captured. The "build" part involved constructing everything from housing to a free and fair election system from scratch. In the meantime, large numbers of military police officers would patrol just like civilian police, bringing long-term safety to the streets.

Meeting the soldier with the blood-filled eyes reinforced my determination to get more directly involved in the war. I wasn't motivated so much by wanting to kill but rather by a desire to protect our men and women. Getting trained and deployed in the RC-26 put me into this role of defender of our side. It also gave me qualifications for two aircraft, which is rare, and a chance to pilot a plane that is much more exciting to fly.

The "more" included a bit of intrigue that came because I was gathering information that would pass directly to Special Operations units, who would race to the location where the technology packed into the plane identified a cell phone known to be used by a high-level insurgent. These were the men who either killed our people themselves or planned and directed attacks or the planting of IEDs. With each success, we neutralized a local leader.

The surge was working. The number of Americans killed dropped by about 80 percent in two years. At the same time, the number of insurgents killed jumped so sharply that two years later the number of enemy fighters we could even engage was reduced by about half. By 2009, our soldiers were able to walk many streets in Baghdad without the full armor they previously wore. Infrastructure projects put power and water services back online. Public markets, which sold everything from tomatoes to toilet paper, became safe, bustling centers of commerce again as shoppers returned. Iraqis and our soldiers chatted amiably on street corners and in cafés.

General Petraeus was transferred from Iraq to central command in the United States in the fall of 2008. Responsibility for the day-to-day conduct of the war would shift to General Raymond

Odierno, who came up through the ranks as an artillery officer, not a counterinsurgency commander. An immediate drawdown of troops would follow, and we would quickly fall to pre-surge levels.

Back in the United States, a flood of news reports and expert analyses fully disproved the claim that Saddam had an atomic weapons program or that his military had stockpiles of lethal gas or intercontinental ballistic missiles. The majority of Americans said that they didn't believe the rationale for the war in Iraq and said the same thing about the invasion and occupation of Afghanistan. President Bush offered a supposedly humorous take on the controversy when speaking at the White House Correspondents' Association dinner. He showed slides of himself searching the Oval Office while saying, "Those weapons of mass destruction have to be somewhere." In time I would hear from a very high-ranking Bush administration official that he thought Bush regretted ordering the invasion of Iraq.

As a lower-level officer, I could have no effect on any big decision made in Iraq. As a Midwesterner who discovered pro-military people expressing skepticism every time I went home, the disconnect between the people and their leaders led me to reflect on how I might better serve. I did believe that my experience in the military, in local government, and as a citizen of Heartland America offered me the kind of perspective that might help. I was also, quite frankly, possessed of an ego sufficient to believe that I should be involved. And so it was that I decided to go home and run for Congress in the election of 2010.

CHAPTER 6

My Cup of Tea

E veryone seems to jump into politics for the same reasons. They say they are patriotic. They have solutions for serious problems. They feel called by the people, the times, God, or the universe. Whether it's spiritual or intellectual, or an example set by family, I count myself among people who feel drawn to politics for the service aspect and to make things better for others.

On May 19, 2009, when I declared I would run for Congress before a crowd of nine people gathered at the Boy Scout Museum in Ottawa, Illinois, I stressed my desire to win so that I could protect our freedoms and, when possible, make life a little bit better for us all. I said, "There're seven hundred thousand people in this district, and they deserve to see a different kind of Republican candidate," adding that I would reach out to everyone, including Black and Hispanic voters who reflexively vote for Democrats but share my values.

But there's another motivator for going into politics that's pretty universal: ego.

No one talks about it, but who raises their hand and says, "Yeah, I think I should help guide the fate of the world's most powerful country"? The only people who do this possess either a healthy ego in the form of optimism and self-respect, or a sick one that represents dangerous insecurity. Ronald Reagan, a sunny optimist, had a healthy ego. The malignancy of President Donald "Only I Can Fix It" Trump's ego was revealed at almost every appearance, from his inaugural, where he spoke of "American carnage," to his petulant last day in office, when he departed without acknowledging his successor.

In retrospect, I recognized that in part I first ran for major office because of my ego, which is like Reagan's and not Trump's. I know this because my desire to serve began in the idealism of childhood, when Reagan was president and he made it seem cool. Like a big leaguer who starts in Little League, I had been training for it since I was a grade-schooler, putting up yard signs for candidates. I had accompanied my dad to political events, majored in political science in college, ran and won a county board seat at the age of twenty, and then managed my father's campaign for state senate.

In 2007, I talked to the press about challenging a well-liked Republican member of the House in a primary election, only to stand down because I didn't think I could win. But it took some nerve to do that. It also required some nerve to have a friend start a website called draftadam.com long before I announced I would run. This gambit did its magic, getting attention from the press and creating the sense that there may be a groundswell of more people than just the two of us. (Or four, including my parents.) But this was a harmless prank and, in the end, meaningless.

When I finally did announce my run for Congress, there would be four other Republicans and no GOP incumbent to take on in a primary because for the first time since 1995 a Democrat held the office. A former state senator, freshman Debbie Halvorson had surfed into office in 2008 on the enormous wave that presidential candidate Barack Obama achieved: 62 percent of the state's vote and an 8.2 percent national win. She had been helped by the lackluster quality of the GOP candidate and by a personal profile that would have appealed to people in the district: she had four children and worked seventeen years as a Mary Kay cosmetics saleswoman—lots of mothers in the area sold beauty products to friends and neighbors—before entering politics. She had been the first woman president of the state senate and had survived a serious cancer diagnosis before declaring for Congress.

Of course, I had my own profile. It included my faith, my prior engagement with the Christian conservative political movement, and my family's farming tradition, which was still ongoing and connected me to the history of the region. Add my status as a combat pilot and my past service as a local official, and I could present a lot of positives. Also, as a first-time candidate, I wasn't burdened by missteps, misstatements, and a record of votes on legislation, which is always a rookie's advantage. I was also moderate enough to announce my support for Obama's decision to send more troops to Afghanistan and to win support from local unions, who almost always went with Democrats.

My moderate conservatism was considered something positive, especially in a swing district where people were willing to be represented by either party. And I think that my similarly moderate demeanor—generally upbeat, respectful, and willing to listen—was helpful too. I smile and laugh pretty easily, and if you don't think this matters in politics, think again. In one experiment after another, people have been shown to be very good at looking at candidates' faces and determining whether they are Democrats or Republicans. People say Democrats are warm, likable, and trustworthy, while Republicans are powerful, dominant, and mature. People separate the two groups accurately and this makes you think they determine their votes on what they read in a person's face. But what if you are sincerely warm and trustworthy but also manage to appear powerful and mature? Based on the feedback I received, I came across as someone with all these traits, which made me a good candidate in a divided district.

Oddly, and this is something I didn't realize at the time, although my crossover appeal worked in my district, it wasn't going to be a permanent asset in the GOP. I didn't fully grasp how the culture war that the Republican Party had begun in the 1990s—with fierce and vocal alarms about the so-called homosexual agenda, cultural diversity, immigration, and liberal sexual mores—was becoming so deeply rooted. I thought this kind of identity politics was anathema to conservatives. We had always rejected the way Democrats seemed to focus on this group and that group, rather than seeking unity. Second, even though I had been raised in a very conservative faith, I respected everyone's religious journey. I did oppose abortion, but I didn't consider the other side to be evil. Finally, I thought I should run on my personal character and policy priorities. To put it a different way, I would campaign not as an angry man determined to stop someone else, but as a trustworthy, decent man with a positive agenda.

At the start of 2009, regular, traditional Republicans were still thriving in Illinois's 11th Congressional District, as they were across the country. In fact, the data from the election of 2008 showed that, if anything, our candidate for president, John McCain, would have helped himself by choosing one of us normies to be his running mate. Instead, he elevated Alaska governor Sarah Palin, whose affiliation with the Christian Right political movement drove a significant backlash. The trouble for McCain was that Palin was never going to soften her positions. Having been raised in an aggressively political Assembly of God church, Palin wanted to join her version of faith with the government and require schools to teach the Bible's creation story—sometime roughly seven thousand years ago God created the cosmos, earth, and all living things in six days. Backers of this "creationism" also say dinosaurs coexisted with humans.

Before and after the election, opinion polls had shown that the more people got to know Palin, the less they liked her. For a large part of the GOP, many independents, and pretty much everyone who considered themselves live-and-let-live Libertarians, the way she blended faith and partisan politics was outside the American tradition. In studies that would take a few years to complete, political scientists determined that she cost McCain 2.1 million votes and helped push many more independents and moderate GOPers to choose Obama over their party's candidate. In an obvious reference to Palin, the editorial page of *The Economist* explained, "For many conservatives, Mr. Obama embodies qualities that their party has abandoned: pragmatism, competence, and respect for the head rather than the heart."

The Economist may have been right about the 2008 election, but I was concerned about trends that had nothing to do with individual candidates like McCain and Palin. I thought we needed to improve our brand to appeal to different kinds of voters, especially younger ones. The age difference contributed to a demographic problem that almost no one in the GOP seemed ready to address—a mortality gap. Both parties had known for a decade that death rates were higher for Republicans. The gap widened substantially to where Republican deaths exceeded 800 per 100,000 annually, but Democrats died at a rate of about 720. Obviously, we were headed in the wrong direction demographically.

While the political class was dissecting 2008, I spent two months of early 2009 on my last extended deployment in Iraq. In the air, I targeted the enemy for the commandos who captured or killed them in precision attacks. On the ground, I kept dodging the occasional mortar round. And since I was all but certain that I would soon announce my candidacy for Congress, I thought about the issues I would stress in a campaign.

Domestically, my big concerns were like those held by most of the country. The worst economic crisis since the Great Depression, which began in 2007 in the financial sector, had become a nightmare. Unemployment was shooting up. Mortgage delinquencies followed the same trajectory. In 2009, only three states saw more foreclosure filings than Illinois. Fortunately, at least for those who feared losing their homes, fewer than 2 percent did, because their depressed values made repossession a losing proposition.

I thought the Democrats had made mistakes in trying to end the crisis, and as I ran, I would point them out. I would reassure people that the Bush-era income-tax cuts, which were set to expire in 2010, would remain, so that families wouldn't have one more challenge dealing with a cratered economy. With so many people struggling, including small-business owners, it was not the time to tax them more.

I also thought that after the federal bailout program of financial institutions, which Bush began with $700 billion and Obama expanded to $1.1 trillion, more should be done to help people who lost their homes in the mortgage crisis. This wasn't the most popular view, because many people blamed the borrowers who wanted too much house for their own good. Out-of-control lenders didn't care if borrowers couldn't repay, however, because they just bundled these subprime loans and sold them to investors who expected a healthy cash flow. I wasn't against saving financial institutions. The economy couldn't function without them. But it was appalling that nothing was done for those who were being forced onto the street because of deals they had made with lending devils.

Most of my domestic policy positions were drawn from conservative orthodoxy, which has always been a necessary counterweight to liberal excesses. Like most Republicans, I thought the need to reform Social Security had become urgent, but despite the other side's claims to the contrary, I didn't want to end it. I wanted tax cuts for businesses that helped employment rise and tax policies that encouraged investment in them.

I deviated from the dominant GOP agenda in my willingness to increase the gas tax, to pay for infrastructure projects that would repair crumbling roads and bridges and update facilities like airports so we could compete in a global market. I also took a more compassionate approach to health care that varied from the simple goal of overturning Obamacare. It was unacceptable to me that so many people lacked access to health care, which is why I proposed a program to put high-quality free clinics in communities that were underinsured and underserved. Yes, this would be a government program, but sometimes we have to use the government to accomplish things that the private sector cannot.

My concerns for domestic issues were sincere, but my passion remained in defense and foreign policy. In Iraq, I had finished what was a kind of apprenticeship in national security and had come to realize that we were repeating the mistakes we were supposedly determined to avoid. During my early 2009 deployment, America began its seventh year in Iraq. This was longer than the time between our invasion of Vietnam and our withdrawal. The strategy that was supposed to save us from getting into another quagmire had failed. We were in another quagmire, and the new president, Barack Obama, seemed determined to repeat the Nixon mistake of stressing a US desire to abandon a job half finished, which Nixon would call "peace with honor." Obama even said that most of our troops would be gone by August 2010. Common sense tells you that this approach—announcing your desperate desire to walk away—is ridiculous. With this information, we confirm for an enemy that will never defeat us on the battlefield that we've lost our will. This is why the Taliban in Afghanistan adopted a saying: "You have the watches. We have the time."

I'm sure that some of Obama's military advisers had told him we needed to maintain the surge, continue to follow the new counterinsurgency manual, fully vanquish the enemy, and truly stabilize the country. But Obama had opposed the war in the first place, calling Saddam a brutal dictator who posed no danger to the United States, and the war a politically motivated adventure. Defense Secretary Donald Rumsfeld's guarantee that the fight in Iraq "wouldn't last any longer" than five months was absurd, as was his deputy's claim that we could cash in Iraq's own assets, most obviously oil, to pay for the war. With the American people getting sick of the war, it was President Obama's turn to be influenced by politics. His choice would become the centerpiece of my military/foreign policy critique of his presidency, and I believed it would resonate with voters who listened to my argument and recognized me as a credible critic.

When the other side wins the White House, attacks on the president drive the very next campaign. It was ever thus. And for good reason. In the seventy years prior, only one president had gained House seats in his first midterm election: George W. Bush, who picked up eight House seats in 2002. This was largely due to the upwelling of support he received after 9/11, which benefited every Republican on the ballot. But in 2010, Obama and the Democrats couldn't count on this kind of cross-party support. This meant that we had a good chance to win the House, end the Democrats' control of both White House and Congress, and block whatever policy we opposed.

If all of this sounds a bit like a game of chess, it is. In fact, it's like three-dimensional chess. At every level—local, state, national—both parties use every means they can to set up districts where their supporters predominate, contest the small number where a race will be truly competitive, and then win the House, or the Senate, or both. The point of this is not to win a game but to win the power to advance your ideas and block theirs. It is power with a purpose. Individual candidates play the same three-level game to win a primary race, if there is one, and then the fall election. Knowing I had to win a primary, which turned out to be a five-way race, I began working all three levels at once.

BACK IN THE DAY—A DOZEN YEARS AGO—LEADERSHIP SUPPORT still mattered in a political campaign, and I went after it at all levels. Locally, I racked up backing from the town and city council people, county sheriffs, treasurers, board members, and GOP county leaders. At the state level came senators and members of the Illinois House. It wouldn't have been fair for the Illinois Republican Party to select one out of us five for an endorsement, but they did give me access to important mailing lists. I know that at least some of my opponents didn't get access to these, because they didn't know to ask for them.

Many candidates also fail to appreciate the importance of momentum. From August 18, 2006, when the local press reported that I had subdued a knife-wielding man outside a bar in Milwaukee and received a national award for my quick response, occasional news items had kept my name before the public. No one could plan an emergency on the street, but almost anyone can publish editorial columns in local papers, as I did, and while the draftadam.com thing was a bit of a stunt, there are many ways to let people know you are considering running for office and to generate some buzz.

I knew I was making progress when I was invited to meet with the National Republican Congressional Committee in Washington. I was met by NRCC chairman Pete Sessions of Texas, an eight-term representative, and House minority leader John Boehner of Ohio, who had been elected to the House ten times. Although they were close in age and experience in the House, the two made an unusual pair. Boehner was a kind of happy warrior, open to compromise in the service of the country's business, and he always knew what should be on the agenda. Born into a family of twelve, he acquired his people skills at an early age. He started work in the family bar at age eight and learned to play pool like a hustler. He was warm, openly enthusiastic, boisterous, emotional, and profane. Legislation he didn't like was "a crap sandwich." He said fellow Republican Rep. Steve King of Iowa was an "asshole." And when members of the GOP caucus wouldn't raise the federal debt limit he told them to "get your asses in line." He chain-smoked cigarettes and, having grown up in his family's bar, loved a drink.

Sessions, on the other hand, was a bit of a hard-ass who seemed much more devoted to power for power's sake. He had said the GOP could look to the Taliban for inspiration about how to mount the political version of an insurgency. Unlike the Taliban, however, he had no serious policy agenda. In fact, at the time we met, his list of legislative objectives was blank. He personally favored a proposal by Steve King that would have denied citizenship to children of non-citizens born in the United States.

One of four children of a prominent Republican attorney and judge who became the director of the Federal Bureau of Investigation, Sessions had solid connections to politics and power. President Clinton had fired his father after he was accused of abusing the perks of his office. The man who signed the report and confirmed the charges was Attorney General William Barr, future ringmaster of Trump administration controversies, who knew how power was wielded. He knew because he had previously served as attorney general for George H. W. Bush from 1990 to 1991. The actions of these two men, one a Democrat and one a Republican, would have been more than enough to put a chip on the shoulder of a future congressman.

Thanks to Boehner's charm, which lightened Sessions's mood, our get-together was enjoyable and encouraging. Both men were deeply engaged in the effort to take over the House and Senate and end the White House's ability to push legislation through, but Boehner was the one who was clearly competitive without the need to hate the other side. He thought Democrats were wrong about most things, of course, but he thought he could work with them. I liked him very much and appreciated them both after they said the NRCC would back me. Boehner told me, "You're what we're looking for." He meant that the party was eager to find younger candidates with the right background and charisma and the poise to campaign and win.

Soon after the meeting, my campaign received a $5,000 contribution from the political action committee run by Rep. Eric Cantor of Virginia, who was Boehner's second-in-command. Having been anointed a "sky's the limit" politician by the conservative *Weekly Standard*, he was also, along with Kevin McCarthy of California and Paul Ryan of Wisconsin, one of three self-named Young Guns with leadership ambitions. They were considered antiestablishment in a time when Boehner was the epitome of the establishment.

After Cantor's PAC sent money, a flood of contributions came from committees operated by other members, including Aaron Schock, a freshman representing Peoria, who was the youngest member of Congress and the first person born in the 1980s to serve on Capitol Hill. Money being the lifeblood of big-time politics, and a way for people to gauge who may be ahead in a race, donations begat donations, and a sort of inevitability took shape around my candidacy. Next came endorsements, mostly from people who called hoping to get on board. We had some stationery made with our campaign letterhead at the top and a list of people who had endorsed me, in tiny print, running down both sides. Every Republican in the district received a letter sent on this stationery. You can bet that each recipient looked down the list and saw names they recognized and respected. About fifty thousand votes were cast in the five-way primary. I received thirty-two thousand of them.

With the pivot from the primary to the general election, campaigning got simpler but far more intense. The race was one of the few that both national parties, but especially mine, considered winnable. Although Debbie Halvorson had broken a fourteen-year Republican hold on the seat, no one in politics believed the district had turned from red to blue. It was far more likely that with an Illinois senator seemingly destined to become the first Black president in history, lots of people, including our voters in the 11th Congressional District, wanted to be part of making this happen.

In January, the residual glow of Obama's victory had led one of the country's most respected experts, Larry Sabato of the University of Virginia, to predict Halvorson would win. Distant as he was from the heartland, I think Sabato was a few months behind what had happened to the public mood since Obama was elected. His expanded aid for the finance industry and second auto industry bailout troubled not just conservatives but also independents and some Democrats who didn't like it when Bush enacted similar policies and didn't accept claims that these loans would be repaid. (Seven years would pass before the government would confirm an $8 billion profit.) In March, Democrats used their majorities to force Obamacare through the House and Senate, and with the president's signature, it became law. Then came an explosion of energy from opponents who had been organizing against the entire Obama agenda since before he took office. It was called the Tea Party, and it would alter GOP politics in ways, it's safe to say, that no one imagined.

Never led by a single person or entity, the Tea Party was a mostly organic protest movement that received significant boosts and encouragement from the deep-pocketed right-wing establishment and from the conservative media. The organic part began in 2009, when a young woman in Seattle who called herself Liberty Belle held small rallies against Obama's effort to bail out the economy and enact health-care reform. In Chicago, tech entrepreneur Karl Denninger was equally outraged by the financial institutions that crashed the economy. Then came the moment when the Chicago Mercantile Exchange cheered TV commentator Rick Santelli as he bashed "losers" who couldn't pay their mortgages. The traders' cheers seemed a little off-key, since the massive federal bailout of financial companies had saved many of their jobs. But the rant went viral and became an important factor in the Tea Party's growth.

The rank and file included mostly older people who had long held deep suspicions of the government. They got their news from radio host Rush Limbaugh and the Fox cable network. These sources described an America under constant threat from an out-of-control government, immigrants, anti-America media, gay rights campaigners, anti-Christians, and a president who may be hiding his Muslim faith and may have been born in Kenya and was therefore illegitimate. On the fringes were self-styled militiamen, 9/11 "truthers" who questioned the facts of that day, and anti-vaccine activists. Some described Obama's election in overtly or subconsciously racist ways.

Critics of the Tea Party routinely said it was fueled by racism. They also said that the involvement of big organizations—Club for Growth, Citizens for a Sound Economy, and FreedomWorks—showed the movement was being exploited by the establishment. According to Jeff Nesbit, who was then a consultant for these groups, they had long planned for a mass movement inspired by the Boston Tea Party. In 2007, the campaign for their ally Ron Paul had called for a "tea party money bomb" to fund hard-right candidates when George W. Bush was president. After Santelli's 2009 outburst, a political consulting company created the Tea Party Express and sent a brightly decorated bus on a national tour, paying to train activists, fund events, and operate websites. FreedomWorks held an expenses-paid Tea Party "boot camp" in Washington and sent teams of professionals to help groups nationwide.

It's important to emphasize that the fervor of the protesters and the growth of the movement could not have been fully manufactured. This became clear to me when the two Tea Party Express buses arrived at a rally in New Lenox, Illinois, and a crowd estimated at six thousand to eight thousand showed up to greet them. Speakers at the rally called for shrinking the government and stopping President Obama's health-care plan. They spoke as if a true disaster, one of many that Democrats planned, was about to destroy the country. Obama had made things difficult for himself by making the false claim, which he may have thought was true in the moment, that under his plan everyone would be able to keep their current doctor. When this was shown to be untrue, people began to question every other claim he made. Leaked legislative drafts suggested the very old could be denied certain care—this was ultimately removed—and contained a provision that penalized people who didn't have health insurance of any kind.

Although I was bothered by their methods and questioned their beliefs, I couldn't help but acknowledge the energy the Tea Party brought to the Republican Party. These people were revved up to vote and their main motivation—the details about Obamacare—was genuine and not being considered as the Democrats rammed it through. But over time the movement evolved further and further away from its original conception. At New Lenox, many of the signs that people held bore messages about issues that had nothing to do with the original Tea Party agenda: false claims that Obama wasn't a US citizen, calls for more religion in government, complaints about the federal deficit, demands for gun rights, and in one case, a call for the country to "outlaw GSEs," which are government-sponsored enterprises, like semipublic agencies that backstop mortgages.

Soon Fox News doubled down on coverage of the Tea Party to draw viewers, sending star commentators Sean Hannity, Neil Cavuto, Greta Van Susteren, and Glenn Beck to broadcast from rallies. Beck's show, which aired in the late afternoon, when many working people weren't free to watch, drew more viewers than all the others. He reached this height by literally screaming and weeping about the end of America and then promoting the Tea Party's potential to save the country.

By the summer of 2009, Tea Partiers were jamming senators' and House members' town halls, which were normally sleepy information sessions, and shutting them down with their own screaming and yelling. At some meetings things got so out of control that the member conducting the town hall fled for fear of their safety, and police dragged people outside. In Pennsylvania, Senator Arlen Specter had to be rescued when protesters began to follow him around. In Florida, scuffles broke out as protesters couldn't enter an overcrowded meeting where fifteen hundred people had filled every bit of space. Those shut out pounded on the doors so loudly that the speakers couldn't be heard. On Friday, July 31, Fox News personality Sean Hannity added a banner to his website that said, "Become a part of the mob! Attend an Obama Care Townhall near you!"

Hannity was one of the trusted sources inside the news bubble occupied by the part of America that would supply the foot soldiers for the movement, which had a little over 10 percent support from the country as a whole; small as this may seem, it represented 13 million votes. As polls and more in-depth surveys eventually showed, Tea Partiers came from the Fox News demographic, which was over age forty-five, wealthier, and more religiously conservative than their generation and the larger population as a whole. Worried that they would pay the lion's share of the health-care bill and receive little in return, they were far more likely to expect life would be getting worse for them. By a great majority, they didn't want tax money spent on funding schools in minority communities so they could come up to par with those in white-majority communities.

Toward the end of 2009, the Tea Party movement was divided by lawsuits, debates over strategy, and the effort by a national establishment group to bind Tea Partiers to a long-term political project. As the internal struggles were waged at the higher levels, people at the protests didn't seem to know or care. In 2010, the same nonreaction followed news that the Tea Party Express had spent a hundred thousand dollars on a 2010 Alaska cruise for staff members.

In my race I made a point of telling would-be Tea Party rowdies, "Let's keep the conversation respectable." This message, which they heeded, allowed me to accept their help while avoiding the negative aspects of the national movement, which was, in fact, known for its tendency to disrupt public meetings and drown out those with different views. As I said in 2009, "Let us begin by respecting one another. Working together in a civil fashion we can fix the system. I am committed to taking care of you."

By April 2010 the Republican establishment had seen polls that showed me running even with Halvorson in our bid for Congress, and contributions combined with spending by outside groups came at a rate that would eventually top $2 million. This was still far below Halvorson's final tally of $2.5 million, but it meant we could stay competitive. As it became clear that our local Tea Partiers were not going to disrupt public events with intimidation tactics, I started using the pronoun "we" to talk about the movement. I also accepted the support of Sarah Palin, who, truth be told, never asked me if I wanted it. This only made the Tea Party folks even more supportive. The Associated Press cited its support in an article about how my campaign had eaten away at Halvorson's lead. But it was about then that things got nastier than I would ever have expected.

An accusation of stolen valor is about one of the worst things anyone can say about a service member or a veteran. Hearing rumors going around about me falsifying aspects of my military service made me furious, and as evidence mounted that one of her staffers had been the source, Halvorson fired him. Next came people carrying signs describing me as a Nazi, which Halvorson condemned, saying her team had nothing to do with it. I believed her. Finally, there were the campaign ads. In a mailer, Halvorson turned my support for letting companies compete by investing abroad in China into the idea that I was either a double agent or a dupe. A photo of me superimposed on a Chinese flag drove the point home. In a TV spot she condescendingly offered the closing line, "Young man, you have no idea what you are doing."

As the former Mary Kay lady bashed away, interest in the race grew. By the time we began a series of debates, our contest had drawn intense public interest. Crowds swelled to five hundred or more, which would have been a very good turnout for a presidential primary candidate. She accused me of wanting to gut Social Security, when what I wanted was to fix its finances for the long term. In her telling, my preference for retaining the Bush tax cuts, to give certainty to businesses, became a handout to the rich. Among the more specific local issues I exploited was Halvorson's refusal, after the Tea Party storms, to hold town hall meetings. There were ways in which she could have done this safely and shown she wanted to hear from the people. Her refusal was a grievous self-inflicted wound.

Throughout the campaign I matched Halvorson's textbook attack with critiques that noted both her status as a career politician and her ties to Obama, whom she supported at every turn. We also argued that she was a puppet of Nancy Pelosi, Speaker of the House, whom the GOP consistently described, accurately, as a California liberal and member of the coastal elites many Midwesterners didn't trust. I could make these points with boilerplate statements and snappy retorts that the party considered on-brand and irresistible bait for the press.

Brand politics explains why for at least fifty years the same clichés have circulated in our campaigns. On the Democrats' side, it's "We want good things for everyone. They want to kill Social Security and Medicare, take food out of children's mouths, exempt the rich from all taxes, and pollute the planet into oblivion." On our side, it's "We're the responsible realists who will keep you safe and relieve your tax burden. Those people hate business and religion, and haven't met a government program they won't double in size every year."

The Republican Party expected every congressional candidate to talk about how we were better at managing the economy, better at stopping crime, better at creating jobs, and better at defending the nation. None of this was fair, but like the Democrats, we were committed to winning above all else. And as I learned, thanks to a powerfully effective pollster and campaign adviser, Frank Luntz, we had some of the best words—time-tested for their effectiveness—to fling at the other side. He was the one who developed the list of attack words—*corrupt*, *pathetic*, *sick*, *incompetent*, *traitors*—that helped Newt Gingrich win the House majority for the GOP in 1994. I wouldn't use the negative ones—well, I may have used the milder negatives like *crisis* and *status quo*—but I grabbed the positive ones like *duty*, *freedom*, and *common sense* for myself.

The moderate language, outreach to voters beyond the Republican base, and bond with the Tea Party gave me the kind of momentum that was noticed outside the district. In mid-October, *Time* magazine included me in a list of "40 Under 40" up-and-coming political leaders. *Time* had not yet fallen victim to the online competition that has made it a shadow of its former self. It was then so highly respected that the article became a subject of local press attention across the district. It seemed a bit strange that publications would consider another publication's article so newsworthy that they would publish articles about an article, but who was I to complain.

On election day, my 15-point victory over Halvorson was surprising only for the size of the margin. Like Halvorson in 2008, I benefited from a big win by my party, which gained control of the House with a whopping sixty-eight-seat gain. You'd have to go back to 1938 to find a bigger win. Our victory party was attended by more than a thousand people, and the next day the local paper was so enthusiastic, it sent a reporter to interview my family. My father said how remarkable it was to consider "this is a little kid we raised." I felt slightly overwhelmed by it all, and I took a moment to remind myself that on this day, the day after the election, more people were interested in what would be on *The Oprah Winfrey Show* than in what I had to say. I also thought about how Obama had graciously noted the "shellacking" he had received and promised to work with our side. I said the same thing.

CHAPTER 7

Crazytown

My serious skepticism about the Tea Party began as I noticed how powerful groups like FreedomWorks and politicians like Rep. Michele Bachmann hijacked it for their own purposes. After the Tea Party's 2010 success, FreedomWorks leveraged its relationship with the movement and began a fund-raising campaign that raised $25 million. This amount was literally twenty-five times more than the organization had ever received in a previous election cycle. It was being spent not on the movement's newcomers, but on establishment Republicans.

Bachmann, whom *Newsweek* called the Tea Party's "Queen of Rage," abandoned the movement's anti-spending stand by seeking extra federal spending for her district. She wasn't alone in playing both sides of the street while retaining her Tea Party cred. However, she made herself extra special by organizing a run for president with the intention of becoming the movement's favorite in upcoming primaries against Mitt Romney, Rick Santorum, Newt Gingrich, and others. Based on my contact with her, I had real doubts about Bachmann's fitness. In one exchange on the House floor, she told me that the son of a friend was a Navy pilot. She noted that I was a military pilot and said something like, "Do you know the Navy has airplanes?" I replied, "Yeah. You know, like on aircraft carriers?"

The queen announced her campaign at an event where Elvis sang "Promised Land" over the public-address system. She said she was running because of "the blessings God and this country have given to me" and made frequent references to faith in the words that followed. This emphasis struck a chord with those who waved the cross at Tea Party rallies. They believed that America should be devoted to their kind of faith and that its laws and government be based on a Fundamentalist view of the Bible. They called their theology dominionism, but their agenda, which stressed gaining control of the United States for Jesus, fit the definition of Christian Nationalism. Believers considered Bachmann, who had said she was an avid student of this belief system, one of their own.

I knew very little about dominionism. But I did know politics and understood that Bachmann must have known her chance of becoming president was nil. This meant she had some other reason for running. Lots of people run for president with something other than winning in mind. They run to advance their ideals or to become famous as they travel the country at the expense of campaign donors. (Bachmann often traveled in a sleek private jet.) They run in hopes of getting a TV job, a publishing deal, or fame to fuel a future campaign or to merit a high-level government job. Surgeon Ben Carson ran for president in 2015 and raised and spent more than $62 million before he quit. Donald Trump made him secretary of the Department of Housing and Urban Development, a job for which he had no qualifications.

The hustles that become apparent as you climb higher in politics shock some of the earnest Mr. and Ms. Smiths who go to Washington and discover the self-serving behavior. For instance, there was Republican Representative Trent Franks, who asked his staffer if she could help him have a baby "the old-fashioned way."

One person I trusted, and who remained trustworthy, was Speaker-in-waiting John Boehner, who was interested not in hustling for fame or money but in solving problems and creating opportunities for people. He was open to old school–style compromise with Democrats and among the factions in our party. He signaled his intent by adding me and another incoming conservative to the group that would guide our anticipated takeover of the House. Congressional freshmen attend a bipartisan orientation, which I intended to go to. Just before the date I finished an Air National Guard training flight, turned on my phone, and saw I had more than one hundred texts from Tea Party people who demanded I go to an event they were having instead. I thought to myself, "I'm no idiot. I'm going to the regular orientation." This crash course covered the basics of how the House works and taught us about staffing, and we sat for photo identification badges, which we would need until Capitol Police got to know us.

The freshman orientation was one of the last truly calm pre-session conferences I would attend. Those in the future would be marked by more debate, conflict, and protests. When I arrived at one meeting at a Florida resort, I saw that the Tea Party had sent people all dressed up like Revolutionary War officers—tricorn hats, knee breeches, blue coats—to protest at the entrance to the hotel and on the beach. It was a strange sight amid the palm trees, especially since they were supposedly Republican voters protesting Republicans they had just helped elect. I thought, "Whatever."

Back to 2011. After Boehner finally took the gavel from Nancy Pelosi in a ceremony that celebrated our centuries of the peaceful transfer of power, Boehner added me to his inner circle, which meant I would help him with the herding-cats work of keeping our members in line on votes he considered crucial. I welcomed the invitation to join Boehner's team because, to be frank, I was not fully resistant to the pull of the attention I was receiving and wanted a bit more. But I was happy mainly because I shared his sense of purpose about government, and I just plain liked him. Easy to talk to and free with invitations to have an after-hours drink and a smoke in his spacious office, Boehner had decades' worth of stories about working on the Hill and his years in Reading, Ohio, and he had plenty of jokes. He wasn't afraid of his high school nickname, Boner. And he wasn't shy about making fun of his own team. In 2011, he began calling himself "mayor of Crazytown." He would say DC was a place "populated by jackasses, media hounds, and a few normal citizens as baffled as I was about how we got trapped inside the city walls." He also joked that he spent every second of every day "fighting one batshit idea after another," beginning with conspiracy theories that insisted Obama wasn't an American citizen.

Looking back now, I can see that Boehner put me on his team to serve as a bridge between his group of traditional Republicans and the Tea Party group and those who were sucking up to them because they believed they represented the future. Boehner recognized the power of the Tea Party trend but was loath to encourage it because it was pushing the GOP further to the right. However, as a talented politician, he was always looking to find common ground with people who sometimes criticized him, like the rising star Eric Cantor, whom he made majority leader.

Unlike Boehner, who was all charm and bonhomie, Cantor was overtly ambitious and generally presented himself as serious, sober, and cerebral. In 2010, he, Paul Ryan of Wisconsin, and Kevin McCarthy of California had declared themselves to be the "Young Guns" of the House. The name had been drawn from the Western movie *Young Guns*, in which three upstarts track and kill their mentor after he murders the rancher who employs them. Released when the three congressmen were between the ages of eighteen and twenty-five, the story of betrayal and patricide fueled the fantasies of a generation who resented the world where baby boomers like Boehner might block their ambitions for decades to come.

Ryan, Cantor, and McCarthy had just published a book—*Young Guns*—to announce themselves as *A New Generation of Republican Leadership*, in the subtitle no less. Usually people wait for someone else, like a journalist, to write the book or article that tells the world that they are the next big thing, but since shamelessness was overwhelming modesty in every corner of life, especially politics, no one should have been surprised. The cover, dominated by a picture of them together, showed their unity, but they let it be known that they had individual roles: Cantor was "the leader," Ryan "the thinker," and McCarthy "the strategist." It reminded me of the Spice Girls—Posh, Sporty, Baby, Ginger, and Scary. As they promoted themselves, the Young Guns waxed alarmist, declaring Social Security already "bankrupt" (it wasn't) and announcing the country was headed for an economic "free fall." Boehner looked at these men who were suggesting he was too soft on the Democrats and were aiming for him, their mentor, and told the press that "the three of them know that my job is to make sure that they're well-qualified and ready to take my place"—he then added, to the laughter of the reporters—"at the appropriate moment."

Boehner understood the Young Guns because he had been in their position once. In 1997, the future Speaker won the caucus election to become GOP conference chair. He then joined a group from the class of 1994's self-declared conservative revolutionaries in plotting a coup against then Speaker Newt Gingrich. Gingrich had recently become the first Speaker of the House reprimanded and fined for ethics rules violations. The filing of ethics charges juxtaposed Gingrich's previous effort to exploit ethics rules to go after one of his Democratic predecessors, James "Jim" Wright of Texas. His original charges against Wright fell apart under scrutiny, but the ethics committee found other issues and Wright felt forced to resign. In using the ethics committee in a political way, Gingrich made use of a weapon previously set aside in a kind of gentleman's agreement. Eight years later Gingrich was targeted with charges that were more serious and, after investigation, stuck. After the vote against him, which more than one hundred Republicans supported, Gingrich seemed weakened. Boehner and two others in the GOP leadership won support for their plan to overthrow him from about twenty young guns of the day. Gingrich got word. He applied pressure to members of the caucus, and they returned to the fold. However, the mere fact that some members had hatched such a plan proved that an era of Republicans eating their own had arrived.

The use of the caucus chairmanship to push for a new level of conservative rule has become routine. Recent chairs have included the religious hard-liner Mike Pence (Boehner thought Trump's future vice president was a "fire-eater"); a Texan named Jeb Hensarling, who openly predicted socialism under John McCain; and now it's today's chameleon, Rep. Elise Stefanik of New York. Once a steadfast critic who refused to say Donald Trump's name, she saw which way the tide was running and became such a loyal supporter that Trump called her "One of my killers." She then won the conference leadership election.

UNLIKE STEFANIK, WHO BEGAN HER CAREER IN CONGRESS AS A noisy critic of her own party's leader, I started with a desire to be part of the team whenever possible and deviate from the House

GOP line only when my conscience, the needs of my district, or reason overcame this commitment. After all, I had been elected as a Republican devoted to the Republican agenda and also for my expertise in certain areas, especially the military. I got a chance to make my stance on military spending known before I was sworn in, as a guest on C-SPAN's *Washington Journal.* It was a most unusual program on a most unusual outlet, which, over the years, had become an authoritative source of political and governmental news. A channel founded as part of the licensing agreement the government made with the cable industry almost fifty years ago, the Cable-Satellite Public Affairs Network broadcasts proceedings of the House and Senate, important committee hearings, speeches, talks, and, in the case of *Washington Journal*, a live TV interview show that allows viewers to call in with questions. Announcers and hosts for C-SPAN play things so seriously, and with such a consistent commitment to nonpartisanship, that comedians and comedy shows like *Saturday Night Live* have fashioned bits in which the network's hosts serve as unblinking foils for callers and guests who say the most outrageous things. One of *SNL*'s skits began with a sober introduction of an address by Surgeon General Joycelyn Elders, played by actress Ellen Cleghorne, after Elders had been fired for saying schools should teach masturbation to limit teen pregnancies. (This really happened in 1994, amid an uproar by religious conservatives.) "Every year, many of our young people graduate from high school completely unable to masturbate," bemoaned the actress playing Elders. "And of those who can, most who can are able to do it only at a fifth-grade level. . . . This is a national shame."

It was a relief to know that the C-SPAN host would never ask me to talk about anything like the "national shame" *SNL* referenced, or any other shame, for that matter. Instead, I talked about the federal budget, arguing that despite my close affiliation with the military, I felt there should be no sacred cows in the effort to cut spending, and that I would vote for the Department of Defense to make reasonable reductions in spending. Two weeks later I was able to offer a specific example in my first speech on the House floor. The Pentagon was awarding a $100 million contract for newly designed and manufactured flight suits. I talked to fellow pilots, who told me there was nothing wrong with the ones we had, and as I said to a chamber that was mostly empty, as it's only crowded for votes and major debates, it made no sense to spend $100 million to redesign a suit "worn by only a few thousand people."

Flight suits were just one example of how Pentagon spending could go awry. No one knew exactly how many civilians worked for the Department of Defense, nor could anyone provide an accurate sense of all the weapons systems being upgraded or developed from scratch. In a report it would complete in 2015, the Defense Department would at last put a number on its personnel count—1,014,000—and estimate it could save more than $100 billion per year with proper management of contracts.

My interest in getting a handle on defense spending was a departure from the image many held of me as a military man and deviated from the agenda of the extreme right, where they brooked no dissent from absolute support for every dime of spending. I rebelled against these expectations with votes to support some initiatives of the Environmental Protection Agency and the National Park Service, which prompted leaders of the Illinois Tea Party to publish letters in local papers declaring me a traitor. The attacks were based on a jumble of misconceptions about the intentions of various interest organizations that they seemed to want people to misunderstand. Tea Partiers noted as proof of my apostasy the low ratings I received from the Heritage Action for America, a political action committee, the Club for Growth, and other organizations that posed as Tea Party partisans. In fact, these organizations had been created by the same people and industries that had maintained the GOP status quo for decades. Former executive branch officials and politicians served as trustees of these groups, and they were run not by renegades but by longtime Washington insiders. Attuned to the political winds, they had begun to market themselves as reliable bastions of the Tea Party, but this pose would change if the movement ran out of momentum.

Ironically, given their anger at me, I remained committed to many of the Tea Party's fundamentals—repealing Obamacare and lowering taxes, deficits, and the national debt. The difference between me and others who shouted about the cause, like Rep. Don Manzullo, a Republican whose district abutted mine, was a sense of duty. As someone entrusted with the well-being of the entire country, as well as my district, I wasn't willing to use intransigence or the threat of legislative chaos, which is destructive in itself, just to make a point.

Both sides of the deficit debate played certain games over and over. Democrats always said we were coldhearted people who wanted to take food out of children's mouths. They said this even when we proposed work requirements for single childless people under fifty-five who received federal benefits. Our side always blamed them for rising national debt when, in fact, we had increased it more in recent years. Together Ronald Reagan and George H. W. Bush increased it from $75 billion to $300 billion. Under Clinton it fell to zero. The second President Bush pushed it to $1.2 trillion. Obviously, there were times when deficits were necessary. This is why I threw myself into helping Boehner strike compromises to break a budget impasse and prevent the kind of costly federal government shutdown that helped Bill Clinton win reelection in 1996.

BOEHNER HAD BEEN IN CONGRESS WHEN THE PUBLIC BLAMED House Republicans, engaged in a budgetary game of chicken, for allowing the shutdown of government services for three weeks. People and communities who depended on government programs began to panic. With the press showing uncompensated White House staffers working deep into the night amid pizza boxes and Coke cans, public sympathy ran toward the Democrats. The crisis contributed substantially to Bill Clinton's reelection, despite a scandal over his extramarital affairs, including one with a young aide named Monica Lewinsky.

Five months into my term, a similar crisis loomed as Tea Party members of the House refused to support a federal budget compromise worked out by our leadership team and the Obama White House. They also threatened to block an increase in the debt ceiling, which allows the government to sell bonds to enable cash flow. If they succeeded, the government would behave like a car engine rapidly losing oil. First would come the shadow of black smoke. Then the car would buck. And at last, it would simply stop.

I agreed that we needed to cut spending and felt it was urgent to reduce the national debt. But I wasn't monomaniacal. I hadn't been elected to blindly serve one purpose, and I had never said I would. It was my job to learn all I could about issues and practice the art of the possible, in a place where 435 people represented the legitimate concerns of equal numbers of citizens. It wasn't my job to screw over half the country to satisfy some sort of political fundamentalism.

I performed my reality check, and it proved that while hacking away at the entire budget might satisfy lots of Tea Party folks, it would also blindside many others. To cite the obvious, current or future recipients of Social Security and Medicare would face benefit cuts, would be required to wait longer for benefits, or could possibly lose the guarantee of future income and care. Less obvious was the threat that future generations could face cuts to all or part of veterans' health care, student loans and grants, and income and services for people with disabilities. Cutting federal mortgage-guarantee programs, including one created specifically for rural communities, would raise the down payment required for home loans and shut lots of people out of the market. Add spending that supports farmers, small businesses, schools, cities, and towns, and you see how simply cutting everything wouldn't work. Similarly, letting the debt ceiling expire and causing the government to default would be the fiscal equivalent of driving drunk with the gas pedal jammed to the floor. No one knew exactly what was going to happen, but it was sure to be very bad.

On the other side of the issue, there were good reasons to believe that there had never been a better time to borrow money to build infrastructure, upgrade military hardware, or invest in economic development. Interest rates were so low that soon central banks in Europe would require that investors pay *them* as much as 0.5 percent for the privilege of letting the banks keep their cash safe. In this upside-down dynamic, foreign government treasuries became a safe but costly haven for people who were afraid of other investments. In the meantime, the United States could sell a seemingly unlimited amount of debt in the form of bonds by paying a maximum interest rate of 1.5 percent. Looking at the usual benchmark of ten-year bonds, this was the lowest rate in history and less than half of what the Treasury had paid in fifty-five years, when Eisenhower borrowed to build the interstate highway system.

It was no wonder that when he talked about the Tea Party representatives who repeatedly blocked his effort to reach budget and debt compromises with Obama, the frustrated Speaker Boehner called them knuckleheads. According to the Speaker, all they wanted was to appear on Fox News, where they would be introduced as "insurgents" and then lambaste House leaders as RINOs (Republicans in Name Only). They got away with it because too many of the voters back home had acquired much of their civic education from pandering politicians and ratings-obsessed broadcasters who had to raise the threat level every day to give viewers the kind of adrenaline rush that kept them coming back for more.

I noticed the media/voter opinion phenomenon whenever I went home to meet with constituents. Many of them began our conversations with the words "Rush says" or "Bill says." "Bill" was Fox News host Bill O'Reilly, who called those who disagreed with him pinheads. "Rush" was Rush Limbaugh, the ultra-Right talk-radio megastar. O'Reilly went so far as to call the American Civil Liberties Union the second-greatest threat to America behind Al Qaeda, and said marriage equality for gay and lesbian people would lead to "interspecies" unions. Limbaugh said that Obama's appeal was limited to the fact that he's Black, and that Democrats were welcoming campaign help from "Islamofascists."

Why would anyone believe that Democrats want to make allies of Islamofascists or that the ACLU is a terrorist organization? The evidence for these allegations was so lacking that some who tuned in were skeptical. But if they went to a certain church, they might be persuaded by the sermons they heard from trusted pastors and visiting evangelists. More and more, preachers were saying that politics was where God's plan for a war between his army of good and Satan's army of evil was being waged. Seen through this lens of faith, liberals were Satan's minions.

The Satan-versus-God alarm sounding in the Tea Party and across

Fundamentalist America didn't generally resonate with Republicans on Capitol Hill. This may have been because it was still a fringe belief. Also, people on both sides were already calling one another Nazis, communists, bigots, and morons. They didn't need religion to turn their opponents into demons. They were already doing it.

Although some older members, and a few of us younger ones, held on to the tradition of regarding the other party as the loyal (to America) opposition, this had long ceased to be the norm. Many Democrats had demonized the GOP, and some had used the word *evil* to describe us. However, the Republican Party's move from the old language of respect to the new rhetoric of moral warfare had been followed by a much larger element of the party.

In roughly two decades, Newt Gingrich's practice of insinuating that Democrats are evil devolved into California governor Arnold Schwarzenegger's casual 2005 comments about how Democrats are "evil" and must be defeated in a "great battle." A year later, political evangelist Jerry Falwell put it differently, saying that for the faithful, Hillary Clinton was more frightening than Lucifer. (Like someone who offers a lame "Just kidding!" after an intentional cutting remark, Falwell said he was kidding.) Sprinkle in books by conservative stars, like Ann Coulter's *Demonic: How the Liberal Mob Is Endangering America*, and it was easy to see Tea Party commentary about a struggle between their politically conservative God and the Evil One who served the left.

Among the Tea Party's religious extremists, belief that political opponents were evil and led by the Devil himself led to a posture of absolute commitment, because God called them to nothing less. The paradigm also provided them with the spiritual solace to accept that those who were trusted to carry the fight in Washington would often fail. Satan's power is immense, they reasoned, and their Tea Party warriors were outnumbered and didn't stand a chance, which was why they were celebrated even in defeat. Back in their districts, supporters would cheer their stubbornness. One of them, my personal rumormonger Joe Walsh, the congressman representing Illinois's 8th Congressional District at the time, was a Tea Party darling who went from the traditionally liberal field of social work into the arms of a movement that opposed pretty much everything to support people in need. He was so assertive on the Tea Party's behalf that he said, "I did not come here to blink. I was sent here to run to the mountaintop and yell to all the world."

As others struck poses, Boehner and those of us on his leadership team negotiated with both the Democrats and our fellow Republicans. As the Speaker and Cantor reached out to House Democrats, McCarthy and I gathered up GOP caucus support for a compromise that would cut $40 billion in spending and $50 billion in taxes from the previous year. It wasn't what we wanted, but it was what we could get. It passed, but with fifty-nine of our members refusing to support it.

A few months after the budget battle we had a rematch over the debt ceiling. This time there would be no good reason for voting no. Nevertheless, a crowd of Tea Party members made a big show of resistance, which sent the stock market plunging. For the first time in history, the ratings agency Standard & Poor's downgraded the country's credit rating. With two days to go before the limit was reached, the administration promised to reduce spending in the future and agreed to a scheme that could force automatic cuts, or called sequestration, in both defense and nondefense spending when the government failed to adopt a budget. This process worried many of us, but ultimately it would never be strictly implemented. In the end, the debt limit would be raised, our markets and credit rating recovered, and a true crisis was averted. Little noticed, especially by the Tea Partiers so desperate to cut spending, was the fact that their obstinance cost the American people more than $1 billion in extra payments to short-term bondholders.

It was about this time when a Fox News reporter—many of their reporters play it straight—hung around to ask me a question after we finished taping an interview.

"Can I ask you something?" he began.

"Sure," I replied.

"Are you bitter yet?"

THE DEAL THAT RESOLVED THE DEBT-LIMIT STALEMATE HAD BEEN worked out a few days before Congress voted, but since it could have blown up in our faces, it had not been announced when I appeared on NBC's *Meet the Press*, which is the longest-running program on TV. I was asked to join a roundtable that included the most famous presidential historian in the country, Doris Kearns Goodwin; NBC's chief foreign correspondent, Andrea Mitchell; former senator Chuck Hegel; and the then mayor of Newark and soon to be US senator, Cory Booker.

As the youngest by at least a decade, the least experienced, and the least well-known of the group, I felt a little like a teenager who's finally invited to sit with the grown-ups at Thanksgiving. If I had any doubt about my status, it was immediately erased by the following exchange with host David Gregory:

> GREGORY: Joining us for his first appearance on the program, Republican congressman Andrew Kinzinger— see, I didn't mess up the name, even though you thought I might—of Illinois' Eleventh District.
> KINZINGER: It's *Adam* Kinzinger, but that's all right.

The question at hand was whether politics in general, and Congress in particular, are broken. Goodwin kicked things off by describing how founder James Madison argued that a vast and varied country required governing through compromise. She pointed out that Lincoln's idol was senator and Secretary of State Henry Clay of Kentucky, who was known as "the Great Compromiser." She concluded that Clay's spirit had disappeared because "the kind of people who come to Washington now don't want to do that. And it's only going to make it worse because the caliber of people gets less."

For a split second I thought, "Is she talking about me?" But then I heard Gregory say, "Congressman, you know, you're new to Washington. Is this what you expected? Is this how it should operate?"

Of course I said no and agreed that the system is broken. "There's no doubt it's become personal. It's become vitriolic and acidic. People need to work together." But then I surprised the others a bit, saying that in private, people in both parties can and do still get along. "I think the American people would be pretty impressed with the kind of discussions that, frankly, Republicans and Democrats have. We get along behind the scenes, you know?" I was confident saying this because I knew that an agreement had been made on the debt ceiling, even if I couldn't discuss it.

The others didn't agree with me at all. Goodwin said that conflict within the GOP had made it impossible for Boehner to lead with the same strength of his predecessors. She made it seem like he had less power to end the bickering and move Congress forward than any Speaker in history. Mitchell blamed the extreme demands of campaigns that left members of the Senate and the House little time to build trusting relationships in Washington. "They don't socialize, they don't form friends even between Tea Party and non–Tea Party, as well as Republicans and Democrats." Booker was blunter, using words like "disgusted" and "angry."

Perhaps it was naïveté—honestly, it *was* naïveté—but in my shiny newness I wasn't going to go along with these cynical veterans. Every generation seems to think the old days were better. "I don't think compromise is failing," I said. "I think when we sit around and say Washington's broken, it's never going to get better . . . we're going to have to accept our place in history? No."

Of course, in referencing "our place in history" as something we shouldn't accept, I unknowingly acknowledged Congress was in a precarious place. We were at risk of reaching an all-time low of animus. However, consciously accepting a diagnosis of paralysis that was only going to get worse would leave me with no reason to even try to do my job. I wasn't going to invite this depressing thought into my mind.

Helping Speaker Boehner complete the budget and debt-limit compromises had put me inside a process that was confusing, maddening and, when it was over, somewhat gratifying. Of course, every new member of Congress experiences similar feelings as they struggle to understand what's going on in the House. It is a place where relationships bend and twist, and you need time to discover who is trustworthy and who must be avoided. And too often, people who could be trusted one day would betray you the next.

I was grateful for the inside view I got as a member of the leadership team because, frankly, I needed the help. I wasn't one of the many freshmen who had experience as a state legislator, or had once worked on Capitol Hill, or had come from a family that had a long history of government service. I was not advantaged in any of these ways. Hell, even the lawyers had a leg up on me, since their vocation was based on the laws, regulations, and legal decisions produced by the state and federal governments.

Unfortunately, the Boehner connection led too many constituents and even colleagues to think of me as a kind of marionette, raising his hand to vote as the Speaker required, whenever he pulled the string. This was not true. For example, when President Obama led NATO's action in Libya, where rebels intent on overthrowing dictator Muammar Gaddafi were being slaughtered by his air force, coalition air strikes tipped the war in favor of the rebels, who would capture and kill Gaddafi in a matter of months. However, American public opinion never favored the action and neither did Speaker Boehner, who said Obama needed Capitol Hill's permission to act. I disagreed. I supported the president and the mission, which, I'm sure, made some people think I was in his pocket. But no one who looked at my criticism of Obama's health-care program and the deception he used to sell it to the American people would ever think I was under his influence. I opposed the plan when it was proposed, objected when it was passed and, after I reached Congress, voted to repeal it many, many times. I was opposed to Obama on taxes—he liked them, I didn't—and I thought he was reckless in trying to impose regulations on businesses. When in 2012 he drew a "red line" to warn Syria's bloody ruler against gassing rebels and didn't act when Bashar al-Assad did it, I thought he had made one of the worst foreign policy blunders in history. And I said so.

My votes to change or repeal Obamacare made me a cruel ogre in the eyes of Democrats and some independents. My support for, say, a long-standing program to help low-income people heat or cool themselves made me part of the nanny state and a traitor to Republicans, who were becoming more and more anti-government. Every one of my actions could prompt an unpleasant reaction. This, I learned, is the life of a member of Congress, who must answer to the people in elections held every two years. Add the likelihood of primary challenges, which were far more common for Republicans than Democrats, and GOP members were trapped in a perpetual campaign state. And for me, in 2012, there was an added not-fun element: redistricting.

ALTHOUGH MOST WILL TAKE THEIR ADVICE, IN GENERAL, STATE officials have no power over members of Congress. The powerful exception comes after every ten-year census, when the boundaries of congressional districts are drawn. As I write, forty of the fifty states give state legislators and governors the authority to change these border lines. Invariably, the party in power, especially in those states where there's one-party rule, delineate the border lines in a partisan way. In 2011, where Democrats ruled, they studied voting patterns to discover where parties were stronger or weaker to map out districts that gave their challengers and incumbents an advantage and made life miserable for Republicans. Sometimes they draw bizarrely shaped districts. This is called gerrymandering, which, if you like history as much as I do, has a perfect backstory.

In 1812, Massachusetts governor Elbridge Gerry, who had signed the Declaration of Independence, drew state legislative districts that resembled a host of oddly shaped animals, including a salamander. Thus, the future vice president inspired writers to call this district a "Gerrymander." Just as happens today, the scheme backfired in many places. Gerry lost support in the legislature and was widely mocked. For example, between reports on the six-week-old War of 1812, *The*

Record of Greenfield, Massachusetts, prayed that one of the animals would, "after having bitten its own tail off, have its head quashed by the whole weight of public indignation."

Much of the public continued to be indignant right up to today, but the gerrymandering goes on. After the 2022 census, Maryland has one district that is called a broken-winged pterodactyl. In Illinois we have an earmuff drawn to give Hispanics, who generally vote for Democrats, their own district. Republicans do this, too, and the party uses exquisitely precise software to favor themselves. Democrats are racing to catch up, building their own computer program. Just like Gerry, the mapmakers seem to fail in about half the places where they seek the advantage, and yet they keep on doing it because, well, the other guys do it.

In December 2011, the map approved in Illinois essentially erased my district, leaving me no option but to go head-to-head in a primary with twenty-year incumbent Don Manzullo. Given the way the Democrats had packed GOP voters into one district, the primary winner was almost guaranteed to win in November. Old enough to be my father, Manzullo was extremely well-known in the district, which curled around Chicago and then up to the Wisconsin line, and he was vocal about his hard-right positions. For instance, he called Islam a "savage religion." This made him a Tea Party darling, and with just a three-month primary campaign, he reached out to them again and again.

In January, Manzullo turned a Tea Party crowd into an amen chorus as he said other Republicans had let them down, thwarting their agenda. He made the false claim that one of his aides had been barred from my recent event, and quipped, "So much for freedom!" and the crowd burst into applause. When it was over, a voter who claimed to have campaigned for me in 2010 told the local paper that I was working "against our Bill of Rights" because he had been barred from one of my events. Just how I might have done this wasn't explained anywhere, by anyone, but nevertheless this person felt free to say I was attacking his essential freedoms. This was his right, naturally, under the First Amendment.

The nonsense that I was attacking the Bill of Rights was matched by the editorials published in the larger papers. One paper said that voters should determine "for themselves" which candidate fit their view of conservatism, and then suggested they let interest group ratings be their guide. If a voter looked to ratings and endorsements from very conservative groups, Manzullo would be their choice, as he racked up official backing from, among others, the Tea Party and the Illinois Conservatives, who cited a letter he wrote opposing the debt ceiling increase before he voted for it.

If my account of the interplay between the incumbent, local groups, and the press has your head spinning, imagine how I struggled against the tide. While Manzullo stressed his experience and anti-Obama obstructionism, I argued that my focus was on getting things done. The *Chicago Tribune* repeatedly called the race "hotly contested," but as election day approached our data suggested we were breaking through. It seemed that in the third-largest metropolitan area in the country, plenty of Republicans wanted practical representatives who weren't yelling about Tea Party priorities and supposedly "savage" Muslims.

In 2008, the district had gone for Obama in the presidential race. On election day, moderately conservative voters comprised 56 percent of the vote and gave me a victory, even though polling done by both sides showed me behind by six points in the last week of the campaign. Manzullo was cranky in his concession speech, complaining that we used "Chicago-style politics," which is Republican code for urban corruption, to beat him. It was likely that many of our supporters went with us because they wanted the best chance to win in the fall. Their bet worked out, as we won in November with 62 percent. In the district, this was almost 10 points better than the GOP presidential nominee, Mitt Romney, and his running mate, Paul Ryan, the aforementioned "thinker" of the Young Guns. Obama and Joe Biden won statewide and nationally, despite all the Tea Party protests and forecasts of a Romney win from media pundits like George Will, Michael Barone, Glenn Beck, Peggy Noonan, and others.

If I were to summarize my takeaway from 2012, it would be this: I thought we had begun to put hyperpartisanship behind us. "I will be going to Washington to get both parties to agree on real progress" was how I put it to the press. Then, before I could be sworn in to serve my new district, the Illinois Tea Party bashed me for an end-of-term vote to preserve GOP tax cuts for 98 percent of Americans while permitting Obama's proposal for a small increase for the top 2 percent. They didn't say anything about how, as one of his last acts in the House, their man Manzullo had voted with me. Given the blatant hypocrisy, I thought that this movement was certain to run out of supporters sooner rather than later. Maybe Crazytown wasn't going to be so crazy after all.

And by the way, Joe Walsh lost to a rising Democratic star named Tammy Duckworth, who was a combat helicopter pilot who had lost both her legs when her Black Hawk was hit by a rocket-propelled grenade in Iraq. Duckworth would eventually fly again. Walsh would never again be elected to anything. If you can believe it, he's now an anti-Trump activist.

CHAPTER 8

A New Normal

I thought the Tea Party might go away after 2012. So did the GOP establishment.

Despite the movement's supposed energy, Mitt Romney and Paul—the thinker—Ryan had been defeated by Barack Obama and Joe Biden. The GOP's election "autopsy" of this loss concluded that we needed to encourage gay, Black, Hispanic, Asian, and younger voters to join us. The report's coauthor warned that ideological "purity" would lead us to doom. Tea Party–style absolutists' opposition to all gun regulation, most environmental protections, and all of Obamacare had to be completely eliminated, or we would never win over a majority of Americans.

Fortunately, the purity thing was emphasized less in the 2014 midterms, as the report advised, and it worked. David Jolly of Florida rejected the Tea Party and won both a special election and the general election, scoring 75 percent in the general. Other moderate candidates, including Dan Newhouse in Washington State, Bob Dold in Illinois, Bruce Poliquin in Maine, and Tom MacArthur in New Jersey, all prevailed with similar policy positions. The reason for their success was confirmed by the nonpartisan Pew Research organization, which reported that in 2010, 50 percent of Republicans had said they "agreed" with the Tea Party. In 2014 the "agree" group had declined to 33 percent.

My 2014 campaign began with a primary challenge from the founder of the Rockford Tea Party, David Hale. Like the movement's leaders nationwide, Hale considered Republicans like me members of "the surrender caucus." Hale had been an effective organizer whose rallies had grown so popular that one newspaper photo from an early event showed some unlikely attendees: three elderly Catholic nuns in traditional black habits who stood grinning brightly. One sister held an American flag. Another clutched a Gadsden flag showing a rattlesnake on a field of yellow and the words "Don't Tread on Me." First used in the Revolutionary War, the flag had evolved into an icon of former Confederate states, where Black Americans generally agreed it had racist undertones. It was commonplace at Tea Party rallies.

Despite the apparent addition of Catholics to the Evangelical/Tea Party cause, and the energy evident at some of Hale's rallies, I won the primary by a three-to-one margin. The Joliet *Herald News* declared KINZINGER POUNDS TEA PARTY RIVAL, with polls showing that even the district's Democrats were happy with me. Their party's sacrificial lamb barely tried in the general election, and I got more

than 70 percent of the vote. The rise of the moderates told me everything was back to normal.

I know; that sounds a bit funny now.

Of course, "normal" is not a precise word. It can define something objective like annual rainfall or the position of the planets. But
where humans are concerned, normal is relative. What's a normal
diet, or weight, or haircut—who knows? We may have once believed
we could answer these questions, but the truth is found in a range.
In politics, normal can depend on your age, or the moment when
you were engaged by a cause of a candidate. For some Republicans,
normal is a mature style. It calls for well-mannered debate, respect
for institutions, and resistance to radical change. For others, who
were increasing in numbers, it is partisan combat in an endless war.

As a precocious kid—at least where politics was concerned—
I became aware of parties, elections, and government at around age
six, when Ronald Reagan was reelected to a second term. I understood that my parents liked Reagan, and I noticed how he was always surrounded by the trappings of the presidency. Air Force One,
the presidential seal, and the Secret Service were inspiring. But more
important was the president's grandfatherly warmth. His amiability
disarmed critics and made you feel like everything was going to be
all right. With emotions outweighing intellect every time, the feelings I experienced watching and listening to the president shaped
my model of someone who could lead all the people.

In contrast with my understanding of the presidency, I knew little of the GOP's congressional agenda and how it was being pressed, and couldn't name but a few members of the House. I was not alone. Most people then had little idea that House Republicans were gradually moving away from Reagan. Even insiders had trouble seeing where they were headed. The facts were obscured both by the number of people you would have to track in order to see a trend and by their rhetoric. Long after they had abandoned Reagan's kinder approach and his spirit of bipartisan compromise, members of the House GOP continued to mouth devotion to him. These words of worship made it sound like nothing had changed, when the reality was that they masked the rage they felt at being in the minority and deprived of real power.

The congressional Republicans' poorly disguised anger violated our political tradition, which depended on the barriers of decency that allowed Washington to get things done. Genuine frustration made sense, since Democrats had controlled the House of Representatives for fifty-plus years. If they were united, the Dems could block anything our side proposed. But since both parties counted significant numbers of moderate members, compromises happened all the time. Nobody would be fully satisfied with these agreements, something that was considered the sign of the best outcome for everyone, including a citizenry that held a diversity of views and interests.

By and by, what House members and senators called "comity" was disappearing. Unseen by the general public, House Republicans were often blowing through the barriers, which eventually made both sides more combative. The GOP's Reaganism and, for that matter, the Dems' good-ol'-boy Clintonism receded. Everyone's main goal became power, which would be used either to ram a proposal through the system or to create gridlock to contain the other side. No one said much about how the corruption of power we Republicans saw in the Democrats (power generally begets corruption) was likely to affect us too.

William F. Buckley's *National Review* embodied the conservative movement in its mission statement to stand "athwart history, yelling Stop, at a time when no one is inclined to do so." Whatever his faults and failings, and they were significant, Buckley is the uncontested father of modern conservative thought, whose cutting debate style was matched by his consideration for others and immense gratitude for his country. His influence was profound and lasted for three decades—until the rank and file of the movement replaced policy and thoughtfulness with ambition.

THERE IS A CHICKEN-OR-EGG PROBLEM WITH THE STORY OF HOW anger consumed right-wing religion. These believers often say they practice "faith" but not a "religion." But by every definition they practice a religion that, like all religions, includes an element of faith beyond reason. The question today is whether certain politicians, preachers, activists, and even marketers of media products ignited the passion that now burns across the country or whether they exploited something that was already smoldering.

Think about the fire that has been burning in a sealed coal mine under the small city of Centralia, Pennsylvania. Ablaze for at least sixty years, the fire was spread farther and faster by the air that rushed in every time the mine has been breached by people digging. Sometimes this happened on purpose, in vain attempts to put the blaze out. Other times it was accidental, as excavators believed they were digging in a safe spot.

If the subterranean fire is the low-level anxiety that has always existed among very conservative Christians, then the preachers, politicians, and others are the diggers who supplied the air that made it spread.

Having attended a very conservative church as a kid and lived most of my life in communities where this religion predominates, I know the worldview shared by believers. The most devout are certain that good and evil are battling all around, even to control their individual souls, and that outsiders are likely to be in Satan's thrall. The less devout are not so animated by the idea of spiritual warfare but do agree that eternal damnation awaits unbelievers and that the faith is the only path to right living. A great deal of variation can be found in this religion, but when it comes to America, few believers dispute the notion that we are special in God's eyes and predestined to fulfill a role foretold in the Book of Revelation's apocalyptic prophecy. For two centuries generations of white conservative Christians have eagerly awaited this end-of-the-world battle between good and evil, because in the end, they will ascend to heaven for an eternal existence of communion with God. In every era, believers considered the idea that they join the political realm in order to hasten their calling.

The history of how today's church leaders, evangelists, prophets, and activists pushed conservative Christians toward a more high-powered and politicized religion is well-known, but the context is less well understood. Prior to the 1960s, for example, many if not most of these Christians avoided politics, rendering unto Caesar what is Caesar's. With few exceptions, pastors were modest shepherds of congregations of hundreds. Many thought that politics was such a dirty endeavor that they wouldn't even vote. The change came first with televangelists who were interested in wealth and power and exploited tax-exempt organizations to live a lifestyle of mansions and private jets. Less prominent entrepreneurial pastors— those who weren't on national television—developed so-called megachurches attended by as many as forty thousand.

The financial and sexual scandals that arose as pastors and preachers gained wealth, power, and fame were inevitable and continue to flare periodically, but since they involve leaders of their *team*, the faithful are ever ready to forgive. For example, consider Jim and Tammy Faye Bakker, who repeatedly preached that God wants his people to be rich, and indeed, wealth marked those who were in his favor. After building an empire that included a national TV show, a twenty-five-hundred-acre theme park and resort, and a life divided between homes in North Carolina and Palm Springs connected by charter jet flights, they fell from grace in the 1990s due to sexual and financial scandals. They were back on TV soon after Jim got out of federal prison. In 2008, he opened his own $25 million TV studio.

I thought the smarmy Bakkers and their sordid story were merely signs of Christian delusion. I didn't know that the Bakkers were part of the larger trend that brought their followers to believe that God wanted them to have both wealth and power, and that in pursuing them they would save an increasingly faithless America.

IF MY EARLY EXPOSURE TO THE CHRISTIAN COALITION INTRO-duced me to the potential for the blending of religion and Republican politics on a large scale, the Tea Party's use of religious and political symbols showed how the hybrid could be weaponized. In retrospect, it's hard for me to believe that I didn't see the depth of what was happening, even in my own congressional district. In ever-increasing numbers, people were approaching me at restaurants, gas stations, and convenience stores to tell me what someone on Fox News had said, to demand that I agree and then get upset if I did not.

On rarer occasions, people pulled me aside to tell me how much they liked what they heard me say on TV. At that time, I was on Fox News so often that people began to recognize me in public places like airports and restaurants. I was, in short, famous, and as I know now, fame is the addictive drug of politics. It can give you a warm feeling of being wanted and needed or make you feel energized and excited. And like any drug, the more you get it, the more you want it.

The initial hook comes with being picked, like a kid who's been riding the bench and is finally sent into a game. It is set as the makeup artists make you look good and give your clothes a quick

brush. The studio crew then treats you like a precious commodity—
Do you want water, sir? Is the earphone comfortable?—and then the
host tries to get the best out of you. Invariably you leave with the
words "That was great" ringing in your ears and the distinct desire
to do it again as soon as possible. You are in the cool kids' club, and
you start anticipating the next TV appearance, which will be another chance for your colleagues to see you and say, "I saw you on
TV. Great job!" Personal attention comes as friends, some of whom
haven't been around for a long time, call you again and again. In a
time when attention is a currency that brings status, opportunities,
and influence, this would make anyone feel like a big shot.

It was easy to look like a winner on Fox, where I knew what was
expected of me and could succeed by offering familiar GOP boilerplate. The party's usual argument technique involved just flipping
the other side's position—tax increases for the rich were job-killing
programs—and then riffing off the central theme. If you were feeling aggressive you could say the Democrats don't care about people
who need jobs or the threat of terrorism. If you were feeling laid
back, you could say they just didn't understand the way the world
works.

Sometimes those of us in Congress didn't drive the subject of the
week; the hosts on Fox or conservative talk radio did. For instance,
I once went on Fox radio to complain about Obama changing the
name of Mount McKinley to its native name, Denali. "People feel
like this president is constantly, like, trying to stick it in our eye," I
said. Then I asked if it happened because McKinley was a Republican. Others echoed the same point. John Kasich, running for the

GOP nomination for president, said Obama "overstepped his bounds." Representative Ralph Ragula called him a "dictator."

My quips about the change of a mountain's name aligned with my party's playbook, which favored, almost exclusively, quick, memorable sound bites and put-downs. The process typically began with a high-ranking party leader in, say, the National Republican Congressional Committee or someone in the media isolating a sound bite and determining how it could be used against the Democrats but also rile up our base. The talking points would be discussed in meetings, phone calls, emails, and faxes. In this case, Obama was bringing the federal government in line with the state of Alaska, which had been using the Koyukon people's word Denali for forty years. The tribal name had been in place before Europeans arrived and right up to 1898, when a gold prospector proclaimed it Mount McKinley to boost his favorite candidate for president.

In our arguments, we ignored the deeper rationale and facts that may have benefited the public. If they heard that Obama was trying to respect Indigenous people, some would have felt good about their country doing something that showed we were very different from forebears who practiced everything from theft, to treaty violations, to genocidal warfare. Instead of being reasonable and admitting there was another side to the issue, we cried "Political correctness!"

The situation took off from there. One of the more extreme voices on the right, the columnist Ben Shapiro, exploited the recent tragic killing of a Black teenager named Trayvon Martin by asking why Obama didn't change the name to "Mt. Trayvon." A fringe website called Gateway Pundit said Obama had made a racist move because President McKinley was white. Like us, Gateway Pundit jumped on the Denali issue because it worked. Had our constituents flooded the offices of their senators and House members to complain about the change? I truly doubt it. What mattered was that we could score points on Fox and, since no Democrats would appear alongside us, run up the total.

I won't lie about enjoying this. I did. Also, the Democrats did the same whenever they could too. In their case, however, they seemed to try to corner us on issues of broader interest, while we went for inflammatory culture-war stuff. They were also less likely to use hot words and phrases. We freely labeled them "San Francisco–style" Democrats, which meant they must be gay extremists.

I didn't use in-your-face tactics because I felt they were not necessary in the conservative ecosphere and diminished my credibility outside it. This more reasonable style brought me invitations from the prestigious big network Sunday shows, where all sides were invited to join the discussion. Democrats generally did quite well, because in this format you needed more than a couple of snappy talking points. When I was invited I studied up and did pretty well myself. I also felt honored to be on the same program as people like fellow conservative Dick Cheney, the liberal Supreme Court justice Sonia Sotomayor, and Democratic congressman Keith Ellison of Minnesota, who was a very intelligent firebrand on the left. These people were all in the group I joined on ABC's *This Week* on a Sunday in June 2014. They were brilliant people, and if you consider the lineup, which found Sotomayor and me in the middle and the others on the opposite poles, it was a balanced and therefore more interesting bunch. The audience was high level too.

The more I got involved in serious discussions intended to iron out policy, the more I hoped we could turn away from hyperpartisanship. We were, according to the data, at risk of reaching a tipping point. Eight percent of Democrats told pollsters they were "consistently liberal," while 9 percent of Republicans said they were "consistently conservative." Neither group gave serious thought to compromise. More concerning was the fact that the portion of the electorate saying they held "mixed" political views had reached an all-time low of 39 percent. Media ghettos represented by Fox on the right and MSNBC on the left seemed to be leading people toward real-life isolation. Fifty percent of consistent conservatives and 35 percent of consistent liberals said it was important for them to live in communities where "most people share my political views."

As these numbers on political division came out in 2014, experts began warning that polarization had reached its worst point since the Civil War. I regarded this with a bit of skepticism because assessments of political division in the period prior to the 1950s—this was about 180 years of history—were essentially anecdotal. Better to resist the civil war alarms until we had a truer sense of what was happening and could put it in a context better grounded in history.

It's possible that I resisted the dire warning about civil strife because the Air Force had trained me to stay calm even if I was at the controls of a tanker that was on fire. It's also likely that this was something that came to me naturally. As a teacher, my mother stayed so calm that her students didn't even think of causing any mayhem. My father could work with anyone, from angry program clients to state officials, without ever getting ruffled. Other than a few episodes involving excessive amounts of alcohol, I had always been the kind of person who rarely got too high or too low. By middle school, I was unafraid of speaking to a crowd, talking on the radio, or publishing my thoughts in the local paper. Nothing seemed to rattle me.

The notion of civil war also seemed far-fetched because I believed that in their hearts, most of the people who seemed so fired up—on the right and the left—knew that the issues they were supposed to think were a matter of life and death, for themselves and for the country, were not. Whether they were riled by ultraliberal broadcaster Keith Olbermann or an entire network in Fox News, surely they understood that these sources were a form of entertainment, intended to stir emotion, and not sincere news broadcasts. Hell, even the personalities said they weren't journalists. My constituents' favorite, Rush Limbaugh, was a comic genius of the radio who kept people hooked with conspiracy theories and cliffhangers. He even said he was an entertainer. Their second favorite, Sean Hannity, considered himself a talk-show host who shouldn't be held to the standards of news reporters. If the Fox News slogan "Fair and Balanced" was a joke—and it was—it would be doubly hilarious if applied to Sean.

ALTHOUGH I TRULY BELIEVED EVERYONE WAS IN ON THE GAME practiced by Sean and Rush, and that their followers were not as agitated as they seemed, I was wrong. Again. In fact, operating like a drug pusher, Fox News was taking over viewers' minds and kept a majority of people in my party hooked with increasingly powerful stuff. A key example was the network's focus on the invented controversy around Obama's birthplace. Hosts kept insisting that Obama may be an illegitimate president, and that he must prove he was a "natural-born" American. They suspected he had been born in Kenya, and they believed that under the Constitution this would disqualify him from the presidency. In fact, Obama had made his Hawaiian birth certificate public in 2011. Besides, the Supreme Court had decided that if your mother or father is an American you are a "natural-born" US citizen no matter where you are born. Case closed.

As I tried to convert my district's "birthers" to the truth, I discovered that mere talk almost never changed anyone's mind. Constituents who felt a twinge of doubt about the birthplace issue sometimes switched to another theory: Obama had forfeited his citizenship when he became an Indonesian citizen as a child. There! See?

Obama had lived in Indonesia from age six to age nine, but no evidence exists to suggest he became an Indonesian citizen. Indeed, the only way he could have lost his status as an American would have been by officially renouncing his American citizenship. Children cannot do this without a consular investigation. Had he done so, some public record would exist. And don't you think someone would have dug it up?

Other nutty Fox claims reported as fact included host Glenn Beck's conspiracy theory about a United Nations document called

Agenda 21. The document is real. It calls for action to deal with climate change to safeguard the twenty-first century. It was signed by more than 175 countries, including the United States under GOP president George H. W. Bush. It is nonbinding and grants the UN no authority in any country. Nevertheless, Beck waved around a couple hundred printed pages and claimed it was a copy of Agenda 21, and said it proved the UN's plan for world domination.

Repeated again and again, Beck's charge plugged into a long-running fear of the United Nations among extreme conservatives. For decades the John Birch Society preached about the UN's threat to our sovereignty. I heard these ideas myself as a young person. The Birchers were so radical, they suspected Dwight Eisenhower was a communist. This kind of position drove them into obscurity in the 1960s. However, their ideas resurfaced in the 1990s and were to be embraced by an increasing number of Republicans who agreed that communists and socialists were taking over the country. In the 2000s, militia groups spread the idea that UN concentration camps were being established to support a takeover of the United States and that flights of so-called black helicopters were evidence that they were searching for sites. In 1996, Helen Chenoweth, a GOP congresswoman from Idaho, said "we have some proof" of the chopper theory. She never produced it, but the claim played well with the paranoia crowd. In 2013, quite a few Americans freaked out over rumors, spread online, that helicopters were flying over potential invasion sites. In 2014, GOP consultant Dick Morris, supposedly a serious man, published a book titled *Here Come the Black Helicopters!*

During this time, John Boehner was calling Fox News network's big star Sean Hannity "a nut" and said that Americans were being "brainwashed" by continuous claims about Obama. But as one of fifty-one people ever to hold this high rank—third in line to the presidency—Boehner had far less public influence than Hannity and his colleagues. Their doomsaying and distortions played on an infinite loop in homes, bars, barbershops, cafés, restaurants, and even some workplaces. The fear and outrage pouring from TVs and radios raise listeners' adrenaline, which delivers a boost of energy as the ancient fight-or-flight instinct is activated. Over time, the phenomenon that experts call an "adrenaline bath" can cause people to have obsessive thoughts—say, about political danger—and develop a craving for more of the excitement hormone.

Ratings proved that millions upon millions were listening to the gloom shows, but the depth of their effect was revealed in one-on-one encounters. In early 2015, after I wrote a newspaper column about nuclear power with my colleague Cheri Bustos, you would have thought I had insulted half the people in the district. The blowback began with people asking how I had the nerve to work with Bustos, a Democrat from our state, on anything. It didn't matter that we were promoting a typically Republican policy to assure that nuclear power remains an energy source into the future. Then came the anger about how the article I put my name to acknowledged the small successes of Obama's efforts to reduce unemployment, help manufacturers recover from the Great Recession, and increase exports. He also defied his party to push increased gas and oil production. I also signed on to the argument that it was important that nuclear power did not emit gases related to climate change and that the damage done by excess carbon would cost as much as $18 billion to fix.

I still disagreed with Obama on many things from health care to foreign policy, which could be seen in the huge humanitarian disaster in Syria, but you can't talk about the future in a rational or constructive way if you don't see the present clearly. Fox said climate change research had been "fabricated," so my interest in reducing carbon emissions was wrongheaded. Eight million fewer Americans were working than in 2009, Fox said, and the United States would need to spend "eight billion dollars a day" on oil that could be pumped out of deposits in the Gulf of Mexico. These were wildly erroneous claims, but they came from people my constituents trusted more than they trusted me.

The decline of trust in leaders, authorities, and institutions was—and remains—a big problem. With the exception of a spike in the late-Clinton/early-Bush years, faith in government has declined significantly for decades. Encouraged by people who want to be the sole source of information for as many as possible, activists tried to destroy trust in science, medicine, education, and the other disciplines. Their efforts worked, as many people came to believe that experts of all sorts were suspect and that truth was impossible to determine. They didn't know that the people pushing them toward cynicism included tobacco company lobbyists who spread arguments that discredited medical researchers and fossil fuel operatives who attacked climate science. Our party took advantage of the political energy these campaigners stoked as people learned to resent experts.

This skepticism drove people to do their own "research" on websites like Facebook, which bases its business on reinforcing users' biases. Cherry-picking sources could bring them to people like the GOP operative Andrea Tantaros, who claimed that prior to the American Revolutionary War, "some guy in Boston got his head blown off because he tried to secretly raise the tax on tea."

Democrats had their own problem with distorting or omitting facts and making specious attacks on Republicans. In campaigning against Mitt Romney in 2012, President Obama unfairly claimed to know that his opponent didn't care at all about the poor and the middle class. In the same year, Obama employed some doozies during his final debate with Romney, falsely accusing him of, among other things, wanting Pakistan to control our anti-terrorism efforts, and charging, in contradiction to the facts, that Romney would have done nothing to help the auto industry through the recent financial crisis.

Although the Democrats' sins were real, to my distress they were not as numerous and outlandish as the ones coming from my side, and I sometimes felt like I was working with people who, in a phrase often attributed to Mark Twain, "refused to let the truth get in the way of a good story." This is why I just didn't rely on many of the talking points memos. More importantly, whatever the unfairness the Democrats perpetrated, it didn't affect people in my district very much. My constituents were motivated by the intramural fight for control of the GOP, which required their constant vigilance so that they could weed out the weaklings, the faithless, and the deceivers. And even though the Tea Party organizations were fading to irrelevance, the issues the movement stressed and the grievances they brought to politics remained, and more people seemed to be motivated by them. Indeed, the tricorn hats would soon be replaced by red baseball caps—emblazoned with Trump's campaign catchphrase "Make America Great Again"— that signaled their support for Donald Trump's 2016 presidential campaign, and there would be far more of them.

WITH THE RED HAT UPRISING STILL SOME MONTHS AWAY, I CONSID-ered the tide of complaints about my deviation from orthodoxy and tried to understand what was happening to people. Though expressed through politics, their feelings were so powerful that I had to think they went far beyond attachments to a party or a candidate or a partisan idea. Whether the source was their own minds or had been wedged into their hearts by the media, these people harbored deep anger and resentments that made it seem that they were in the midst of a collective identity crisis. This made sense if you recognized they were white, middle-class, conservative Evangelicals and Fundamentalists who lived in rural communities and felt like the country, which was dominated by coastal cities and suburbs, was ignoring them and quickly abandoning the values of the heartland. Conservative Christians almost never appeared in TV shows or films, and when they did it was as corrupt evangelists, heartless parents, or mean-spirited Elmer Gantrys. When they traveled to the coasts, middle-of-the-country folks felt like they got second-class treatment. Worst of all, their problems never seemed to rise to the top of the public agenda.

The sense that faith was in decline in the Christian belief system was supported by the facts. The number of Americans who identified as churchgoing believers had declined in every year since 1990. By 2011, the number of unaffiliated, agnostics, and atheists exceeded the Evangelicals. This shift included baby boomers, their parents, and their children. From a conservative Christian point of view, these changes indicated that the church was being reduced to the "remnant" that the Bible predicted would be left just prior to the Apocalypse. Those who were part of the remnant believe they are the only true Christians in the world. Thus, everyone else—mainline Protestants, Roman Catholics, even moderate Evangelicals—was not.

Key to the way many felt was the pain caused by the decline of high-paying manufacturing jobs, which once helped male wage earners support their families on their own. Matched with rising competition from women and members of racial and ethnic minorities in the workplace, the 1950s lifestyle favored by the men in this cohort seemed to be disappearing. Considering how women were increasingly outnumbering men at colleges and universities, the future looked even worse, according to them.

One truly remarkable fact that went unnoticed until 2015 and the approach of another election was the rise of so-called deaths of despair among white working-class people, especially those in their early fifties. In this group, the rate of fatalities due to alcohol, drugs—especially opioids—and suicide had risen from forty per ten thousand people in 2000 to eighty in 2015. This was a uniquely American problem—no other country was seeing such a spike—and it affected mainly men in the age and skills group most likely to have lost top factory jobs without finding new employment with comparable pay. Unable to keep up with many peers, let alone their own fathers who had worked during the heyday of US industry, they lost their sense of purpose, identity, and relevance in a society where their talents and strengths were consistently being devalued.

As so often happens, the factors that set the conditions for outrage on the right—feeling ignored, fearing the future—did the same on the left. This was evidenced by the so-called Occupy Wall Street protests by young people whose futures had been thrown into darkness by the economic catastrophe that began in 2007 and intensified in 2008. The movement that emerged from the first protest, which disrupted life in New York's Financial District for more than a month, was far less organized than the Tea Party. It was not aided by the organizing, logistics, funding, and training the Tea Party received from wealthy organizations. "Occupy," as it was called, never advanced much beyond sit-ins and marches intended to highlight complaints about corporations and rich people who paid little or no taxes and government officials who did nothing to help the young people in the movement. This leftist "Tea Party" declined as participants grew to full adulthood and other pressing matters kept them busy. The spirit would rise again with independent senator Bernie Sanders's 2016 presidential campaign, but even there it was too small to even attract and hold the attention of the press.

The Occupy and Bernie people also failed to incite the level of energizing outrage provoked by the Tea Party/Trump people because in general their activism left out a key incendiary component: race.

I have thought long and hard about the issue of race and the early Tea Party and also about what I can and should write about it here. Let me say from the start: I think very few Tea Partiers were consciously racist. The time has long passed since racism became established as such a marker of ignorance that even those raised in homes where it was heard and acted upon have refused to talk and act this way themselves. However, there is such a thing as unconscious bias. Everyone has it, to one degree or another, and given the ancient instincts toward tribal safety it's all but impossible to eradicate. I doubt that even the Dalai Lama could pass the most widely used bias test. (Want to try it yourself? Visit https://implicit.harvard .edu/implicit/.)

The racist element of the Tea Party was sparked, as much as anyone can tell, by Barack Obama's election in 2008. For many it wasn't the thought of Obama's race, per se, but a fear that his rise to the presidency foretold their own declining status. And it wasn't just Obama's election that stoked these fears. Some Tea Partiers were also affected by the changing racial and ethnic makeup of the country, which brought them in contact with new cultures and communities. (All this has been documented by many serious studies, including one done at the conservative Stanford University's Graduate School of Business.)

Harder attitudes were revealed over time as extremists who once stayed away joined the Tea Party and brought racism with them in full force. By the end, Confederate flags and racist slogans were common at Tea Party rallies. One of the worst signs read "American Taxpayers Are the Jews for Obama's Ovens." Others showed Obama as an African tribesman and, as if to prove that Tea Party protesters feared declining status, the slogan "Obama's Plan = White Slavery."

One little-appreciated problem with the attitudes reflected in the rally signs was the way they affected the Republican Party. Orange County, California, Republicans were swamped by controversy when a party committee member who was also in the Tea Party distributed a cartoon showing Obama as an ape. Mega-donor Joe Ricketts, father of the billionaire Republican governor of Nebraska, Pete Ricketts, apologized publicly after racist emails he exchanged were uncovered.

To say that the bigotry sparked disappointment in me is an understatement. As the Tea Party normalized extreme attitudes within the GOP, huge numbers of Americans would turn their backs on us, including plenty of conservatives. This was one of many reasons that made it easy for me to endorse Jeb Bush's candidacy for the 2015 presidential nomination. As governor of Florida, he had established himself as a calm, effective leader whose status as George W. Bush's brother was a good thing and not the source of resentment voiced by his critics. He was also the favorite, but this would change as sixteen others joined the primary field, making it the biggest ever seen in either party. Included were some of my least favorite members of Congress, who were among a handful of extremists who seemed prepared to sabotage every effort to get things done while, at the same time, screaming about gridlock.

The first of the kings of obstruction was Jim Jordan of Ohio. When I was first sworn in, Jordan was a regular conservative. Known for his peculiar (defiant?) habit of never wearing a jacket except when on the House floor, he had become the very model of an angry political warrior who bullied witnesses and tried to bully colleagues. He often stretched the truth to and beyond the breaking point. If he ever backed anything put forward by the Democrats, I'm not aware of it.

Next up was Raúl Labrador. Obsessed with social issues, like rolling back the Supreme Court rulings permitting gay marriage, Labrador of Idaho was never a moderate or traditional conservative. He had expected a GOP "revolution" and was perpetually frustrated because the House often gave the Tea Party types less than they wanted. He clearly reviled anyone who supported Boehner and believed he was supposed "to represent the fear and angst" of angry voters. I never heard him talk about anything outside politics.

Then there was Mick Mulvaney. He was ruthless in his pursuit of a Libertarian agenda, which included slashing everything in the federal budget, including defense. The member from South Carolina believed Republicans shouldn't speak to any lobbyist representing clients who didn't give Republicans campaign donations. He reveled in disrupting the federal budget process.

And finally, there was Kevin McCarthy. Determined to one day become Speaker of the House, McCarthy was a political windsock, always shifting to join what he imagined was the trend of the moment.

Labrador and Mulvaney were in my freshman class in Congress, (Jordan was one term ahead of us) and though we wouldn't be close friends, I could get along with each one of them. Others, not so much. When I arrived, Ron Paul of Texas was beginning what would be his last term. He was perpetually out of sync with the caucus and, in fact, with generally accepted political reality. Paul nominated himself for Speaker, getting precisely one vote. On trips across the country, he campaigned fervently to return our currency to the gold standard. Of the nearly seven hundred bills he authored in his career, precisely one became law. It authorized the sale of an unused federal customs house in Galveston.

Paul was joined on the nut tree by Louie Gohmert of Texas, who was isolated both in his beliefs and as a member who rarely interacted with others in the House. He loudly presented bizarro notions including the "fact" that an oil pipeline in Alaska made caribou friskier, and he believed that in time he would be regarded as an American Winston Churchill.

On the Senate side of the Capitol, Texan Ted Cruz and Ron Paul's son Rand—the nut doesn't fall far from the tree—were guys who looked at you as if they smelled something bad, which meant they had supremely punchable faces. An oily, sneering manipulator who was in the running to be the most disliked person in Washington, Cruz was an Agenda 21 conspiracy believer. But he took things one step further than most. He said the UN intended to end all private property rights and to force rural residents into cave-like "Hobbit houses."

Cruz and I sometimes appeared on the same TV news programs, and I loved to argue with him. He always appeared to be winging it, confident that his superior intellect would win the day. It rarely did.

Rand Paul was his father's ideological match—aggressively strange—but was better at wearing an I'm-not-nutty costume. He was, however, very good at baseball. One year we had a pleasant talk in the dugout as we participated in the annual GOP versus Democrats game. When I later spoke out against his proposal to cut defense spending by 30 percent, he acted as if I'd killed his dog. As his baseball buddy, I was supposed to support him.

Setting aside Gohmert, who truly was in a category of his own, most of the Capitol Hill characters I thought were the worst of my party were, in fact, its future. McCarthy would soon become the GOP's minority leader in the House, which meant he would be ranked second among Republican officeholders in all of Washington. He was still determined to be Speaker and would eventually succeed. Jordan was destined for a major role in several high-profile investigations and chairmanship of the prestigious House Judiciary Committee. Cruz and Paul would both declare runs for the presidency, which, as the whole world now knows, became, pardon the expression, a shit show.

You know what happened in the 2016 election. But let's review it briefly. Businessman Donald Trump, infamous for bankruptcies, a tabloid sex scandal, and his verbal abuse of everyone from entertainer Rosie O'Donnell to Jimmy Carter, entered the race in June 2015. As the former host of a reality TV show, he commenced to suck up all the attention in the campaign. He did it by saying nasty things about immigrants, the press, the voters of Iowa—you name it—and pasting insults and nicknames on other candidates as if he were an insult comic.

When my candidate Jeb Bush got his turn as a target, Trump called him "low-energy Jeb" because he was a thoughtful person who, unlike Trump, spoke in complete sentences, with respect for others, and as if questions posed at debates were serious. This was what I liked about Jeb. He was a statesman, not a showman, and he had good plans; I especially liked his options for addressing immigration humanely. Unfortunately, as Trump poked him with outlandish false criticisms, no one paid much attention to the policies Jeb tried to discuss. Instead, the main postdebate topic became "Why doesn't he punch back?" With so many candidates, the debates took on a circuslike atmosphere, with Trump, a seasoned performer, acting as ringmaster.

As every one of his opponents struggled to figure out how to respond, Trump intimidated them. A significant number, led by Senator Lindsey Graham—"a stiff," said Trump—dropped out months before the voters had any say. At times voters seemed mesmerized. Despite calling the state's voters stupid, Trump almost won the Iowa caucuses. Rand Paul, whom Trump called "truly stupid," did so poorly in that contest that he exited the next day. Jeb, whose family summered in neighboring Maine and had always enjoyed support in New Hampshire, took aim at its first-in-the-nation primary. He spent lots of time there and started to get momentum, but it was far too late. He got just 11 percent support. Trump got 35 percent.

Given how many voted for someone else, you could say that the people of New Hampshire were not all that enthusiastic about

Trump, and this reflected long-standing sentiment in the country as a whole. Trump's 35 percent of the Granite State vote was equal to historic polls of his popularity as an entertainer, when surveys found that the majority of people were turned off by his noxious attitude and behavior. But what Trump understood was that in a world of many options, his one-third support was more than enough to prevail, whether it was in the TV ratings or in a multicandidate election campaign. That's what happened in New Hampshire, which caused Chris Christie ("a little boy"), Carly Fiorina ("horseface"), and Rand Paul to drop out. In the very next primary, in South Carolina, Trump was nicked a bit. Rubio and Cruz both grabbed a bit more than 22 percent, but Jeb mustered less than 8 percent and dropped out.

Depressing as it was for someone who liked Jeb and was becoming more alarmed by Trump every day, I expected the result. I had been in the so-called spin room after the South Carolina debate, where journalists gathered to hear what candidates and their supporters—called surrogates—had to say. As Jeb's surrogate, I was a rather lonesome presence. I looked around and saw reporters who'd ignored me swarming in one corner of the room. At the center of the swirl stood Donald Trump, spinning better than anyone. He was the only candidate who had bothered to perform his own spin (others felt it undignified) and he was selling himself hard as the winner of the debate. The reporters, whom he insulted daily as purveyors of "fake news," couldn't get enough of it.

With Bush dropping out, my best anyone-but-Trump option was

Rubio. After we texted a few times, I decided to back him publicly and went to meet his campaign people in Washington. In retrospect, I should have been worried that it had been so easy to text with Marco. No one running for president should be that available. The press had been reporting that he was rarely seen in the early primary states, had almost no local operatives in these states, and that his team had concluded that traditional campaigning was not a good investment. Better to focus on press appearances and social media. However, press reports and social media attention come only after you distinguish yourself from the pack. To do that, you must get in front of people.

Meanwhile, at rallies that grew ever larger as people recognized them as entertainment, Trump got people excited in ways the press couldn't ignore, for fear they would miss being there when things got ugly. I say ugly because Trump, who couldn't be nice even when handed a baby, dealt only in mockery, derision, and menace. This maniacal style, which had not been seen before in modern American politics, threatened to turn every crowd into a mob.

Anyone who has experience performing before crowds that come anticipating excitement knows that just about any audience can be whipped into a dangerous frenzy. In partisan politics we all know how to control this dynamic, for safety's sake and out of a commitment to our tradition of hard-fought campaigns. Trump instead toyed with the emotions of his followers, pushing them from anger to rage and occasionally moving them to violence. What reporter would turn away from a Trump event and risk not seeing this?

• • •

As you know, in the end Donald Trump chewed up "Little Marco" Rubio and "Lyin' Ted" Cruz months before the Republican National Convention. Having called Trump a "sniveling coward" and endured, in return, attacks on his wife, Cruz would soon make up with Trump and seek to become his best friend in the Senate. Thus, his words "sniveling coward" were revealed to be what psychologists call a "projection" of his innermost thoughts about himself.

At the convention, Cruz was literally booed off the stage by Trump's followers, who were encouraged when their man gazed stone-faced over the spectacle and pumped his fist at them. I knew I was witnessing the first cult of personality to ever seize control of a major party, and the humiliation of a senator who was one of the worst people to occupy the Senate since Republican Joe McCarthy of Wisconsin, who ruined many lives with his witch hunt of the 1950s.

For his part, Trump had succeeded in converting millions to his cult and threatening the destruction of the party by trashing norms, abandoning the cause of democracy, and dividing the country in ways that made me feel politically disoriented. I had begun to realize the Trump effect when I attended the Illinois state convention earlier in the year and saw a huge number of people wearing Trump regalia and talking about how it was now their party. Many turned their backs on me, and I reciprocated by quickly giving up on them. The freeze thawed a bit when I gathered my partisan feelings to give a talk calling for people to get behind the cause to defeat Democrat Hillary Clinton.

At the national convention I entered an environment where it seemed like half the people were decked out in Trump-inspired clown costumes, including face paint and toupees resembling his unique swooping comb-over. Outside the convention, dozens of men patrolled with automatic rifles, and a guy who called himself "Vermin Supreme" stood with a large rubber boot on his head and made an incomprehensible speech using a bullhorn.

The business of the convention included removing a long-standing platform plan that supported Ukraine against Russian aggression. Here again was another example of Republicans making a situation that Obama had screwed up—he did nothing when Moscow seized Crimea in 2014—worse for no good reason. Only later would we all learn that this deal benefited Trump's campaign manager, who was in hock to one of Vladimir Putin's billionaire cronies to the tune of tens of millions of dollars. The second worst thing that happened at the convention—chants of "Lock her up!" referring to Hillary Clinton—occurred about every hour. The third was Trump's bizarre entrance on the first day of the convention. He appeared in silhouette, shrouded in fake fog, and then seemed to walk on water as he stepped forward through bluish light. All of it seemed to have been borrowed from former pro wrestler The Undertaker and the singer Beyoncé, who both make use of the same stage tricks.

I LEFT THE CONVENTION BEFORE TRUMP WAS FINALLY NOMINATED and became the 2016 GOP candidate. In the campaign that ensued he was so easily offended, and quick to play the victim, that I judged him to be as weak as a person as he was strong as a performer. Weeks and then months passed with him falling into one controversy after another, and voters in my district began asking me when I was going to endorse him. As he welcomed Russia's support, attacked immigrants, including the parents of a Muslim soldier killed in Iraq, and insisted the election would be "rigged," I decided I could not support him.

When TV footage of Trump declaring that as a celebrity he could "grab" women "by the pussy," his campaign went into a tailspin. Added to more than a dozen allegations from women who said he sexually harassed and even assaulted them, "Pussygate" confirmed my choice to stay away from Trump. Other prominent Republicans abandoned him, but then former New York City mayor Rudy Giuliani came to his defense in the media and predicted that some big news about Hillary Clinton would break in a matter of days.

As a former United States attorney for New York, Giuliani was, and remained, a confidant of many FBI officials whose experience investigating Bill Clinton and others had left them with extremely negative views of Hillary. The big news about her came from their agency. For years House Republicans had considered Clinton's use of private computers to conduct State Department business a scandal, and the controversy had been used against her in the campaign. Then, true to Giuliani's prediction, the FBI announced it had discovered some Clinton-related emails in the laptop of a congressman named Anthony Weiner, who was under criminal investigation. These were being reviewed, said the FBI, and thus the email issue was back on the table. Two days prior to the election, FBI director James Comey announced nothing significant had been discovered in the Weiner trove, but this announcement came too late to be of much use to Clinton.

The emails issue had, in my mind, been serious but not as egregious as my colleagues claimed. However, Clinton's other problems, including her role in various scandals involving her husband's presidency, her handling of the attack on America's diplomatic mission in Benghazi, and the sense of entitlement she seemed to bring with her to every public moment, made it impossible for me to vote for her. Terrified of what Trump could mean for the country, I endorsed no one and contemplated a write-in choice.

By Election Day, with polls showing the candidates essentially tied, I knew my own reelection was assured because the Democrats didn't even field a candidate. As someone certain to win a seat in Congress, I didn't think my rejection of Trump made me a pariah. I believed that many other Republicans considered him beyond the pale, and since they couldn't abide Hillary Clinton, they had either left the presidential line on their ballot unchecked or written in someone they admired.

AT THE END OF THE DAY, I WENT TO THE GRUNDY COUNTY GOP watch party, which was in the basement of the Fraternal Order of Eagles Aerie in the small city of Morris. The basement was as you'd imagine it, a space of less than half a basketball court with a low ceiling and a massive bar in front of a TV with several neon beer signs. It smelled a little of hops and the fried-fish dinners that were served there every Friday night. As I circulated, almost no one spoke to me and some turned away as I approached them. Finally, I saw an elderly woman named Betty who had always been a supporter. My encounter with her went something like this.

"Hi, Betty. How are you?"

"If he loses," she said angrily, "it's your fault."

I had had enough. "Oh, you think it would be me and not the fact that he's a racist idiot?"

She snapped back with something about how Trump is not a racist and neither are his supporters.

"Betty, you're way smarter than this," I said. This she likely felt as an insult, and I wouldn't blame her.

Then, out of the corner of my eye, I saw Betty's husband approach.

"Okay, guys, okay," he said. "This is over now."

Having discovered I was persona non grata, I left to watch the returns at home. I thought I knew what was going to happen in the election and what would happen to me in the coming months. Trump would lose. The fever would be broken. America would begin to heal.

Oh, how little I knew.

CHAPTER 9

Carnage

Donald Trump claimed one and a half million people attended his swearing-in ceremony.

Gimme a break.

I attended the ceremony, which took place on the West Front of the Capitol, and sat about five rows up, with a full view of the crowd. It filled the space in front of the reflecting pool and then about three grids of the National Mall. To my eye it was much smaller than the 1 million I saw gathered at the second Obama swearing-in; his first had been attended by a record 1.8 million.

Trump's claim was absurd but it was not the most upsetting element of inauguration weekend. That distinction went to his theatrical behavior at the moment during the swearing in when he took part in the 220-year-old, peaceful-transfer-of-power ceremony that shows our democracy in action to the world and fixes the burden of the presidency on a person who, until the oath is spoken, cannot feel its weight. In his demeanor Trump seemed less like an authentic leader and more like an actor performing in the opening scene of a big-budget film that might be called *The President*.

This phase of the event began with the arrival of the VIPs, who took their seats to the strains of hymns and marches played by the Marine Band. Among them were congressional leaders, Supreme Court justices, departing president Obama, and former presidents Jimmy Carter, George W. Bush, and Bill Clinton. It was a procession of both power and history.

The music stopped right before a presenter with a powerful baritone voice announced the entrance of the vice president–elect Mike Pence and those responsible for arranging the event. Then he deepened his voice and said, "Ladies and gentlemen, the president-elect of the United States, Donald John Trump."

Marines in their dress uniforms—blue coats, white belts and caps—opened the two brass doors at the top of the steps and stood perfectly tall as they held them in place. Donald Trump emerged from beneath the canopy that extended about fifteen feet from the door with his overcoat and suit jacket unbuttoned to show his white shirt and his trademark extra-length necktie. It's likely that no president-elect had ever arranged his clothes so casually. I checked later, and all those who were photographed had buttoned up. In the audience, those who failed to consider this bit of swagger were probably distracted by the red tie that cascaded over his belly and landed six inches below his belt. It acted like a red arrow sign at a car wash, directing attention not to the line of cars waiting to be cleaned, but to his genitals. As a man exquisitely attuned to image and stagecraft, nothing in his appearance—not his dyed golden hair, nor the orangey skin—was unintentional, most especially the tie. His tie was *always* longer than everyone else's. Even when it wasn't red.

Trump stopped at the top of the stairs to raise a single fist, making himself look like so many autocrats pictured in history books. He then proceeded slowly down the carpeted stairway, enjoying every tick of the thirty seconds he took to descend twelve steps and walk the same number of steps to reach the front row. There he received a no-contact air kiss from his unsmiling wife, Melania. He greeted the Obamas, and Vice President Biden, and then took his seat at center stage.

Thirty minutes passed as the assembly heard various invocations and prayers. Music came from the University of Missouri Chorale, the Mormon Tabernacle Choir, and the Marine Band. Trump took the oath of office, vowing to uphold the Constitution, and then stood, for the first time, at a podium decorated with the presidential seal. Where Kennedy urged Americans to ask what they could do for their country, and Reagan promised we could preserve "this last great bastion of freedom," Trump painted an America in darkness. The speech would become known, immediately, by his phrase "American carnage."

In a blessedly brief address, Trump bragged of his election by a movement "the likes of which the world has never seen" and contrasted this with a landscape he called "American carnage" in the form of lost jobs, declining incomes, and poverty. His personal theme—the unrivaled quality of his support—was an unseemly boast belied by the facts. Forget the world. Trump's popular support wasn't even in the same ballpark as the groundswells that elected the likes of LBJ, Reagan, or even William Henry Harrison. Set aside, if you care, the fact that he lost the popular vote by almost two million. His margin of victory in the quirky Electoral College had been so slim that it ranked 48th out of 56 in history.

Trump's other theme, economic "carnage," drew on conditions caused by the Great Recession, which was sparked in 2007, and ignored seventy-five straight months of job growth, a gross domestic product rising faster than it had in five decades, and the previous year's 5.4 percent jump in household income. Also, the rate of poverty had dropped for two years in a row and sat at near the median rate for the previous fifty years of 12.5 percent.

As he ended with unenthusiastic shout-outs to faith and unity, Trump had proved he favored stagecraft over authenticity and fantasy over facts. He offered his final phrase, "God bless America," and jutted out his chin, furrowed his brow, and again raised a fist. He held it higher than he had before and shook it at the crowd. After turning to shake hands with nearby dignitaries, Trump stopped as he reached his chair and turned back to face the crowd. A seasoned stage pro, he knew how to milk the moment. He hopped back onto the platform that elevated the podium and threw *two* fists in the air. Just like Rocky Balboa. The cheering from the crowd grew a bit louder.

I applauded with no enthusiasm, as did Senate Majority Leader

Mitch McConnell and Speaker of the House Paul Ryan. Trump and Obama shook hands and clasped each other's left arm for emphasis. They spoke briefly, with Obama saying generously, "Good job." First Lady Melania Trump, who throughout the ceremony had smiled only when her husband looked at her directly, maintained a stern expression and offered him only a nod and two or three words as he approached her. In time it would seem that the new First Lady knew something of what was to come.

THE TWO THINGS I REMEMBER ABOUT THE 2017 ANNUAL REPUBLIcan legislative planning retreat in Philadelphia are that Donald Trump talked and acted just like the person you saw on TV during the campaign, and that I got . . . hmmm, what's that term . . . oh yes, shit-faced. In fact, I got as drunk as I have ever been. And only now am I coming to understand the reasons.

First of all, I was shaken by the sight and sound of Donald Trump giving a speech in person, which was an experience I had avoided until this moment. During the campaign he had said, "I can be more presidential than anybody." He could have chosen to present himself as presidential and thereby calm our fears. Instead, he chose to talk like the guy who also said, "I could stand in the middle of Fifth Avenue and shoot somebody and I wouldn't lose any voters." He repeated ridiculous claims—Mexico will pay for his border wall—and announced as fact that "Democrats are determined to replicate the most catastrophic failures of world history right here in the United States."

As I listened I thought to myself, "Is this really our president?" I knew we had elected some bad ones, but this guy was worse than Franklin Pierce. Trump's main strength lay in acting like some sort of demonic cheerleader, rallying people to his side. However, this shadow charisma was a superpower, which established a hold on the vulnerable. Ever since his nomination, and especially since his election, magic worked on the Republican Party—my party—as well as it worked on individuals. The bond was so tight that nothing he could do or say would break it.

It's hard to do justice to the inanity of Trump's remarks. He began with some grade-schooler comments about Philadelphia as the cradle of American independence. What followed was a word salad of campaign themes, bragging about executive orders, and sudden non sequiturs. At one point he stopped and blurted, "Paul Ryan and other leaders in Congress and I, and Mike Pence—how good a choice was Vice President Mike Pence?" Then, like a Vegas performer pointing at a star in the audience, Trump swept his arm toward Pence and commanded, "Stand up." In a preview to the many servile Pence moments to come, he did as told, to a smattering of applause. "Everybody loves him," said Trump.

Repealing Obamacare was one of the few policy goals the new president mentioned and here, too, he veered into the strange. Republicans had been promising to roll back the health-care program for five years. He wanted to be the one who fulfilled the pledge, because he was the one who had said during the campaign, "We'll have so much winning you're going to get bored with winning." However, he seemed to know his support on this issue was soft, so he suggested we do nothing for two years because premiums for the program would rise so high it would collapse on its own. Talk about hedging your bets.

In a later health-care policy discussion, which we held among ourselves, Tom McClintock of California explained the doubts held by lots of Republicans. "We had better be sure that we are prepared to live with the market being created," he said, because "that's going to be called Trumpcare." To make the point crystal clear, he added, "Republicans will own it lock, stock, and barrel, and we'll be judged on that."

McClintock's remark was secretly recorded and then released to the press. This practice, which gave the leaker some currency with a journalist, was typical of current-day politics. Today you have to assume that members of the House routinely record supposedly confidential gatherings and, if they believe they come off well, share them with the press.

At the retreat no one said anything that might be deemed critical of Donald Trump, nor would anyone mention that in the twenty months since campaigner Trump first promised a better and cheaper alternative to Obamacare, there was no sign it was even in development. He did better with his proposed $1 trillion infrastructure program, but he would never actually push to see it become law. Like his supposedly wonderful health-care plan, infrastructure would forever remain in the yapping stage. The blather would rise during seven so-called infrastructure weeks—remember him sitting behind the wheel of a semitruck and pretending to drive?—that never amounted to anything tangible.

Of course, at the start of every presidency, the party that holds the White House imagines not meaningless talk, bickering, and false starts, but a string of achievements justified by the supposed mandate granted by the voters. However, with presidents elected on the slimmest of margins in the popular vote—and sometimes, as in Trump's case, with minority support—the idea of a mandate is a bit of a stretch.

Fortunately for us, after the 2016 election the GOP retained control of the lower chamber. A similar result came in the Senate, where we lost two seats but held on to the majority. This meant the good guys—both parties consider themselves the good guys, by the way—would have to act fast and stick together before the electorate gave the bad guys the congressional majority in 2018.

In the meantime, Republicans in Congress and across the country gathered behind Trump and gave him extremely high levels of support. One could have hoped that this move reflected what writer James Surowiecki argues in his book *The Wisdom of Crowds*, that the public does a good job of making judgments and choosing a direction on the basis of choices made by large crowds. Indeed, he says that crowds are generally wiser than individual decision-makers because they accommodate the experience and judgment of many minds working at once. It's sort of like when scientists tap a huge network of personal computers to work on big problems. The wisdom of crowds may explain why voters intuitively toggle back and forth between the parties and often give one the legislative branch and the other the executive. Something inside them wants to limit the degree to which one party can change things. It's the notion of checks and balances, enshrined in the Constitution, expressed by the people.

Unfortunately, the wisdom of crowds can be blocked by devices like the Electoral College, which may be why only one other developed country, Ireland, uses this system and, like us, accepts that the chief executive may be chosen by the minority. This reality permits the reelection of the same chief executive, which explains in part an aspect of the retreat that was even more distressing than Trump: my colleagues' essentially unanimous conversion to his political cult.

One after another, members I respected and who I knew considered Trump a mean-spirited buffoon made it clear that they were behind him 100 percent. Unsurprisingly, the Freedom Caucus led the way, reacting to Trump in the way that superfans would react to the presence of Taylor Swift. But this rush also included nearly all my friends. A good example was Billy Long of Missouri, who was in my class of 2010. He had worked to regulate and reduce diesel emissions, improve rural broadband service, and fund suicide prevention programs. These priorities did not reflect Trump's priorities, and Billy abandoned them once it became clear that Trump would ruthlessly wield his power and punish wayward Republicans for their disloyalty. Just look at how he *humiliated* senator, former governor, and former GOP presidential nominee Mitt Romney by dangling the secretary of state job at a much-photographed "private" dinner and then picking Rex Tillerson, the chief executive officer of ExxonMobil. Tillerson's qualifications began and ended with his status as Vladimir Putin's best American friend. Just four years earlier he had signed a $3.2 billion deal to explore for oil in the Russian Arctic. Soon after this, Putin awarded him the Russian Medal of Friendship.

Trump expected that Tillerson would make US-Russia relations his top priority. This confirmed that what the president would dismissively call "this Russia thing" was in fact a serious concern. It also moved me to call for a government program to counter Russian disinformation that threatened our democracy. Among the specific targets I thought we needed to counter were the troll farms and the Russian government's Internet Research Agency, which had bombarded US social media with lies to help Trump and harm Clinton.

Fewer than a handful of Republicans in Congress were as receptive as I was when it came to the Russia thing. This didn't mean I had lost all hope for the immediate future. A handful of adults remained at the top ranks of the government. The courts were also in a position to impose some limits on Trump, and despite his ferocious campaign to discredit them as an "enemy of the American people," the press could potentially investigate and publicize the inevitable scandals that would emerge from within the administration.

As I calibrated my view of the future, I had to adjust for the very real possibility that the snail's-paced court system would do little to moderate Trump, as well as the certainty that under GOP control, there would be no legislative oversight of the administration.

And the press? The country had long been divided between conservative and liberal media sources, which left precious few in the middle, absorbing reality-based reports. This wasn't the Watergate age, when every major outlet worked to limit bias and present serious reports. It was the Fox News/MSNBC age, and this meant that fully half the people would be denied the fullest truth on any issue of consequence.

A splintered press. A captive Congress. A legal system designed to move in increments. No wonder I left the crowd at the retreat, found a place to drink, and kept at it until I could barely navigate to my room.

THE ALCOHOL PRESCRIPTION FOR MY PSYCHIC PAIN WORKED AT the time, but it was not worth the physical pain I felt when I woke up. It got worse when I rolled over, checked the clock, and realized that I was supposed to meet a crew from CNN in ten minutes. Through prior experience, I had learned how to wash, jump into clothes, and take off at a run no matter how I felt. I went through this routine and met up with the TV team in time to put an earpiece in and do a mic check with the control room in New York. Then the field producer announced there would be a delay.

"You're on camera and the control room can see you're really sweaty," she said. "We're going to hold you for fifteen or twenty minutes so you can cool off."

Although I can't recall now anything I said in the interview, I had obviously played it safe because no one at the retreat said anything about it to me afterward. And no one said a word about my bloodshot eyes and the little pauses I needed to take so that I could kick my brain into gear after a question was posed. Of course, this may have been because most of them were either in the same condition I was the night before, or they had been there and done that and would never judge me for looking a little green around the gills on TV.

Everyone in the national politics business knew that the Washington inhabited by members of Congress—especially younger members of Congress—was about as alcohol soaked as a college fraternity, except that most of the booze is free and it generally comes with the best food in town. Think of *Animal House* but with expensive whiskey instead of beer, aged steaks instead of pizza, and no cash required. Some of those who indulge are social drinkers who know their limits. Others are alcoholics who have an incredible tolerance. If you doubt my reference to addiction, check the twenty-four-hours-a-day schedule for Alcoholics Anonymous meetings in the capital.

But addiction and pleasure drinking don't explain why so many members of Congress, especially the younger ones, imbibe so heavily. The real reason is their insecurity. Despite the clichés, a great many people who run for office are not natural glad-handing extroverts. They are, instead, perpetually uncomfortable introverts trying to prove something to themselves or others. In high school they were the kids who were rejected by the popular crowd but signed up for the debate team so they could stand up for themselves, at least verbally. Many believe they will overcome their insecurity with their election only to discover there are popular kids in the House, too, and they are hard to impress. The Freedom Caucus was full of these awkward but also envious people who inevitably revert to type, becoming desperate to be liked. And it showed.

There's also the money factor. Those who come to Congress without independent wealth find it hard to resist freebies. This is why expensive DC restaurants are often packed with small groups of members in the company of lobbyists who are delighted to fatten people who wield votes in the House. I use the word *fatten* here in a deliberate way since, just like college students, members of Congress typically gain a "freshman twenty" pounds thanks to these meals and alcohol. I did, and it took a year of concerted exercise to get rid of them. One side benefit: the gym is a great place to meet and talk with colleagues without fear of being recorded, as you might be on the phone. I mean, who can hide a taping device in the towel that's wrapped around their waist?

Thanks to working out, I could continue eating high on the menu several nights a week, all for the price of talking with someone who wanted to influence me. But since my interests and their interests were often aligned, and lobbyists are hired for their pleasant personalities, this price doesn't seem that high.

Sometimes the perks of office go beyond Washington to include international trips for official and unofficial business, which become opportunities to have a good time. But of course, when you put dozens of what I'd call "baby congressmen" on planes and buses, unexpected things are going to happen.

In my freshman summer I joined a fact-finding tour of Israel. Most of our daylight tours were spent with government officials who showed us defense facilities, areas where they struggle to maintain security, and examples of the country's wealth and development as well as its areas of vulnerability. Israel is surrounded by potential and actual enemies and is isolated as a functioning democracy. It needs American support. In the years since it was founded, the country has received more money from America than any other country. Today it flows at a rate of $150 billion annually. This is perhaps the biggest reason for the Israelis to stand as eager hosts for an endless stream of American finders of fact. It's not a matter of tolerating us. They want to strengthen the US-Israeli bond by impressing us with on-the-ground experiences. When you see how many members of Congress return from these trips as pro-Israel hawks, you understand that this kind of tourism for the powerful works extremely well. However, I was already very pro-Israel before the trip.

On the last night of the trip to Israel, we were invited to celebrate at a restaurant on the shore of the Sea of Galilee. It was free, of course, and our hosts even sent a barge to anchor offshore and serve as a platform for technicians who launched beautiful fireworks. Like so many places in Israel—Jerusalem, Hebron, Bethlehem—the mention of our destination evoked in me and others the religious element of our own identities. The Sea of Galilee is the lake where Jesus was baptized by John the Baptist. It's where, according to Scripture, he walked on water and where he fed a multitude of people with a small supply of bread and fish that miraculously never ran out.

After a dinner that began with several shots and included fine wines and after-dinner drinks, we followed through on a plan for a swim that we'd concocted earlier, with one change driven by the booze. Because the sea meant so much to many of us, we wanted to commemorate this moment by going in. Instead of respectfully wading in, the alcohol convinced us we could jump in in our underwear. Ignoring my poor swimming ability, I got thirty feet out from shore and started to panic. My anxiety caused me to throw up in the water (classy!) and I shouted for help. I can't recall who came to my aid, but someone did. When we reached the beach, I could see the guys on the security detail had taken off their ties and jackets so they could jump in if necessary. Fortunately, it didn't become quite such a dire situation.

The following morning, some of my colleagues began expressing their fear that our swim would become public. Talk of scandal began. We could imagine the headline—CONGRESSMEN STRIP AND SWIM IN SACRED SEA. Our shared anxiety meant that no one spoke of the escapade until months after we were home, when an article appeared in *Politico*. The story got out because Republican Dave Schweikert, running in a primary against Ben Quayle, had been on the Israel trip and leaked it.

After Galilee, I vowed to attend only events where I could talk to people about the needs of my district and the hosts could aid us. If I went abroad I would stick to business. Stay out of the water. And I wouldn't let myself drink too much. I did this in my day-to-day life at home too.

ONCE I CEASED TO BECOME A PARTY-HARD PAL FOR OTHER FRESHmen, I dedicated myself to being a good Team Player. The Team

Player label belonged to members who build independent political action committees, raise substantial amounts of money, and then distribute the money to other members facing tougher elections. Good Team Player status also requires voicing support for everyone in the party and holding back critical thoughts. Thus, I complied with what Ronald Reagan said was the "the eleventh commandment" for good Republicans. Democrats have their own loyalty practices, which explains why Bill Clinton was impeached but not convicted on charges of perjury and obstruction of justice related to a sexual affair with a White House intern. Before Clinton's impeachment, it was Republicans who steadfastly supported Richard Nixon as the Watergate scandal grew and grew until the point where it got so bad he resigned from office to avoid the shame and save the country from the political trauma of an impeachment. Nixon should have stayed in office, according to Trump, even if the decision led to a national political crisis worse than Watergate.

For a couple of years, Trump avoided being tested like Nixon. Back then, the scandals of the Trump administration generally involved minor financial corruption of cabinet members. Although the volume of these financial and ethical scandals was unusual— seven in the first year alone—none of them registered strongly with the public. This was, in part, because Trump governed and practiced politics so chaotically that people struggled to keep up, let alone grasp the import of any single event. Whether he was issuing lies via Twitter or threatening the North Atlantic Treaty Organization, or continuing to deny the Russia scandal, Trump kept the entire nation focused on his bizarre or troubling behavior and wondering what would come next.

Although this was partly attributable to his nature, I believe it was also a deliberate strategy. The method was once explained by Trump adviser Steve Bannon, who used the football expression "flood the zone" to describe it. In football, it means sending so many offensive players to one area of the field—a zone—that defenders can't keep track of them. With Trump, the zone was the time and energy people could devote to keeping track of him. He flooded the "zone" with so many lies, distractions, and absurdities that those who tried to defend themselves would fail.

Looking back, it's astounding to see how many people and institutions Trump disparaged. Early in his presidency, I was appalled by his attack on key allies like NATO. No organization has been more essential to keeping the peace than NATO, and, since Trump had been aided in the 2016 election by Russian operatives, there was no way to ignore the possibility that his effort to wound NATO was a thank-you to Putin for all his help. This idea gained more traction when Trump emerged from a meeting with the Russian dictator to say Putin had denied election interference and that he had no reason to doubt his claim.

The idea that Trump and the Russians had a political partnership was something my party fought with a determination that matched the resolve our forebears brought to fighting communism and the expansionist goals of the other Soviet Union. Members of my party understood that the current regime in Moscow, run by a former Soviet spy, Vladimir Putin, was just as eager for empire as the old USSR and had recently demonstrated it by launching an unprovoked invasion and occupation in parts of Ukraine. They also knew that one of Trump's campaign advisers had spoken with Russian officials about getting some assistance, and that the campaign employed a manager who had worked in Moscow and Ukraine as a political operative and owed almost $20 million to one of Putin's oligarch buddies. This came out after the Republican National Convention withdrew its long-standing commitment to support Ukraine against Russian aggression.

As my GOP colleagues in Congress lined up behind Trump on the Russia issue, I stuck with my position in support of Ukrainian independence and security. The mood in the caucus turned paranoid as Trump sent out thousands of social media messages to seventy million followers, who responded to those by attacking other politicians, including Republicans, as if they were calls to political combat. Any talk of Trump's deficiencies—the man was truly unfit for his office—occurred in private between those who had made certain they shared the same perspective.

It stunned me to see how supposedly mature men and women in Congress trembled at the thought of being targeted by a tweet or Facebook post. It reminded me of an episode of the original *Twilight Zone* called "It's a Good Life." The program revolved around a monstrous mind-reading boy named Anthony who possesses the superpower to destroy all with just a thought. Set in the one community left on earth, it shows the excruciating efforts adults make to avoid even thinking something negative. It ends with Anthony still in charge, making the grown-ups do whatever he wants.

Terrified of Trump's ability to destroy their careers, twenty-six House Republicans, the most since 1972, retired before they would have to run for reelection in 2018. This spared them the indignity of losing to a Trump-backed primary challenger and relieved them of the stress of life in a place where the safe topics for conversation were baseball, the weather, and Trump's successes, the few genuine ones which included tax cuts, judicial appointments, and smaller measures like the creation of a medical-care hotline for military veterans.

On the Senate side of the Capitol, two Trump critics whose terms were ending, Bob Corker of Tennessee and Jeff Flake of Arizona, resigned rather than face difficult primaries. In his farewell remarks on the floor of the Senate, Flake spoke of his personal frustration with gridlock and a politics of anger and his alarm over Trump. "There are times when we must risk our careers in favor of our principles," he said. "Now is such a time." He warned of the Senate's "complicity" with the unacceptable. "I rise to say, enough."

Flake was unlikely to be reelected, which Trump's allies pointed out as they skewered him as a traitor. Others said that he should have braved the fight on the chance he might win and return to join those who said they stayed in Congress to do what they could to either counter or guide the wayward president. The latter assumed that he wanted to be guided toward more reasonable behavior.

Speaker of the House Ryan and Senate Majority Leader McConnell tried to coach Trump in the ways of governing, which really can't be done by picking fights, ignoring your own advisers, and believing in your own infallibility. "Mitch McConnell and I spoke quite a bit in these early hours," Ryan would eventually tell *The New York Times*. "I put out this massive Gantt chart with McConnell's consent. Every time he [Trump] put out some crazy tweet or tried to get Congress off its agenda, I'd always say, 'No, remember, we have this Gantt chart, and this is what we're supposed to be doing now.'"

The chart used horizontal bars to indicate each of several projects—traditional tax cuts, deregulation, etc.—and vertical lines showing deadlines for the steps needed to achieve each one. It was a useful tool, but it was pure Egghead Ryan to use the formal name of the thing as he discussed it.

Eggheads irritate a lot of Americans, including members of Congress. They come across as smarter-than-thou types. (Exhibit A = Barack Obama.) But if Ryan drifted into this super-nerd territory as he explained the approach, it didn't mean he and McConnell hadn't done extremely important work. They also played the political magic trick of using false praise and support to disguise their real intent. Since the president's main currency is ass-kissing—he likes to smooch and *be* smooched—this move gave them the best possible chance to exert some influence.

In the meantime, Trump would use his timeworn tactics of threats, punishment, and charm to continue indulging his instincts. As so many reported after visiting him back in his New York days or in Washington, Trump could be exceedingly charming, even fun to be around. He loved giving people tours at the White House, impressing them with the button he used to summon a Diet Coke whenever he wanted one.

Trump displayed his childishness with more important guests too.

As FBI director James Comey noted in his book *A Higher Loyalty*, the White House kitchen was on notice that the president should always be served twice as much ice cream as anyone he invited for a private dinner, and to watch him interact with champion athletes when they visited—he offered the Clemson University football team a buffet of fast food—you would have thought he was an eight-year-old at heart. This was something his ex-wife Marla Maples said she found charming in him.

I found Trump puzzling, deluded, self-indulgent, and cruel. At one meeting with him, I expected the cold shoulder because I had opposed his candidacy for president. Instead, in what I learned was one of his hallmark moves, he tried to win me over. He told the others in the room that I dressed very well and was terrific on TV. Since he was addicted to cable news, often flipping from channel to channel, I understood that Trump had seen me, and I knew that he valued performance above all else. Remember, he became nationally famous playing the mogul/host of the reality show *The Apprentice*, where his catchphrase was "You're fired!" But in the moment his reaction to me was puzzling.

In another visit to the White House, a group of us tried to discuss the Chinese company ZTE, which was selling US communications technology to Iran and North Korea. The company had shipped microprocessors, routers, servers, and the software to help both countries build entire networks. The original agreement that permitted China's *own* receipt of the US technology, which Silicon Valley companies had pushed hard to complete, had been extremely controversial. Federal experts had determined that the equipment could be rigged to collect data that might be transferred back to the seller. Given the Chinese government's partial ownership in ZTE, the data could be used for all sorts of nefarious purposes, from industrial espionage to the capture of government data. Over the course of a US investigation, begun before Trump was president, we had discovered that ZTE executives kept the sale to North Korea and Iran secret even from their auditors. This suggests that the Chinese government was involved. With their repeated declarations of hostile intentions toward America's allies, nuclear weapons programs, and terrorism, Iran and North Korea were among the most dangerous nations on the planet. The world depended on us to contain them. With our sanctions came a warning that those countries who evaded them would be excluded from all trade with the United States. The sanctions worked, as Iran and North Korea were forced to go without, or pay black market prices for, essential commodities and goods.

President Trump had campaigned on the promise to be tough on China, which manipulated currencies and unfairly subsidized exporters, but he said he wouldn't crack down on ZTE because he had promised China's president, Xi Jinping, that he would go easy on the company. In fact, Trump had agreed to drop all sanctions on ZTE because Xi had complained about job losses, which he somehow linked to the history of Western aggression against his country going back more than a century.

This problem was a classic example of the complexity of our relations with other countries. Trump's desire to govern by personal relationships made things even more complicated. Years later, then national security adviser John Bolton would write about it, saying that Trump "said he had told [Commerce Secretary Wilbur] Ross to work something out for China, Xi replied that if that were done, he would owe Trump a favor and Trump immediately responded he was doing this because of Xi." This is not the way to protect America's interest via diplomacy. But it satisfied Trump's self-indulgent instinct.

This instinct continued to be on full display when I went to the White House to talk with Trump about continuing to aid and protect the Syrian, Iraqi, and Turkish Kurds, who occupied refugee camps on the border with Turkey. Kurdish fighters had been our fierce allies in northern Iraq and continued to be a great source of intelligence. Unfortunately, they had also been engaged in a long-running struggle to gain political control of ethnic enclaves in Iraq, Syria, and eastern Turkey. I certainly opposed any effort to widen this conflict to Syria and felt that the Kurds deserved our aid, if not because it was humane, then because we owed them.

However, Turkey's prime minister, Recep Erdogan, who had evolved from a democrat into an autocrat, called Trump on a Sunday to request that the US troops stationed to protect the Kurdish camps in Syria be ordered out of the country. A self-avowed admirer of strongmen, who considered Xi, Erdogan, and others to be friends, Trump acceded to the request. To my horror, the Turks attacked the Kurds in Syria as soon as our soldiers departed. Estimates of the number of Kurds killed ranged as high as five hundred, with wounded estimated at fifteen hundred. This included many civilians who were killed and wounded as they fled. Their blood was spilled as a result of Trump's cruelty.

YOU WOULD THINK AN EXPERIENCE LIKE THE ONE I HAD WITH Trump over the Kurds would have prepared me to vote to impeach him for his betrayal of Ukraine. Hell, the Ukraine issue was already, well, hot as hell, when he granted Erdogan's request. And as the Democrats investigated the scandal and then conducted hearings, I was inclined to vote to impeach him, which would be the equivalent of an indictment, which would be followed by a trial in the Senate.

With any other president, the story of an impeachment would be locked in your memory. In the 242 years since America claimed its independence, only two presidents had been impeached. Andrew Johnson was impeached but not convicted in 1868. The outcome was the same for Clinton in 1999. Both benefited from the constitutional requirement of a two-thirds vote for conviction, and it was this high bar, posed against the support Trump had in the Senate, that gave me pause. If I voted to impeach him, I would have invited a primary challenger who would definitely win the nomination and end my tenure in the House. Like everyone else in Congress, I believed that my presence truly mattered. "Indispensable" was too strong a word to attach to this belief. It was more like *not dispensable*. This was an attitude I tried hard to develop, and if I ever lost it, people in my family were sure to call me on it. Based on my interactions with them, many of my colleagues chose not to perform this kind of reality check. Spend a few days among them and you would notice it too.

When I say the decision to vote for impeachment gave me pause, I don't mean I believed that Trump had done nothing wrong. He had held up vital military aid, which the United States had promised to Ukraine for its fight against Russian invaders, on the condition that the country's newly elected president, Volodymyr Zelenskyy, help him push back against the Russia election interference controversy. Trump preferred that Kyiv, not Moscow, be shown to have interfered. He also asked Zelenskyy to investigate the son of former vice president Joe Biden to help prove that he had leveraged his father's office to receive payments from a Ukrainian energy company. By that time, Biden was already the front-runner in the race for the Democratic Party's 2020 presidential nomination.

As a former actor and comedian, Zelenskyy had played the comic role of a man who bumbled into his country's highest office. When he was actually elected, it was mainly because voters saw their choice as a protest against widespread corruption. Zelenskyy was overmatched in the call, in which Trump said, "I would like you to do us a favor" in exchange for the assistance. In a transcript of the call, Trump sounds every bit like a gangster and Zelenskyy like a beleaguered leader desperate to keep the Russians, who had already seized the Crimean Peninsula and part of the Donbas region, from advancing further. (This is why he needed the promised American matériel.) Instead, Zelenskyy was met with the demand that he

target Joe Biden, whom Trump believed would be his 2020 opponent, and come up with evidence that Biden had leveraged his status
as Obama's vice president to shake down Ukrainian businesses.
Zelenskyy did not say "no" in a direct way, but he would not do what
the American president asked him to do.

Trump's scheme was aided by a team of clownish figures who
held no government position. Lev Parnas and Igor Fruman were
Ukrainian businessmen who had bought their way into Trump's
orbit with substantial campaign donations. They became partners
with Rudy Giuliani, who, after winning international approval for
responding to the 9/11 attack as New York City mayor, squan-
dered the goodwill with continuous attention-seeking and pursuit
of enormous fees for political consulting. He had once chased
Trump's nomination to the position of secretary of state. The closest
he would come involved announcing he was "President Trump's attorney" to gain access to European officials and undermine the real
diplomats.

The Ukraine scandal was revealed by a whistle-blower who was
supported by other witnesses but vilified by Trump's loyalists in
Congress at every turn. The Democrat-held House first used the
intelligence committee to investigate by conducting hearings in a
secure, below-ground spy-proof room called the sensitive compart-
mented information facility (SCIF). Generally restricted to members of the committee, the SCIF was open to others because of the
nature of the proceedings. But their numbers were limited by the
size of the room. Some of my more extreme colleagues would storm
the SCIF and violate its security. A few moderates disappointed me

by joining in. Some of them told me it was an easy way to signal support for Trump without serious repercussions.

As the impeachment vote neared, I criticized Trump for stirring anger and fear (a habit of his) by saying the push constituted "treason." He retweeted fundamentalist pastor Robert Jeffress's warning that it would cause "a civil war–like fracture." Jeffress was one of several religious leaders who exalted Trump's hideous ways. Nationally prominent preacher Franklin Graham, for example, abandoned his father Billy's famous and effective neutrality to become a shameless Trump supporter. He declared Republicans who stood against Trump to be like "Judas," which would make the profane and immoral president Jesus Christ. When the treason and civil war comments were made, I felt obliged to push back, noting that since presidents are supposed to keep the country the *United* States, these statements were "beyond repugnant."

Trump's behavior, the testimony of dozens who met with House committees, and documentary evidence did add up to a compelling case for impeachment, but supporting it would require an act of rebellion that I wasn't ready to make. The Democrats gave me and others an out as they rushed to finish their report and ask for a vote before the Christmas break of 2019. They justified the decision by saying that January 1 would mark the start of 2020 and another campaign for president, and they didn't want to make the issue more complicated by delaying. On the other hand, Republicans could say that every year is a campaign year, practically speaking, and that moving so quickly indicated a lack of seriousness.

I never defended Trump against the charges and left open the possibility that I could vote to impeach. But with every other Republican voting no, I couldn't imagine standing as the lone member of the caucus voting with the Democrats. I did know that the other Republican who gave serious thought to a yes vote, Liz Cheney of Wyoming, had finally decided to vote against the articles of impeachment. The timing and flaws in the case put to the House by the Judiciary Committee made it easier for me to march with my side. Besides, there was no chance that the House managers who would prosecute the case would get two thirds of the votes.

The result in the Senate was what I expected, with one minor twist. Mitt Romney of Utah voted to convict Trump on the charge of abuse of power. In the process, he became the first senator to vote to convict an impeached president of his own party. He was, in this case, a greater renegade than me.

Do I regret not taking a similar stand and accepting the consequences? When I think of what followed, I do. If I hadn't buckled under the pressure my colleagues brought to bear, I may have given cover to others who were on the fence. We, in turn, could have demonstrated to the country that the system is not as broken as they think. Instead, I played along, hoping Trump would be chastened. He wasn't. In fact, things would get much worse. So yeah, I regret it. As he might say, I regret it "big time."

CHAPTER 10

I Am a Traitor
(and I'm Okay with It)

Chris Krebs: Dude, I think there's going to be violence.
Kinzinger: On January sixth?
Chris Krebs: One hundred percent.
Kinzinger: I think so too.

—December 2020 text exchange with Trump
administration chief of US election security

On the day when the crimes were committed, an emergency alert system that had rarely been activated in my time in Congress alerted us to an active threat against us. A second alert came within an hour. Urging members and staffers to shelter behind locked doors, I hunkered in my congressional office. The massive door to the reception area, typically wide open, had been locked against the mob that was roaming the Capitol. They were pounding on doors and breaking into some offices, where they began rifling through desks and cabinets. My gun rested on my desktop. I prayed that I wouldn't have to use it. I wasn't afraid, but I was shocked and horrified by events that were almost unimaginable.

I also realized that the party that once held my loyalty was gone. It had been replaced by a fascist cult of personality built upon decades of ever more extreme partisan politics and cultural warfare. It had all come to this, I thought. It had all come to this.

THE REPUBLICAN PARTY HAD STARTED DOWN THE ROAD TO THE January 6 attacks even before the November election results were in. On the day after people went to the polls, with key states yet to finish counting, Trump's former secretary of energy, Rick Perry, sent a text to White House chief of staff Mark Meadows that began "HERE's an AGRESSIVE [sic] STRATEGY." He went on to note that states could reject the electors chosen by the voters and send pro-Trump ones to Washington for the formal meeting of the Electoral College, where, as in every prior election, a pro forma count would be done. The whole mess would then "go to SCOTUS," added Perry. SCOTUS is, of course, the Supreme Court of the United States, and the implication was that with a conservative majority, including three justices whom Trump appointed, he would have a good chance of being declared the winner.

Twenty-four hours after Perry's text, with the vote count yet to be finalized, the president's son Donald Trump Jr. wasn't willing to wait for his father's loss to be announced, per modern tradition, by the Associated Press. Instead, Junior texted Meadows to give him a list of states where Republicans held the governorship and controlled the legislature and could simply certify an Electoral College count different from the voters' choice. "We have multiple paths," he wrote. "We control them all."

One of the paths involved telling Republicans in the states to organize alternative electors pledged to Trump. These states would stand by and, if one of the many lawsuits filed by the president's campaign succeeded, crash the Electoral College meeting in Washington, DC. Party activists went along with the scheme, declaring themselves electors in six states, which together held seventy-nine Electoral College votes. This number would give Trump a five-vote win in the national count and the reelection he desperately craved. But as the Trump campaign lost every legal challenge, the alternative electors' initiative fizzled. Several of Trump's advisers, including Attorney General Bill Barr and Secretary of Labor Eugene Scalia, counseled him to accept defeat.

Unfortunately, one of Trump's defining characteristics is his refusal to give up on getting what he wants. Another is his willingness to win by any means necessary, especially if it is so complicated that it catches the other side by surprise.

The search for another extraordinary measure led Trump and his team to target the very final act of the election, which must occur on January 6, when the US Congress accepts and records the state certificates that communicate their electoral count results. A single constitutional scholar, John Eastman, had advised Trump that the presiding officer of this ritual, Vice President Mike Pence, could accept the pro-Trump certificates from states where Republican control of the legislative and executive branches permitted them to override the will of the voters to give him their Electoral College votes. Should Pence refuse to act, members of the House and Senate could object to the certification of specific states. The rules required one senator and one member of the House to object. In this event, both houses of Congress would hold a debate of up to two hours and vote on whether to accept the certificates that would turn a loser into a winner.

When they learned of what Trump planned, GOP creatures in Washington and in the states joined the cause with the enthusiasm of a bunch of high schoolers who thought they had figured out how to hack a teacher's computer to get the answers to the final exam. Thirteen senators and more than one hundred representatives put themselves into this game, declaring that they would raise objections. There was only the smallest chance that the challenges would work, but those who backed them would enjoy the president's favor and, presumably, the support of Trump voters back home.

I went to several meetings where I tried to get House members and senators to stand against this plan. I met with one senator in his little hideaway office, a pleasant perk of life in the upper chamber, thinking that because he had been defeated in November, he would want to help cool the country off. I think I was right about where his heart was but wrong about his head. He was afraid to stand against Trump because he might one day want to run for governor, or even a higher office, and it could cost him a nomination. Like all the others, he wasn't going to risk his political career by doing the right thing.

Of course, no one comes right out and says, "I hate Trump but I'm going to stay quiet because I'm a coward who won't follow my conscience if it looks like it'll cost me something." What they do is agree with you without really agreeing and worm out of making a commitment. You can press for a clear answer, but remember, these are politicians. They are experts at giving nonanswers to direct questions or creating an escape hatch by saying something like "As of this moment I agree with you but . . ." You can fill in the blanks yourself, I'm sure. Then, when they take the easy way out, they hide behind the folks back home, falling back on the idea that they are elected to follow, not lead.

What too many could not appreciate fully was the way that the Electoral College report scheme would raise the expectations of the 74.2 million who had voted for Trump, most of whom believed, despite Biden's vote total of 81.2 million, that they had been robbed of a victory. These people had heard Trump's claims of fraud and seen them confirmed by people in right-wing media. They had been excited by Trump's call to attend a so-called Stop the Steal rally for the same day—January 6—that the Electoral College votes would be accepted. "Will be wild!" he promised on social media.

When I considered that Chris Krebs had told me that law enforcement thought January 6 would bring violence, I decided to take a stab at getting my colleagues to back away from the plans to tie up Congress's receipt of the votes with their objections. I did it on

January 1, 2021, on a conference call that connected every House Republican who wanted to participate, or at least listen to the caucus's plans for the future.

Liz Cheney was the first to speak. She argued that January 6 would be a dark day if House members indulged in the fantasy that they could overturn the election. They didn't have the right to, she said, and doing so would push them further from true, small-government conservatism than they already were. Liz followed her warning with a twenty-one-page paper that proved that neither Congress nor state authorities held the power to overturn the election. Citing legal rulings, including decisions made on Trump's postelection suits, she refuted the very concept of challenging the counts in all the targeted states, from Arizona to Wisconsin. I was not one of the 175 members of Congress who were lawyers—you read that right, 175 are lawyers—but you didn't need a law degree to see that this was a brilliant document. Citing the Constitution, the law, and precedent, she made it obvious that there was "no basis to object to the electors in any of the six states at issue."

After Liz spoke, McCarthy immediately told everyone who was listening, "I just want to be clear. Liz doesn't speak for the conference. She speaks for herself." This statement wasn't necessary. Everyone knew she was speaking as an individual member and not from her position as chairperson of the caucus. Jumping in to emphasize the obvious was unnecessary and disrespectful, and it infuriated me.

I spoke right after McCarthy got in his little dig.

"Look, I know these people," I said. "I know what's going on in social media, and it looks like the sixth could get really bad. People are saying that if they are convinced the election was stolen it's their patriotic duty to use violence." If a substantial number of House members and senators announced they would object to counting some state's vote, Trump's people would come expecting to celebrate a political miracle. If it looked like they weren't going to get one, they would try to force the issue. Whipped up by a Trump rally performance, they were likely to let loose the anger they had felt since the election was called for Biden. I finished by calling on McCarthy to say that as minority leader, he wouldn't join the group opposing the Electoral College states. He replied by coming on the line to say, "Okay, Adam. Operator, who's up next?"

McCarthy's rude and dismissive tone was typical of his style, which was notably juvenile, especially when compared with his predecessors'. Paul Ryan had made policy arguments that he hoped would bring the caucus together behind real ideas. John Boehner was equally committed to an agenda of getting things done but did it with genuine warmth and humor. Both men understood and accepted that sometimes a member of the caucus had to go his or her way. No harm, no foul. McCarthy was much more like an attention-seeking high school senior who readily picked on anyone who didn't fall in line.

I went from being one of the boys he treated with big smiles and pats on the back to outcast as soon as I started speaking the truth about the president who would be king. He responded by trying to intimidate me physically. Once, I was standing in the aisle that runs from the floor to the back of the chamber. As he passed, with his security man and some of his boys, he veered toward me, hit me with his shoulder and then kept going. If we had been in high school,

I would have dropped my books, papers would have been scattered, and I would have had to endure the snickers of passersby. I was startled but took it as the kind of thing Kevin did when he liked you. Another time, I was standing at the rail that curves around the back of the last row of seats in the chamber. As he shoulder-checked me again, I thought to myself, "What a child," and felt some anger and thought to say something. Instead, I just chalked it up to the immature behavior that he favored and that had become more and more common inside the chamber.

In the few days between the Republican conference call and January 6, I realized why the Trumpists seemed so familiar. They were fundamentalist in their politics, just as people I knew as a kid were fundamentalist in their religion. They believed that life was a drama in which good and evil battled for control, and that they, who stood for good, had no choice but to engage in the fight. In the religious version of Fundamentalism, confidence in the Bible as they understood it was the foundation of one's identity. In this political fundamentalism, it was Trump's word, not the Word of God, that mattered.

The most dangerous of Trump's followers practiced both religious and political fundamentalism, which meant that the word of God and the word of Trump were equally motivating. They struggled against both the evil represented by Satan and the one represented by wayward Republicans. These Republicans are, to the Trumpists, like apostates to Fundamentalists. They were worse than Democrats because they had heard the truth and should believe. In that way Trumpists were similar to Islamic fundamentalists, who wage battle to create Islamic states where government operates on the basis of strict religious dogma. In this scheme, McCarthy and others could be considered mullahs who would handle day-to-day affairs and discipline those who committed relatively minor transgressions against the state and Islamic orthodoxy. Trump could be considered the equivalent of the chief ayatollah or supreme leader, who would inspire and rule on the biggest issues.

Unfortunately, Fundamentalism generally evolves toward more restrictive rules and greater power for the person at the top until eventually you reach the point of authoritarianism. Since the Trump movement was extremely right wing, fascism was the logical destination, and proof of this could be seen in the movement's symbols— Confederate flags, for example—and heard in hateful rhetoric at events like the 2017 Unite the Right rally, where young men paraded with torches and chanted, "Jews will not replace us." More recently, Hitler had come to the mind of a freshman representative from my home state, and she didn't hesitate to mention him at a gathering of women activists.

"Hitler was right on one thing," said Mary Miller. "He said, 'Whoever has the youth has the future.'"

I'M AN AMERICAN MAN FROM THE SMALL-TOWN MIDWEST AND A well-trained military officer. I believe that stable, law-abiding people have a right to own guns for their personal safety. I have a Ruger LCP for this very reason. It's made for self-defense. On January 6, 2021, given Chris Krebs's warning of impending violence and my own fear of a rally crowd becoming a violent mob, it made sense to have it ready.

Except for the more than usual number of red ballcaps with the Trump slogan Make America Great Again, I saw nothing out of the ordinary on my short drive to the Rayburn House Office Building. The sun peeked in and out of the clouds. The temperature was in the high twenties, and wasn't expected to rise above forty, but this was normal for Washington in winter. At Rayburn I got friendly waves from the three Capitol Police officers on duty and found my parking space underground. I switched off the car, unsnapped my seat belt, and took the Ruger out of the glove compartment. Although at 10:00 a.m. the MAGA presence was negligible on the Hill, I knew that could change after the planned rally on the Ellipse, a huge lawn next to the White House, which is also called the President's Park.

My office, which was on the second floor, was unlocked when I got there. Considering the unpredictability of the day—I expected violence—I had given almost everyone the day off, so the place was quiet. The few staffers who were present would go home at around noon. The House's only business would be the opening and receipt of the Electoral College results from the states, so there was no need to keep people there for a full day. Besides, as the moments passed and tens of thousands assembled on the Ellipse, I felt myself growing ever more alert. It was a little like the intuition I felt before mortar shells landed at the air base in Balad.

The House floor was where I could talk with colleagues and get a feel for what was about to transpire, so I put on my COVID face mask and walked along a pedestrian tunnel that connects Rayburn with the House side of the Capitol Building. When I reached the floor at about 12:30 p.m., Speaker Nancy Pelosi was making a fuss about everyone keeping distance from one another, another pandemic measure, and asking members to go to the gallery that overlooks the floor to reduce crowding. I was in no mood to be pushed around, so I decided I would return to my Rayburn building office where I could just watch the proceedings on the live TV feed from the House Chamber. This is generally how House members function. They spend key moments in the chamber but otherwise work in the office, knowing that when votes are called they'll have time to get there.

At around this time the police discovered unexploded pipe bombs in front of the building occupied by the Republican National Committee and the one housing the Democratic National Committee. The buildings were blocks away, but an alert came through the emergency system of loudspeakers and small radios. It said that while the Capitol complex was safe, it was recommended that we avoid walking outside. This got my attention because I had rarely heard an announcement come through the system before. But I had heard similar warnings in Iraq about mortar attacks that never came or struck feebly short of our bases. I wasn't going to panic over this one.

As I walked the tunnels to Rayburn, I received a call from one of the people in my office. He reported that the office of the Architect of the Capitol, who oversees such things, wanted me to move my car. Apparently, the spaces had been reassigned with the swearing-in of new members. My new space was adjacent to my old one, but for all I knew someone was raising a stink about their specific spot, so I went to the garage and moved the car before going upstairs. On the way back to the office I saw a police officer holding her radio up to her ear. She looked very upset.

"What's happening?" I asked.

"They're using bear spray."

I knew she was talking about the mob at the Capitol, so rather than quiz her, I decided to see what I could learn by texting other members and watching the TV news channels. However, when I walked into my office, I looked out the one window that offered any kind of view of the Capitol. I could see a small park called the House Triangle, and beyond it a portion of the West Front lawn. A stream of people was headed for the building, marching like a small army in civilian clothes.

"This has got to be on television," I thought, and used the remote to switch on the screen. The cable networks hadn't yet begun to broadcast live, so there was very little I could learn from them. When I called my wife, Sofia, she told me to go to the C-SPAN website, where they had live feeds from several cameras inside the Capitol building.

Sofia and I had met about two years prior, when she worked for the Department of Homeland Security. She's whip-smart, beautiful, fun, and due to her upbringing in El Salvador, a little bit exotic. We fell in love in a short time. On January 6, we had been married for just a year, and though most members' partners would be terrified of what was happening, she was calm. Part of this may have been due to her growing up in El Salvador in an era of violence. She also had confidence in my ability to defend myself. Besides, the marauders were focused on the Capitol, not the office buildings.

But the main reason Sofia was calm was that she had spent years working at the highest level of government and trusted the security of the Rayburn Building. She had worked in Boehner's office, and as a press official for both the Department of Homeland Security and for Vice President Mike Pence, who had Secret Service protection. We didn't have the equivalent special security units, but still, the Capitol Police were effective, and no one had ever breached the protection they maintained at the many buildings occupied by House members and staff.

At around 12:45, CNN began to show interactions between a few dozen Capitol Police officers and elements of a crowd already in the thousands. The officers stood inside an arc of low steel barriers that looked like bike racks, facing screaming, spitting madmen who wanted them to move over. Soon the barricades were pushed aside, the officers retreated to new positions, and the crowd surged. With attackers approaching on two sides of the building, the police had more than they could handle. On one side a siege began as an enormous horde of men and women pushed to enter a lower-level entrance guarded by thirty or forty officers.

When I looked at the security-camera view of Statuary Hall, which is about forty feet from the House Chamber, I was astonished to see that the police did not have control of the building. I heard shouts and saw a trickle of people with their Trump flags and

Confederate banners come into view. Soon people were pouring in. At about 2:45, rioter Ashli Babbitt would be shot as she tried to force her way through the doors to the chamber. She would die, on the floor, in a pool of blood.

As they got their cameras up and running, the news channels showed a sprawling mass of people outside the building and tear gas wafting over them. Trump had promised eighty-eight million Twitter followers that events that day "Will be wild!" His former White House adviser Steve Bannon had predicted "All hell is going to break loose." It was happening as they promised, and I knew that the Capitol was being overrun by people who connected with, and had begun expressing, something far beyond political anger. It was evil.

Trump fit my definition of dark power. But I thought this was a rare trait, and that when it came to everyday people—my constituents, people you might meet on an airplane, even Trump's fervent followers—I was sure there was some basic goodness guiding their behavior.

Now I felt my faith in humanity draining from me. Civilians playing soldier in tactical gear—helmets, bulletproof vests, and other body armor—wielding bats, toxic sprays, Tasers, and battering rams made from two-by-fours were waging a medieval battle against the police, threatening the lives of the people inside, and showing no sign that they felt there was a limit to their actions. In short, in that moment, I no longer felt that people were basically good.

As the afternoon wore on, I texted and talked with colleagues in the House Chamber who hadn't heard what was going on—the walls are very thick—and then were suddenly rushed to safety. Rep.

Jaime Herrera Beutler, a good friend, came to my office and told me what it was like to have been evacuated. Fortunately, she had been on the floor of the House. People whom Pelosi had sent to the gallery as she enforced her social-distancing rule had to wait for security officers to reach them, enduring minutes that must have felt like hours as they hid between rows of seats. Some texted and called their loved ones. Others prayed for rescue. Eventually officers got to them and cleared an escape route.

Jamie and I were dumbstruck as we watched what was happening and saw recorded video of Trump's rant at the noontime rally. Trump had said that because the election had been fraudulent, they could respond according to "different rules." Protesters would have to be "very strong," he said as he announced he would join them on the march to the Capitol. In response the crowd chanted, "Fight for Trump! Fight for Trump!" The idea was for a mass of Trumpists to march with him to the Capitol and demand that Congress refuse ballot results from key states. "We're not going to let that happen," said Trump. Then they attacked, and Trump waited for 187 minutes, watching it all on multiple televisions, until he sent out a social media message.

Trump's mob had stopped Congress from finalizing Joe Biden's victory, but only temporarily. To her credit, Speaker Pelosi gaveled the House back into session at 9:00 p.m. that night, determined that we finish the work that the Constitution prescribed for January 6. To their shame, a group of 61 Republicans led by one of the most bizarre and ridiculed people in Congress, Paul Gosar of Arizona, objected to the acceptance of the state's votes. Six senators led by

Ted Cruz joined the objection, with the result that two hours of debate would ensue before majorities in both houses accepted the states' votes. Eight Republican senators and 139 GOP members of the House, including Kevin McCarthy, voted against accepting votes from one or more states. However, the requirements for debate and voting on objections were met only in the cases of Arizona and of Pennsylvania.

It must be said that no real evidence of meaningful fraud or irregularities had been identified in any of these states, and the House members and senators who voted against accepting submissions knew it. (In fact, most of the irregularities that were identified involved people who supported Trump, not Biden.) And yet, after being run out of the building by attackers who accepted the lies about fraud, these politicians were so eager to please Trump—or afraid to cross him—that they still couldn't do the right thing. So it was that the delays caused by debates over objections meant that the work wasn't finished until a little after 3:00 a.m. on January 7.

In finishing its duty, Congress demonstrated our democracy's resilience. But there was no cause for celebration, as many continued to play to the mob and its leader despite enduring some of the institution's darkest hours. Trump eventually accepted that he had run out of moves, pledging a peaceful transition of power. But he also said that he would continue to "fight to ensure that only legal votes were counted."

"While this represents the end of the greatest first term in presidential history," he tweeted, "it's only the beginning of our fight to Make America Great Again!"

Some took Trump's statement as a concession, but you should

read it. He said he would continue to fight to ensure that only legal votes "were" counted. This word choice indicates that he wasn't ready to set aside the fantasy that he had been cheated, even though one investigation after another had turned up no evidence. The problem was that too many people were eager to join him in this fantasy and, certain that the press and every other government official couldn't be trusted, were not open to reconsidering their views. In Trump they trusted. And no one else.

Trump would never accept responsibility for what happened on January 6. Fortunately, even in the midst of the attack, one of my Democrat friends, whose office was on the same floor as mine in the Rayburn Building, was already getting to work on a document that would begin an accountability effort. David Cicilline of Rhode Island, who would be joined by Ted Lieu of California, sat in his office drafting a single article of impeachment that would be proposed to the House as soon as possible. Had I known they were doing this, I likely would have gone down the hallway and asked to join them, because at that moment I, too, knew that something had to be done.

Of all people, Kevin McCarthy expressed similar feelings in the week after the attack, saying, "The president bears responsibility for Wednesday's attack on Congress by mob rioters. He should have immediately denounced the mob when he saw what was unfolding. These facts require immediate actions by President Trump." McCarthy told an interviewer that he had had an extremely heated conversation with Trump during the attack. And in a private conversation, which would be recorded and released to the press, Senate Minority Leader McConnell had said that Trump should be driven out of politics.

Sadly, the outrage didn't last. As days passed, McCarthy's anger waned. When he learned that the Democrats were going to bring another impeachment effort against Trump, he said he could support censure—the congressional equivalent of saying "Naughty boy!" to Trump—but not impeachment. McConnell said that it wasn't necessary to impeach Trump because he would leave office in a matter of days. Of course, impeachment and conviction were two things that might have kept Trump from seeking federal office again. But nothing in the Constitution indicated he couldn't run, if he had the nerve.

If McCarthy and McConnell had pushed hard with Republicans, both impeachment and conviction would have happened. Instead, they checked where the wind was blowing, detected that Trump's followers were still sailing with him, and backed off.

To say that McCarthy and I moved in opposite directions is an understatement. On the day after the attack, as workers continued to clean the Capitol of everything from shattered glass to human waste, I became the first Republican to call for Trump's removal from office. I asked that Congress remove Trump by invoking the Twenty-Fifth Amendment to the Constitution. The amendment sets a process for removing an incapacitated president, which almost everyone assumed required members of the cabinet to act first. It doesn't. As Jamie Raskin of Maryland had pointed out more than a year before, Congress could establish its own committee to investigate and report on the president's condition. It could then begin the removal process.

Although Raskin could irritate you with an occasional I'm-smarter-than-you display, he was a professor of constitutional law who was extremely intelligent and as passionate as anyone when it came to our founding document. I trusted his scholarship and believed the evidence of Trump's incapacity was undeniable. This is why I made a video calling for his removal and posted it on Twitter. I said, in part:

> Sadly, yesterday it became evident that the president has not only abdicated his duty to protect the American people and the people's house, he invoked and inflamed passion and he gave fuel to the insurrection that we saw here. . . . All indications are that the president has become unmoored not just from his duty or even his oath, but from reality itself.

Viewing it from the distance of a couple of years, I see in my video calling for Trump's removal a man who appears to be both certain and distressed. My face betrays the effects of the long day and night we had just endured. But if there was any sense of lingering trauma, it was a mild and fleeting thing compared to the effects suffered by those who had been under more immediate threat.

Members of the House who were in the chamber, staffers who barricaded themselves in Capitol offices, the police who fought hand-to-hand combat against the surging mob—all these people, and others, suffered far more than I did.

With my call for the president's removal, which would be overtaken by events, I understood that I was inviting the wrath of Trump supporters. It came immediately from across the country and from people in my district, who called me everything from a traitor to, well, I'd rather not repeat the words here. None of this surprised me, except for the letter written by my dad's cousin Karen Otto and sent to me, my parents, and various GOP leaders around the state on behalf of several people in my extended family. The letter called me "a disappointment" to the family "and to God." The word *disappointment* was underlined three times. God once. It declared, "[Y]ou go against your Christian principles and join the devil's army."

The letter was the product of a mind overtaken by the politico-religious complex and emptied onto the page. References to the "devil's army" and "King David" and God's interest in me, and Trump's declarations of faith being offered as proof of his worthiness, show how my cousin connected herself to the movement's belief that their mission is supernatural as well as secular. A comment she made to *The New York Times*—"I wanted Adam to be shunned"—invoked another religious term. In her letter she also gathered with her the conservative broadcasters, mostly from Fox News, whom the Trump base regarded as the equivalent of Christ's apostles.

I AM A TRAITOR (AND I'M OKAY WITH IT)

You should be very proud that you have lost the respect of Lou
Dobbs, Tucker Carlson, Sean Hannity, Laura Ingraham, Greg
Kelly, etc. and most importantly in our book, Mark Levin and
Rush Limbaugh. It is now most embarrassing to us that we are
related to you.

The list of broadcasters cited by my cousin comprised a who's
who of racist, misogynistic, and just plain nasty broadcasters. Limbaugh had used racial slurs against President Obama, made homo-
phobic comments, and said that women should be banned from
juries when "the accused is a stud." Tucker Carlson had called Iraq
"a crappy place filled with a bunch of, you know, semiliterate prim-
itive monkeys"; Dobbs decried the number of women who "have
become breadwinners," adding that it is "a troubling statistic."
Laura Ingraham had mocked Parkland school shooting survivor
David Hogg, who became a gun regulation activist, for having his
application for college rejected by some schools.

Considering the media company my cousin kept and trusted, I
wasn't much affected by her letter or by many similar ones that
arrived—some anonymous, some signed by constituents—that accused me of being a traitor, a dupe of the Democrats, or a socialist.
In fact, I was a truer Republican and conservative than those who
had fallen victim to a man who lied to their faces—election fraud!—
to the point where he incited the Capitol riot. I estimate that prior to
the rise of his cult, most of them had never been more than casually
engaged in politics. The rest, including public officials, were just
riding the bandwagon, afraid of being left behind.

THE TWENTY-FIFTH AMENDMENT RESOLUTION CALLING FOR
Trump's removal passed, with my "yea" vote the only one coming from
a Republican, and I knew this meant I would be challenged and probably defeated in the next primary election. But it would turn out to be
symbolic, as Raskin's call for a congressionally led removal process was
not accepted. Instead, the House appealed to Vice President Pence to
lead the effort. When he refused, impeachment became the only option. It was scheduled to go to a vote the very next day, January 12.

In the five days before final acceptance of the state's electoral votes,
nine other Republican House members committed to voting for the
one proposed article of impeachment, which alleged the crime of "incitement of insurrection." We became the core group who supported
one another and encouraged colleagues to consider defying Trump
and the party as we would. About ten others expressed sincere interest.
Two of them were Mike Gallagher of Wisconsin, whom I considered a
good friend, and Nancy Mace of South Carolina, whom I didn't know
very well. I thought there was a strong possibility that Mace and Gallagher would be moved by the arguments made by the members in
favor. Rep. Jim McGovern, a Democrat from Massachusetts, com-
mented on how we were debating "in the actual crime scene," and Terri
Sewell, a Democrat from Alabama, observed that "blood is on this
house" and "we must do something about it." My friend Jaime Herrera Beutler moved the Democrats to applause when she said, "My vote
to impeach our sitting president is not a fear-based decision. I'm not
choosing a side, I'm choosing truth. It's the only way to defeat fear."

No one on the Republican side could make a serious case in opposition. Kevin McCarthy complained that no time had been devoted to an investigation, as if he hadn't been forced to flee the mob and had then said Trump was responsible. Others talked about how little time was left in Trump's presidency, which would come to an official end on January 20, and called for "unity" instead of the division that would be caused by a second impeachment.

But there is no impeachment statute of limitations related to the end of a president's term. And how, one should ask, is unity possible without accountability?

Impeachment was approved by a vote of 232–197, and even without Gallagher, Mace, and others, we ten Republicans constituted the largest number of representatives from a president's party ever to vote for his impeachment. The price would be high, but we knew this and couldn't justify voting any other way.

I was encouraged, though, by some phone conversations I had with donors who were important financial backers of the GOP. They considered the public's outrage and the long-term effect of the videos of the attack playing over and over in the media and had concluded that the survival of the Republican Party was at stake. I agreed. So did other individual donors. Perhaps most important, many of the corporations that also donated to GOP campaigns and political action committees announced they would pause giving to the 147 members of the House who voted against accepting ballots from one state or another after they had been forced to seek shelter as the battle waged outside the door to the chamber.

Known collectively as "Downtown," because that's where they kept their offices, these companies could, when banded together, exert real influence. Included were, among many others, Microsoft, Toyota, and American Express. I recognized that their stand might mean that money could be available for an organization that would try to counter extremism in the party. In that moment I thought, "Why shouldn't I build an organization devoted to mainstream politics?" It could be open to Democrats, Republicans, and independents who were willing to put country first, ahead of party. It could also reach out to the press, educate the public, support members who took the center lane, and even field candidates. If we created the right structure, we could develop a kind of matrix covering key issues and principles to determine which candidates fit a Country First profile—pro-democracy/opposed to gridlock—that Downtown could use to determine where to put their money. The candidates would get access to funders. Downtown would get a chance to take a stand for democracy, and the country.

Knowing I couldn't do all the work needed to get a serious effort off the ground, and that a one-man band is always a bad idea, I contacted every other Republican who voted for impeachment, and each one seemed open, initially. Together we would have the moral authority to set up the organization and seek support. And since we were all devoted to the idea of putting the country first, that's what we would call it: Country First.

WITH THE SENATE TRIAL OF THE IMPEACHED PRESIDENT YET TO occur, you might have said we jumped the gun on Country First.

After all, it was possible that in some alternate universe Trump could be convicted. We knew, of course, that in this universe it would never happen. Being the tactical and political genius that he is, Senate Minority Leader Mitch McConnell managed to delay the trial of Donald Trump until after Joe Biden became the forty-sixth president. On Biden's inauguration day, the sulking Trump refused to attend his successor's swearing-in, as every president in memory had done, and instead indulged in some pathetic pumping at the departure ceremony held at Joint Base Andrews. His hand never got higher than his shoulder. In a twenty-minute address, he bragged and lied, praised his own family for how hard they worked, and ended with the strange suggestion that the people in the small crowd "Have a good life."

When the impeachment trial was finally conducted, the House managers, led by Jamie Raskin, had presented their case in a way that avoided the droning repetition of the managers in the first impeachment. Raskin and his team also had the advantage of access to countless hours of video and thousands of still images, and they chose key images and sections of video to show the senators who sat as a jury of one hundred. Included was never-before-seen footage of Mike Pence being spirited away from the Senate when the attackers were within feet of the chamber, and video of Mitt Romney being redirected by Capitol Police Officer Eugene Goodman, who had single-handedly delayed the arrival of rioters who were close behind.

Although presiding officer Senator Patrick Leahy had admonished them to pay close attention, Republican senators were especially disrespectful of the proceeding. Senator Tim Scott of South Carolina spent time studying a map of Africa. Josh Hawley of Missouri read a newspaper with his feet up on the chair in front of him. Rand Paul made a sketch of the Capitol. Others made a mockery of their pledge to act as impartial jurors. Mike Lee, Ted Cruz, and Lindsey Graham went behind closed doors to consult on strategy with Trump's lawyers. Democrats misbehaved, too, but in minor ways. There were nudges and words exchanged, but they did not show the contempt that Republicans did.

In closing for the prosecutors, Jamie Raskin quoted Tom Paine, the great pamphleteer, saying, "Tyranny, like hell, is not easily conquered. But we have this saving consolation: The more difficult the struggle, the more glorious in the end will be our victory. Good luck in your deliberations."

In his closing for the defense, Trump lawyer Michael van der Veen insisted, "At no point did you hear anything that could ever possibly be construed as Mr. Trump encouraging or sanctioning an insurrection. The act of incitement never happened. He engaged in no language of incitement whatsoever on January sixth or any other day following the election." Van der Veen also said that Trump's behavior was no different from that of Democrats who supported Black Lives Matter protests that followed the police killing of George Floyd in Minneapolis. In fact, Democrats, including Biden, had said the violence that broke out at some of the BLM demonstrations and marches was unacceptable.

Van der Veen's misrepresentation was typical of the Trump defense, which often appeared bumbling, especially when compared with the House managers'. However, they were in a sense playing with house money, because only a few Republican senators, notably

Mitt Romney of Utah, Susan Collins of Maine, and Lisa Murkowski of Alaska, were certain to join the Democrats and vote to convict.

When the clerk called on Republican senator Bill Cassidy of Louisiana to cast his vote for impeachment, he surprised me with his response: "Guilty." With the clerk working alphabetically through the roster of senators, Cassidy's vote was one of the first, so it seemed that as many as six or seven other Republicans would join him. At this moment I began to wonder whether Senator McConnell might somehow indicate that it would be all right for his members to vote to convict. McConnell had seemed riveted by parts of the prosecution's case. And I knew that the managers held on to the hope that McConnell might make a dramatic move until the voting passed the point where it would be possible for seventeen GOP senators to vote to convict.

McConnell did not, unfortunately. Despite winning an impressive majority—the vote was 57–43—the managers failed to reach the sixty-six votes required to convict. Nothing is worse for lawmakers than to lose a historic battle and then hear that your main opponent agreed with your moral stand. This was why, when it was over, the managers would drink whiskey and not champagne.

After the vote, in a speech given to the Senate and the tens of millions watching on television, McConnell offered a scathing review of what happened on January 6, including calling the attackers terrorists who "had been fed wild falsehoods by the most powerful man on Earth. . . . There is no question that President Trump is practically and morally responsible for provoking the events of the day."

McConnell went on and on, decrying the behavior of the attackers and Trump and then excused his own vote to acquit, and those of every senator who joined him, with the argument that "the question is moot because former President Trump is constitutionally not eligible for conviction." This notion has never been tested and is hotly debated in the legal profession. Besides, it took a lot of cheek, nerve, chutzpah, gall, and, dare I say, balls for McConnell to talk this way since he personally blocked the consideration of the case until Trump departed. An impeachment trial could have been accomplished before that event, but he said no. It was one of those strange episodes where a politician tries to have it both ways. McConnell had spared Trump with the aid of rules that were tilted in his favor—just as thanks to the Electoral College he had been decisively defeated in the popular vote but won the presidency anyway. He had also declared himself outraged by what Trump had inspired and suggested that of course he deserved to be punished.

BUT TRUMP WAS NOT CLEAR OF EFFORTS TO HOLD HIM RESPONSIble. Speaker Nancy Pelosi floated two ideas for a bipartisan group to investigate and report on January 6. The first called for a blue-ribbon commission made up of prominent and esteemed former officials who would investigate and produce a report. Its appeal, and its lack of appeal, depended on the same factor—its resemblance to previous commissions like the one convened in response to the September 11 terrorist attacks. The prominence of those appointed signaled that Washington was serious, but the commission had worked largely out of public view and its report didn't generate much public interest. Commissions were, it seemed, where issues were sent to die. For this reason and others, the idea of a commission of wise men and women simply fizzled.

Pelosi's other idea for an investigating panel attracted much more interest, especially as she proposed that it include five House Democrats and five Republicans. With the power to establish a committee in her hands, and hers alone, Pelosi could have planned one that Democrats would dominate.

Unfortunately, months would pass before the commission idea was formally shelved and the House focused on the committee idea. Then more weeks would go by as the two parties haggled over how it would work. This slow process that often governed important decisions surely annoyed some freshman Democrats, who had yet to serve sixth months in the House and knew that the Capitol attack had been the gravest domestic assault on democracy in history. But this is just how the Congress works. With 435 members and a vast and far-flung population to consider, the institution grinds slowly. Unfortunately, the pace favors those who would block an effort like Pelosi's. It gives members the chance to retreat from their positions and to pressure others to join them at the barricades.

With the passage of time, and threats to marshal his followers against them, Donald Trump reestablished his dominance over the GOP and Republican members came to heel. Kevin McCarthy abandoned the righteous anger he had expressed in January and excused Trump, saying he had responded to calls for him to help stop the attack. Other members said the attackers had behaved more like tourists than rioters. Some House Republicans, and eventually the Republican

National Committee declared the riot "legitimate political discourse" and said that Democrats were engaged in the "persecution of ordinary citizens." (They soon revised the statement to indicate that violent attackers were not the ones they were defending.)

In the same caucus meeting, the members formally rebuked Liz Cheney and me for supporting Pelosi's investigation agenda, forcefully denouncing Trump, and condemning those who stopped the certification of the election. The rebuke was not unexpected. We had already been censured by the national party committee. I was being attacked by Republicans all over the state of Illinois. Liz faced even more ferocious criticism in Wyoming. On February 6 her state party delegates would vote 66–8 to formally censure her because, as Darin Smith, whom Cheney had defeated in a primary, said, "We need to honor President Trump."

On Capitol Hill we experienced the kind of shunning seen in Fundamentalist churchgoers' treatment of the excommunicated: There's no fury like the fury they feel toward the expelled. For me it began with my support for a Twenty-Fifth Amendment examination of Trump's fitness. It was then when Trump true believers, who had previously been friendly when we shared space in an elevator or on the floor of the chamber, turned into stone. After my impeachment vote, other Trumpists whom I considered to be friends would literally turn their backs when I approached. Eventually, the only people who treated me with any warmth were the others who had backed impeachment. We had to be a bit careful about how we interacted, lest our colleagues think we had become a dangerous cabal plotting against them. This was a special concern for those in the group who still felt connected to the party and imagined having long careers in elected offices.

As time went on, I began feeling less and less interested in staying in Congress, and I knew that the increasingly authoritarian party was abandoning traditional conservatives like me. Besides, I was more interested in the work of Democrats who labored to set the House's institutional response to January 6.

I kept a close eye on this activity while working on Country First. Donors, most of them liberals, sent us money, and our bank account quickly grew to $250,000. The others who had voted for impeachment seemed genuinely interested. Peter Meijer, from Michigan, suggested we work with the Downtown donors to identify members who were pro-democracy and worthy of their campaign contributions and those who were not. "I'm gonna work on it," he promised. "Definitely." I even got encouragement from the group when I talked to them about forming a GOP Democracy Caucus. Imagine what would have happened if this had become a reality. How would anyone explain why they didn't join?

When Meijer stopped talking about the authentication idea, I should have realized I could be abandoned by people I regarded as partners. Instead, I was surprised as one by one, people stopped talking to me about the organization. Then, the House members who had been brave enough to support impeachment lost their courage. Many of them blamed aides who warned of political suicide.

It was hard to credit these excuses. Politicians often fib about taking the advice of their staffers, or when the aides do say what they think, their bosses give too much weight to their advice. As workers whose jobs depend on the boss's reelection, staffers have an incentive to think more about what works politically instead of what morality and duty to country demand. Despite their experience with a mob that seized control of the Capitol, forcing them to flee, fearing for their lives, they weren't willing to stick by their promise to make a bit of history by breaking with the party and launching a real defense of democracy.

With so many in the House becoming mini-Trumps, I didn't think moderation was possible. I had witnessed the futility of this pursuit when Trump was still in office and I encountered two of his top officials pursuing this goal in vain. The first was retired Marine general John Kelly, who would last less than sixteen months as Trump's chief of staff. At the midway point, an exhausted and exasperated Kelly invited about five of us congressional Republicans to a private breakfast at the White House to discuss the war on terror and, more specifically, what was happening in Afghanistan. Kelly arrived looking gaunt and exhausted. It was 8:00 a.m. and he could barely stay awake. He told us he was trying as hard as he could but was "barely holding it together." I was surprised by the level of Kelly's distress. He clearly suffered from political shell shock.

The problem with Trump, from a chief of staff's perspective, was that he preferred to do everything informally and on his own with minimum staff engagement. Consequently, Kelly and others regularly discovered that Trump had considered advice from this crony or that social contact at his Mar-a-Lago resort and was serious about acting on it. The work of diverting Trump's attention away from terrible ideas and directing him to fulfill his duties obviously took all of Kelly's energy.

On another occasion, John Bolton invited some of us to support him in protecting the Kurds in Syria. The group included, among other people, Liz Cheney, Dan Crenshaw from Texas, and Richard Hudson from North Carolina. Once we got to the Oval Office, I could see that Trump was impatient, and Bolton was desperate for someone to get through to him. A plain-spoken intellectual, Bolton strained to remain polite even as Trump seemed uninterested. The Kurds had fought and died for us in Iraq, said Bolton. They were continuing to provide great insight into politics in the region. Nothing we said worked, and I left with two lasting impressions. One was the despairing look on Bolton's face as Trump kept struggling to focus. The other was when Trump said of the Kurds in Syria, "Why would I give a fuck?"

In the House, increasing numbers of Republicans gave no fucks about Americans who disagreed with them on any issue—one was enough to disqualify you permanently—or about our international role, or the state of our democracy. Bigoted against those who are different in any way, fascist in their approach to domestic power, and vulnerable to conspiracy theories, they were direct descendants of fringe groups like the John Birch Society, which was created by a group of extreme right-wingers who were among the wealthiest people in America. The Birchers' antiestablishment attitude is echoed by the people who now controlled the GOP.

Proof of the growing influence of the extreme right in Congress came when Nancy Pelosi invited Kevin McCarthy to be an equal partner in a genuine effort to understand what had occurred on January 6. An even number of Democrats and Republicans could sit on an investigating committee, work together, and report on their findings. Any hope that the sides could reason together disappeared as McCarthy then nominated to the committee five staunch supporters of Donald Trump, including three who, after being driven into hiding by the attackers, returned to the House Chamber and helped drag things out by voting against accepting results sent by several states. One of these three, Jim Jordan of Ohio, was an attack dog masquerading as a representative, whose reason for being seemed to be disruption, obstruction, and the destruction of bipartisan cooperation.

Not as unhinged as, say, Louie Gohmert, Jordan was a fiercely intelligent guy who had mastered the art of the "When did you stop beating your wife?" kind of interrogation of witnesses who came to testify before his assigned committees. He was also willing to break the rules by talking well past his allotted time during hearings and floor debate, and by interrupting his Democrat colleagues. If you were a Democrat, you considered Jordan to be one of the most obnoxious people in Congress. In picking him, McCarthy had responded to Pelosi's outreach by slapping her hand.

Never shy about wielding her power, Pelosi said that Jordan and his similarly partisan colleague from Indiana, Jim Banks, would not be accepted on the committee. The other three Trump supporters were accepted, but Pelosi asked McCarthy to name two more to fill the five GOP seats.

Had he been willing to compromise, McCarthy could have had a direct line into the committee's work. If things went well, he could claim credit and stand as a mature and honorable leader. If he didn't like what happened, he could have encouraged his members to push back and make the process go the way he wanted. Hell, if he wanted to prove to Trump that he was his man, he could have turned the committee into a target he could lambaste for months on end. Instead, he rescinded his nominations, leaving in Pelosi's hands the power to shape the committee as she saw fit.

After Pelosi had given Liz Cheney one of the Democrats' spots on the committee, McCarthy immediately talked of taking away her committee assignments, including a coveted Armed Services Committee spot. Cheney was not the type to worry about whether Kevin McCarthy liked her. In the previous year, when Trump was leading attacks on Anthony Fauci, who led America's scientific response to the COVID-19 epidemic, she openly defended him. The Freedom Club immediately convened so that Jim Jordan could bite her the way he bit Democrats. His buddy Andy Biggs of Arizona fumed about how Republicans who were bothered by Trump should keep silent about it. The fact that she wouldn't keep silent did make Liz different from those who knew Trump was more than borderline crazy and stayed quiet because they thought they were serving the country by trying to moderate him.

I first heard that Speaker Pelosi wanted to put me on the January 6 committee on the afternoon of Liz's appointment, when my neighbor across the hall, Democrat Jamie Raskin, wandered over, looking for me. I wasn't there, but I contacted him as soon as I got his message. Speaker Pelosi wanted to name me to the committee, he told me. This weekend. "What would you say?" he asked.

It was an offer I had expected would come. My fear for our democracy, anxiety about Trump's charisma, eagerness to establish a permanent record of January 6, and my sense of duty required that I accept, although I absolutely didn't want to. I told Raskin yes and expected Pelosi would call in the coming hour or two. I waited and waited through the day, into the evening, and through most of the following day. I finally heard from her on Sunday morning, after she had gone on the national TV show *This Week* to tease the idea. This speculative comment and then the interviews she would do after the appointment was made official would give her two bites from the publicity apple—the favorite food of politicians—and schooled me on just how assertive she can be. Pelosi would show me more about how power politics is played when she promised to keep her hands off the committee and then demanded the Democrats defer to her on every major move.

They would comply.

CHAPTER 11

Do Your Job

They finished installing the black steel perimeter fence encircling the Capitol on January 9. It was seven feet high and, due to its design, impossible to scale. A symbol of our democracy's state of crisis, it rose and dipped with the slope of the famous hill and fully separated the people from the People's House. My heart sank every time it caught my eye. Then, just as the committee to investigate the attack was formed, crews began to dismantle it. You had to wonder whether the barriers between the people and the truth about January 6 might also be removed.

The process began slowly, as we needed to hire a staff sufficient to investigate, conduct interviews, and analyze hundreds of thousands of pages of text, including documents, correspondence, and memos. This required approximately 100 lawyers, investigators, managers, and support staff. Add the work done by members themselves and aides from our legislative offices, and there were a good

120 people involved. Even with all this manpower, and some modest document-processing technology, the staff struggled to keep up with the volume of material as interviews and documents came pouring in. Eventually we would amass more than a thousand interviews and a million documents along with hundreds of hours of staff-reviewed video. The recordings capture actions from more than a hundred vantage points provided by security cameras, individuals' cell phones, social media posts, and footage shot by news crews and documentarians.

Denver Riggleman, a former Republican member of Congress who had been defeated in a primary by a Trumpist and had previously worked in data management, volunteered to help manage the data. He would work on the hundreds of thousands of text and phone records we received from witnesses and carriers. These weren't recordings of actual conversations or messages, but rather records of which numbers were connected and when. It was technically possible to put the phone numbers together with certain people, map out the times they connected, and compare these with key events—prosecutors do this all the time, only with far fewer data points. This information would help us determine not only who contacted whom, but allow us to ask intelligent questions of the people who made these connections. Rather than ask, "Did you, Mr. Z, ever reach out to Mr. Y?" we could say, "We know that on this date you called Mr. Y five times. Why?"

After a couple of months' work, Riggleman came up with a way to streamline the process, but developing the software would be expensive. Like a million dollars expensive. The decision on whether to pull the trigger on this idea stalled. Then, with phone companies likely to begin erasing records that were more than a year old, a general practice for some, the whole idea was dropped. To say Riggleman was disappointed is an understatement.

I am certain that the million-dollar decision was made in Speaker Pelosi's office. In fact, despite her pledge to keep her hands off the process, it became clear early on that she couldn't resist stepping in. This was something the Democrats on the committee seemed to accept, as if the Speaker had practiced this kind of leadership ever since she became congressional Democrats' top leader in 2003, which meant her caucus had nearly two decades of experience with her heavy hand.

Of course, the Speaker doesn't say she will exert her power whenever the mood strikes. In fact, when our committee first came together, she called us into her office and said, "I believe in you guys. I am not going to be involved. I am going to let you do your work." Then she assigned one of her aides, Jamie Fleet, to be her eyes and ears inside our offices. Fleet was a smart guy who understood and even sympathized with our concerns. However, when I asked him to lend a hand on a separate issue, he didn't help. And with the Democrats folding their cards every time, Pelosi got her way whenever she wanted to, though thankfully it didn't happen all that often.

The Democrats on the committee included Chairman Bennie Thompson of Mississippi, Stephanie Murphy of Florida, Jamie Raskin of Maryland, and Elaine Luria of Virginia. They were joined by three members from what everyone called Pelosi's California Mafia, including Zoe Lofgren of the Bay Area, Adam Schiff of Los Angeles, and Pete Aguilar of Riverside. I was one of the two Republicans in the group. The other was Liz Cheney.

Although we had five high-powered lawyers on the committee, the group came from varied backgrounds. Luria was a Navy vet. Murphy had worked in the Pentagon and as a business school professor. Aguilar had served in California governor Gray Davis's administration and been mayor of Redlands, California. Thompson had been a schoolteacher. I came to respect everyone on the committee. Adam Schiff and I had a prior relationship that became even more effective. As a Republican, I had been told to hate him because, well, he was such an effective and dogged questioner at high-profile hearings. Suddenly on the same team, I came to appreciate his intelligence, generosity with other members, and his sense of humor. Our friendship was solidified, I think, when I referred to myself as Adam Junior and to him as Adam Senior. (After all, he *is* older than me.) From that point forward we were easygoing friends.

Bennie was such a calm leader that it sometimes seemed like he wasn't leading at all. What I realize now is that he was a kind of Zen master at collegiality. He was respectful, attentive, and never brushed anyone off. However, he seemed to know that things had a way of working themselves out. But if he had a flaw, it was that he was just too nice to reporters, who have their ways of cornering members whether they want to talk or not. They lurk outside the door to the chamber and in the hallways outside members' offices, or just cruise the tunnels that connect the office buildings to the Capitol. Most are decent enough, even if they are always looking for the quote that might cause controversy. For some reason Bennie just couldn't walk past these people, so whenever he had microphones thrust in front of him, he responded politely. This caused a bit of trouble because every time he was asked the big question—When is the committee holding public hearings?—he tried to answer with something optimistic. This meant that from the fall of 2021 to the start of hearings in June 2022, it seemed as if the start date was being pushed back every few months, though this wasn't the case.

We divided the committee staff into five groups tasked with conducting the vast majority of interviews and gathering all the documents. However, it was decided that the committee members would participate in the interviews of high-level witnesses, including some that occurred in public sessions. These involved the president's top advisers and those who participated in advocating for the gathering of outraged Trumpists and guiding events on the ground as the attack began and progressed.

We also settled on the documentation we wanted to deliver to the American people so that no one would have much doubt about the who, what, how, and why things happened as they did. Our model became, for lack of a better term, the must-watch limited series seen on streaming TV services. Our "series" would run for eight "episodes" and be accompanied by a sprawling written report, with thousands of endnotes, like the ones typically produced by investigating committees.

As the "hosts" of the series, we were each assigned episodes that we would conduct as chairpersons. I was chosen to conduct the fifth hearing because it would focus on the way so many public officials broke their oaths, and others, who knew better, participated in a coup attempt unworthy of people who considered themselves patriots. I was chosen because I am not an attorney and we hoped that people would be able to grasp the legal concepts if they were expressed by a nonlawyer.

My second assignment, which I shared with Elaine Luria, would be a hearing that would delve into the day of the attempted coup and, most important, the 187-minute span between Trump becoming aware of the attack on the Capitol and his call for its end. In this case, I believe that Elaine and I were assigned because we were both military members who had taken and kept oaths of office and knew how to act in a crisis. The president, in contrast, didn't know how to act in a crisis and had ignored his oath. We were not attorneys, and what was called for was a down-to-earth telling of a story that required no lawyerly touches. This was especially true when it came to Trump's refusal to act to stop the violence. Having planted himself in front of cable news, he knew what was going on. GOP leader McCarthy even called to beg him to act, and he refused.

As much as the public hungered for the compelling story we needed to tell, we on the committee were determined to complete the work in an orderly way. As anyone who watched the hearings could see, Liz was the most forceful and fully informed member of the committee. She left no doubt that she saw the grave danger that Trump represented, and that the January 6 attack was the product of all his lies, inflammatory rhetoric, and irresponsibility. (If I were qualified to diagnose Trump with a mental disorder, I'd offer it here. Instead, I can just say, in colloquial terms: the guy is nucking futs.)

Within the group, Liz often refocused us when we drifted away from the central issue of the coup, but she could do this in a sandpapery way that left some people feeling sore. Actually, she probably rubbed every one of us the wrong way at one time or another. This was because she was intense and blunt—and better informed. In these ways she was a lot like her father, the former vice president. He wasn't exactly lovable, but he was extremely effective. Like father, like daughter.

At the start of 2022, when we seemed a bit stalled, the chairman organized a one-day retreat at the Library of Congress to deal with friction in the group. The world's largest library, it occupies four enormous buildings, but the most famous one is the imposing, late-nineteenth-century structure that occupies an entire city block facing the East Front of the Capitol. It took eleven years to build. The outside is heavily ornamented with features borrowed from the Paris Opera House. Visitors climb past the famous statues of Neptune's Court to enter on the second floor. The inside of the library is dominated by an enormous circular main reading room. A key scene in the film *All the President's Men* reveals the grandeur of this room with an overhead shot that offers a view from a rising perspective until you see more than a hundred desks arranged in the big circles split by eight aisles that from a height look like rays of the sun.

At one point during the meeting, Liz suggested we visit the reading room reserved for members of Congress. As we faced one another around a table, we couldn't help but be affected by the original handwritten copy—one of five in existence—of the Gettysburg Address, which had been brought into the room at Liz's request. I won't say that we faced a challenge remotely like the one Lincoln confronted, but we were dealing with an event that was unique in our history—a coup attempt inflamed by a president—and the American people, including those of future generations, would judge our response.

Here I would like to quote a blog post by Library of Congress staffer Donna Sokol, who describes a mosaic titled *The Law*, which dominates the room. At its center a woman representing Law sits on a throne. Sokol writes:

> The right side of the mosaic shows three figures—Fraud, Discord, and Violence—that represent the result of a lawless land. Fraud covers herself with her robe to hide the truth of her unlawful activities. Discord holds two dueling snakes, whose confused entanglement will lead to the demise of each by his own venom. Violence is clad in a helmet, clutches a sword, and keeps a burning torch nearby. On this trio's side of the throne, we see two discarded items—a law book and the scales of justice, representing their disdain for the law.
>
> The left side of the mosaic represents what happens when the rule of law functions well: Industry, Peace, and Truth. Industry is a young man who holds a hammer with a wheel sitting beside him. Peace holds an olive branch and wears a crown of the same, symbolizing peace. Truth, unlike her foil, Fraud, is unashamedly uncovered and holds lilies, which in this scene symbolize innocence. On their side of the throne, two doves represent peace—the result of a lawful existence.

The mosaic described precisely where we stood as a committee. On one side we confronted the evils of fraud (Trump's lies), discord (created by his enablers), and violence as it was perpetrated by his followers on January 6. We had reached the point where we needed to sharpen our focus. Liz, who had identified Trump as the most dangerous leader in our history, wanted us to make him central to every chapter in the story we would tell. No one would argue this point, but some wanted to pay special attention to related problems.

Jamie Raskin, for example, thought we should zero in on how the Electoral College system permitted Trump's scheming. The college had been created to balance the power of states with larger and smaller populations. Though it was essential to national unity at the time, this method clearly violated the one-man, one-vote essence of democracy. The founders also set conditions for the confusion Trump sowed by prescribing a drawn-out process for gathering and certifying results. This may have made sense in the era of Paul Revere's ride, and it worked—until someone devoted only to his own power used the weeks between the election and certification to convince half the country that evil was afoot, and tens of thousands became so agitated that they felt forced to act.

This is as good a place as any to note the way Trump created an alternate reality occupied by his followers, who were primed to make themselves into action-figure heroes. First Trump had, for at least five years, periodically spread doubt about the election system. After he lost in 2020, he sold the Big Lie about how the worst had come to pass. His prophecy had been fulfilled. Primed to believe, filled with patriotic fantasies, and perpetually enraged about the government, his most extreme followers felt the moment to act had come. But like Fundamentalists who rally behind a preacher reading Scripture they don't understand, Trump's marauders were ignorant of current events, American history, and the Constitution, yet full of false righteousness. They put on their costumes—combat gear, Revolutionary War getups, Trump regalia, and even costumes modeled after cartoon characters—and became a snarling, violent mob.

I wanted to join Jamie in focusing on how the Electoral College opened the door to tragedy. I was sympathetic to his belief that the Electoral College should be abolished but I didn't want to go that far. Pursuing this reform to deal with a background factor would distract from our effort to tell the truth of January 6. The same was true, but to a lesser degree, of Stephanie Murphy's desire to focus on the security vulnerabilities revealed by the attack. The Capitol Police had failed to understand the threat and hadn't deployed a big enough force. Those who were on duty lacked the proper equipment, and their communications and coordination broke down almost immediately.

But when you consider all the factors in the police response, it becomes harder to criticize. Unlike the District of Columbia police, who deal with demonstrations and the threat of civil disorder almost every day, the Capitol Police had never seen anything remotely like what happened on the first Wednesday of 2021. On their side stood perhaps a hundred officers, lightly armed and increasingly alarmed. On the other side raged a mob big enough to fill the local NBA arena and was, in toto, better armed than the officers. Capitol Police were certain that many in the crowd carried sidearms and knew that drawing their own weapons, or firing a warning shot, could spark an out-of-control gun battle. With no arrangement for arresting and holding people who committed crimes, the Capitol Police acted heroically, delaying the mob until everyone inside could escape or find secure shelter.

But Liz was concerned about focusing on the police, which could easily devolve into a blame-the-victim scenario. More than one hundred officers had been injured. One had died as a result of his injuries. Two had committed suicide just days after their traumatic experiences. The police had already put improvements in place and were working on more. Besides, as a Cheney staffer would later explain, her view was that "the Capitol didn't attack itself."

It was relatively easy to reach consensus in the intimate and inspiring environment of the library room. We decided that while both the problems of the Electoral College and concerns about the defense of the Capitol would be discussed, neither would become the focus of intense scrutiny or recommendations. We also began addressing an important question: Would the report contain a series of direct recommendations, or would it stop with analysis and conclusions about what happened before, during, and after the riots?

ALTHOUGH DOZENS DEFIED SUBPOENAS AND REFUSED TO SHOW UP, the witnesses who did appear before the committee could be divided into three groups. The first, most of whom refused to answer questions, citing their Fifth Amendment right against self-incrimination, were those I would describe as Trump-infected zombies. The man's words had taken over their brains, like parasitic worms, rendering them pathologically loyal and incapable of independent thought.

The best example of a Trump zombie was Roger Stone, who took the Fifth more than seventy times. Stone is an especially repulsive figure who has pursued the attention of the political press for more than fifty years. Part of this shtick involves dressing in outlandish outfits: if you look online, you'll find him in clothes that make him look like Mr. Peanut. He toned it down for us, but still wore an ultra-wide-collared shirt and a silver silk hankie tucked cavalierly into his suit jacket's pocket. He is a man who often appears accompanied by thuggish young bodyguards, and his cowardly refusals to engage with us were entertaining.

Another zombie was John Eastman, the law professor who advised Trump that Vice President Mike Pence could interfere with the Electoral College certifications. He cited the Fifth 150 times. Given his national reputation for making unorthodox legal claims, Eastman's avoidance came across as more pathetic than amusing. Everyone knew, of course, that he had reversed himself on the Pence issue, first telling Trump that there was nothing the vice president could do and then arguing that Pence could, as he presided over the largely ceremonial certification process, simply set aside enough state filings to cast Biden's election in doubt. The only explanation he could have made, if he had spoken, would have landed him in an intellectual trap where he would have had to answer for what was an obvious play for Trump's favor. I couldn't help but wonder if Eastman imagined he would be appointed attorney general should the coup attempt succeed and the president somehow manage to stay in office.

The second group of witnesses were what I would call partial zombies. The Make America Great Again worms were present, but there were corners of their brains that were less infected and allowed for some independent thought or courage. One partial zombie, Rudy Giuliani, dodged questions about his participation in spreading the Big Lie. His memory failed at many convenient (for him) moments. He also veered into some irrelevant comments—an attack on Hillary Clinton was one—and offered, without evidence, conclusions about "massive [election] cheating" in places like Philadelphia. Giuliani also explained that in the many calls he made to Trump on the evening of January 6, he urged him to keep fighting to block the certification. All in all, his testimony featured so much deflection and distortion that it confirmed the general public's belief that the once great leader who rallied New York amid the devastation of 9/11 had become the blithering servant of a man who never deserved his attention.

The third and last group of witnesses included men and women of integrity who had been part of the Trump team, either inside the administration or in his political operation, and who had shown some spine as the January 6 attack approached and then occurred. In contacts with higher-ups and in several cases the president himself, they had warned against inflaming his supporters, and during and after the rally they had begged their superiors to do something to stop the riot at the Capitol.

Truth-teller Cassidy Hutchinson, aide to chief of staff Mark Meadows, told us that White House officials understood that contingents of the violence-prone Proud Boys and Oath Keepers were going to be at the rally on the Ellipse. She said that on the day of the rally Trump had complained that people were slow to pass through weapon-screening magnetometers and wanted the safety screening suspended because he believed they had not come to hurt HIM. One of the most appalling stories she told, a secondhand tale that was later confirmed, was of Trump's demand that he be driven to the Capitol after the rally. When security officials refused, citing the risk, Trump reached from the back of the car, grabbed the driver, and repeated his demand. It didn't work.

A second truth-teller, Trump's former deputy press secretary Sarah Matthews, testified about how in the early stages of the attack Mark Meadows heard desperate pleas—from aides and outside advisers—that Trump call off the horde but remained in his office because, he would say, the president "wanted to be alone." Meadows had been looking at his cell phone screen when White House lawyer Pat Cipollone rushed into his office to demand that something be done to stop the riot. Minutes later, when Matthews passed by Meadows's office, she saw that he was still absorbed by his phone.

The testimony about Meadows was consistent with the man I had known in the House, where he had represented a North Carolina district from 2013 to 2020. Consummately ambitious, Meadows had been the leader of the Freedom Caucus and one of Kevin McCarthy's key allies. He was also the kind of politician who would slap your back in a playful moment and then stab you in it the next. Bizarrely, or perhaps not so bizarrely, he had sold land in Colorado to a wacky creationist group who opposed earth science and the theory of evolution and falsely claimed that a bunch of homeschoolers had discovered a dinosaur there. As their film about the discovery sank into the oblivion reserved for extremists, Meadows stood by its creators. Meadows was an intelligent guy. He had to know the claims in the film were hokum. But the stand bonded him with politically powerful Fundamentalists, and that was what mattered to him.

MOST MEMBERS OF THE COMMITTEE VIEWED THE DEPOSITION VIA video conference connections due to the rules of social distancing put in place to deal with the pandemic and so that we could view the proceeding from our district. I still loved my hometown and district, despite the harassment I faced when I went to public places.

Video would replace in-person work when we began telling the story of January 6 in public hearings that attracted millions of TV viewers. Each hearing began with opening statements by Chairman Thompson and Vice Chairperson Cheney. In every case, while Thompson calmly forecasted the shocking testimony that would follow, it was Cheney whose words were the most cutting.

Cheney speaks with her father's bluntness and adds a level of scathing insight so marked by common sense that no one could possibly miss her meaning. "President Trump is a seventy-six-year-old man," she said in one hearing. "He is not an impressionable child." In the same hearing she said, "Donald Trump cannot escape responsibility by being willfully blind."

Although she was unyielding in her comments about the investigation, Cheney showed a soft side in dealing with the honest and therefore risk-taking witnesses, especially after sessions were gaveled closed. In one iconic photo from the day of her testimony, Cassidy Hutchinson is shown closing her eyes, a smile on her face, as Cheney gives her a hug.

Although you may think that experienced members of Congress question witnesses in response to their statements or speak spontaneously when they get the chance to offer their own comments, this is not true when committees conduct complex investigations. As I got ready to chair the fifth hearing, which would focus on the Justice Department and January 6, I was grateful for the formal preparation we went through. It went along the lines of what I would expect that casts do before a live TV broadcast like, say, *Saturday Night Live*, with read-throughs and tweaks done around a table and then rehearsals in the Cannon House Office Building Caucus Room, which is the largest meeting space on Capitol Hill.

With millions of people tuning in to the televised hearings, it wasn't long before the investigation gained cultural relevance. In October 2022, *SNL*'s "cold open" focused on the committee, which was described as a bunch of "monotone nerds." To my delight, I made it into the sketch, where the actor playing me begged to have one of the cupcakes "Bennie Thompson" brought to reward us at the end of the hearing. "I" returned to reveal I had stolen a cupcake and then presented all the witnesses who had informed Trump that he had lost the election, which included a German shepherd. "I" also got to mispronounce my own name and join the cast shouting, "Live from New York, it's Saturday Night." The committee had, it seemed, become culturally relevant.

I was a little nervous as the hearing approached but was calmed by the knowledge that I had gone over the material time and again. We had practiced and, most of all, my colleagues had my back. Before I began presenting evidence, I said, "I remember making a commitment, out loud a few times and in my heart repeatedly even to today, that if we are going to ask Americans to be willing to die in service to our country, we as leaders must at least be willing to sacrifice our political careers when integrity and our oath requires it. After all, losing a job is nothing compared to losing your life."

During the hearing we on the committee showed how the top officials in the Department of Justice had resisted pressure to support Trump's demands. (He asked them to declare the election "corrupt" and then, as he said, to "leave the rest to me and the Republican Congressmen.") As I presented the evidence, the committee staff played accompanying video from depositions of various witnesses, who backed up what I said. The video made the presentation easier to follow and spared people from sitting through the type of drawn-out questioning that takes place in live testimony where, let's face it, members often compete for time, so they can raise their profile in the media and show the folks back home that they are important.

Some of the most damning videos dealt with a lower-level Justice Department official named Jeffrey Clark, who promised to conduct investigations that he was sure would find widespread fraud. However, he could only do this under a new attorney general. Who might that be? Jeffrey Clark recommended Jeffrey Clark. Remarkably, for Trump, Clark didn't get the job.

Anyone who doubted the connection between the Trump team's

scheming and the January 6 attackers only had to look at the clip we played of a MAGA man standing outside the Department of Justice building on his way from the Ellipse to the Capitol. "Do your job! Do your job! Do your job! Do your job! Do your job!" he shouted. "Live in DC, we're marching to the Capitol. We are at the Department of Justice right now telling these powers to do their job!"

"Do your job" was repeated by Rep. Louie Gohmert in a montage of extreme-right members of Congress—Paul Gosar, Jim Jordan, Mo Brooks, Matt Gaetz, and others—who warned, among other things, that on January 6 patriots would begin "taking down names and kicking ass." Although I had seen all this footage before, seeing it presented in a hearing room filled with people and knowing it was being viewed across America and around the world gave me chills.

As the fast-paced hearing ended, I believed we had displayed, in a convincing fashion, the many ways that Trump had tried to corrupt the Justice Department so that he could use its work as a cover for subverting democracy. He had pressured Attorney General Bill Barr to announce a big investigation of voter fraud (Barr refused), and he had insisted that if his successor would do it, he could just "say it [the election] was corrupt and leave the rest to me and the Republican congressmen." Barr's successor, Jeffrey Rosen, also refused. Trump then tried to install a flunky in Rosen's job and was thwarted only when he learned that top justice officials would resign if he did.

Trump had, throughout his life, used legal proceedings like lawsuits to lend credibility to his claims. This had worked, at least when it came to attracting the attention of reporters who, eager for a story, would happily aid the charade. This time, however, Trump ran into people of integrity who demonstrated that many officials understand they owe allegiance not to one person, even if he is the president, but to the office they hold and the nation. With the stakes far higher than simply a publicity war, people he tried to push around did, in fact, do their jobs.

CHAPTER 12

The Final Hearing

My personal experience of January 6 was never far from my mind as I prepared to present, with my colleague Elaine Luria, the eighth and final scheduled hearing. We were expected to recap the evidence displayed in the previous sessions, sort of like the final episode of a TV series, and reach important conclusions. We telegraphed our overall point by calling the session "Dereliction of Duty."

I was certain this title was apt, just as I was certain that as a Republican who'd agreed to join the committee I was doing the right thing. But it wasn't an easy thing. Indeed, as I went back and forth to my district, at home in Illinois I would experience the kind of shunning that religious sects impose on wayward members and had to deal with threatening letters, which were all the more upsetting because they were sent to our home, and sometimes addressed to Sofia.

One especially vile letter, from a supposed person of faith, was addressed to my wife. In it he or she wrote, "Although it may take time, he [I] will be executed. But don't worry You and Christian will be joining Adam in Hell too! We find it blasphemous that you name the son of the Devil Christian!" The excessive punctuation and oddly placed capital letters made it obvious to me that he or she was copying Trump's style. So, too, did the hypocrisy evident in the promise of murder offered by a person expressing the outrage of "God Fearing Christians."

Less odious, but just as addled, were the sudden moves against me by a party I had served for twenty years. Dozens of county chairpersons condemned my impeachment vote. Two Trump supporters declared they would challenge me in the next Republican primary, and protesters staged rallies where, among other things, they said they wouldn't even support me in a race for dogcatcher. A GOP consultant flew to the district and announced he would train activists in ways to defeat me. Others who had stood up to the bully president endured the same hostility from local party officials. It should be noted that many of these party leaders had come to power in the Trump years, replacing more traditional Republicans. If they wanted to keep their positions, they would have to carry his water.

All of this antipathy had moved me to announce I would not seek reelection. I became the second of the ten pro-impeachment House Republicans to take this step. As I explained the choice, I said, "My passion for this country has only grown. My desire to make a difference is bigger than it has ever been. My disappointment in the leaders that don't lead is huge. The battlefield must be much broader, and the truth needs to reach the American people across the country."

Trump's response—"2 down, 8 to go!"—reiterated his commitment to end the congressional careers of every Republican who had voted to impeach him and reminded everyone else that they would face the similar treatment if they failed to show Mafia-style loyalty to the big man. The press response focused on whether I might run for Senate or governor, or even president, seeking to capitalize on the respect I was getting from moderates and liberals. To do this as a Republican would require winning a primary, and I stood a snowball's chance in hell of succeeding at that. The other option called for a run as an independent, and that, like most independent candidacies, might be nothing but a folly. As for the presidency, I thought, "You can't be serious."

In the end, I decided against running for any of the offices people suggested for me. I was burned out in Congress, so the Senate didn't seem like a good option. Could I even imagine myself in the governor's mansion or the White House? No. Besides, I had a new son, Christian, and a partner in Sofia, who were overdue for my presence. There was also Country First, which was developing quickly and would help continue my efforts on the side of democracy. And of course, the January 6 committee continued its work, putting me in a position to explore the violent attack I felt affected me personally.

WHEN ELAINE AND I SHARED THE PRESENTATION RELATED TO THE 187-minute gap, people seemed most impressed by witnesses who described how Trump had stayed in a dining room near the Oval

Office, watching TV, speaking to outside advisers (there were two calls with Rudy Giuliani), and receiving but ignoring reports on the violence being carried out in his name. As various Fox News hosts, including some in my angry cousin's pantheon, implored him to act, Trump resisted, preferring to simply watch his troops fight, like a mounted eighteenth-century general watching a battle from a hilltop. Of course, presidents aren't supposed to sit on their hands when they witness a disaster unfolding. This is why the theme for the evening was "Dereliction of Duty."

As I noted during my narration, "He [President Trump] told Mark Meadows that the rioters were doing what they should be doing, and the rioters understood they were doing what President Trump wanted them to do." Meanwhile, the president's daughter Ivanka and son Donald Jr. sent messages begging him to call off the mob. Trump didn't just do nothing. He actively refused to accept a call from the Pentagon, which was in the middle of an effort to mobilize the National Guard.

One of the more satisfying bits of evidence we were able to present showed Senator Josh Hawley, outside the Capitol, raising an encouraging fist toward the crowd gathering for the attack. Hawley was committed to vote against certifying results in several states. This gesture riled the crowd and would be replayed over and over in various media outlets. Ignored was a video, which we showed, in which Hawley is seen literally running from the mob. Rarely had a before-and-after display depicted both a man's urge to fight and the man in flight.

One of the most damning pieces of evidence showed how Trump edited a statement he made on the day after the riot, when the country was reeling from what it had witnessed, and much of the world stood aghast at the spectacle of a great democracy brought low. It shows he had crossed out the comment that he had been "sickened" by the violence and the words "you do not represent me." No more "prosecuted to the fullest extent of the law." Added was a lie about how he deployed the National Guard (he did not). In a video outtake he says, "I don't want to say the election is over, I just want to say Congress has certified the results without saying the election is over, okay?" That is what he did.

In my concluding statement I summed up what I had learned, and what I feared:

> Whatever your politics, whatever you think about the outcome of the election, we as Americans must all agree on this. Donald Trump's conduct on January sixth was a supreme violation of his oath of office and a complete dereliction of his duty to our nation.
>
> It is a stain on our history. It is a dishonor to all those who have sacrificed and died in service of our democracy. When we present our full findings, we will recommend changes to laws and policies to guard against another January sixth. The reason

that's imperative is that the forces Donald Trump ignited that day have not gone away.

The militant, intolerant ideologies, the militias, the alienation and the disaffection, the weird fantasies and disinformation, they're all still out there ready to go. That's the elephant in the room. But if January sixth has reminded us of anything, I pray it reminded us of this: laws are just words on paper.

They mean nothing without public servants dedicated to the rule of law and who are held accountable by a public that believes oaths matter—oaths matter more than party tribalism or the cheap thrill of scoring political points. We the people must demand more of our politicians and ourselves. Oaths matter.

The Definition of Courage

The extremists who attacked the Capitol on January 6, 2021, seemed to believe that they were the truest example of patriotism: They shouted about protecting the country and the Constitution and waved scores of American flags. However, these were far outnumbered by banners featuring the name Trump. Deluded by his lies, the people who rallied behind the flags were sure that the president whom they worshipped had been cheated out of reelection by traitors. So it was that they had sought to overturn our election. Unable to reject the lie about a rigged election and ignorant of the country's history, founding documents, laws, and values, they turned to violence on behalf of a would-be tyrant.

Although many Republicans remain fervent Trump supporters, today there is reason to hope the fever is breaking. According to the most recent polls by CNN, Republican support for Trump, once over 70 percent, is down to 52 percent. Support among all voters is 37 percent.

More than five months after I left Congress, I find myself feeling calmer and better able to take a wider and more optimistic view of the country. My family is living in Houston, near Sofia's parents, where the days are getting longer and the morning sun shines brightly. In fact, it seems every day since I got out of Congress has gotten brighter and longer. This adds to my feeling of hope. I see that the vast majority of Americans are not obsessed with politics. They are interested in their families and communities. They greet one another with kindness and look for common ground.

You don't realize what a toll Congress takes on you when it's your day-to-day life. I suppose it would be similar to fighting in a ground war: you adjust, survive, and maybe even thrive. But when the guns go silent, a new reality overtakes you. After Iraq, I entered a different battlefield and never had the chance to take inventory of my life. A physical fight had transitioned into a metaphoric fight in the halls of government.

The day after I was out of government, the guns fell silent, but they still rang in my head. It is an adjustment to realize you no longer have to comment on every issue or fight every online battle. It takes time to understand that. But every day those battle scars become more faint. Congress members gain not just a title, but an identity. Everywhere you go people see you as the title, and everything you say in public and private has to be screened in your head before you speak the words. After all, anything can get out and destroy not just your job, but your whole person. Most interactions inevitably become a discussion of politics. It's just par for the course.

Every former member of Congress I knew used to tell me, "Trust me, there is life after here," and now I truly understand that. Being able to be a father and a husband is amazing, as is the freedom to make plans outside of the fickle schedule of the House of Representatives or being hostage to one crisis after another. Every August recess and Christmas break were on the chopping block as we careened to some deadline. If the American people would keep a running list, they would notice that the same script is run year after year.

Maybe I will run again someday; right now I don't know and honestly don't really care. But I now know one thing: I don't need it. I don't need the pressure and the long weeks away from home. I'm emerging from the shadow of service. My eyes are still straining to adjust, but I can begin seeing the summer. And it feels great.

MEANWHILE, THE SYSTEM IS DEMONSTRATING THAT WHILE THEY may move slowly, our courts can bring justice. Elmer Stewart Rhodes III, who led a group of attackers who belonged to the so-called Oath Keepers organization, was found guilty of sedition and was sentenced to eighteen years in prison. The head of the group's Florida chapter, Kelly Meggs, was sentenced to twelve years.

Rhodes, you may recall, is the Yale-trained lawyer who began the Oath Keepers within a few months of Barack Obama's election.

The name refers to the oath military personnel and police take to defend the Constitution and many of its members are former and active duty members of the military and law enforcement. Dozens of them showed up at the Capitol on January 6 and many of them joined a tip-of-the-spear operation that had been devised and directed by Rhodes; they led the assault on the Capitol building.

Rhodes was a big fish, but he was just one of more than one thousand who have been arrested for January 6 crimes. Several others had also been convicted of sedition. Donald Trump, as he embarked on his 2024 White House run, was considering the notion that Rhodes and others deserved presidential pardons.

Trump himself faced a number of legal problems, which seemed to be weighing on him. He showed less of his usual grandiosity and pridefulness. Trump appeared at the Criminal Court in Manhattan and became the first former president ever to be arrested, fingerprinted, and charged in a criminal proceeding. He was charged with thirty-four felonies related to a $130,000 hush-money payment to adult entertainer Stormy Daniels in violation of campaign finance laws. The formal accusation also included dozens of charges related to his business practices, including the falsification of records.

Shocking as it was, the New York criminal case was just one of the many legal battles Trump faced. Among them were, briefly put:

- A criminal trial on his alleged crimes relating to his apparent mishandling of top-secret documents. (The indictment included more than thirty counts related to national security law violations and obstruction of justice.)

THE DEFINITION OF COURAGE

- A grand jury recommendation for multiple charges related to his election interference in Georgia.
- A New York State lawsuit alleging years-long business fraud.
- A verdict against him in a suit alleging sexual assault and defamation.
- A lawsuit alleging incitement to riot filed by Capitol Police officers and House Democrats.
- A civil suit alleging fraud in multilevel marketing schemes.
- Possible indictments recommended by the House Committee to Investigate the January 6 Attack on the United States Capitol (the committee on which I served).

The criminal and civil cases showed that the judiciary was trying to hold Trump accountable for crimes related to the January 6 attack, as well as for previous misdeeds. Nevertheless, 60 percent of Republicans still believed Trump's lies about fraud in the election he lost to Joe Biden, which had motivated the January 6 attackers.

Amid all the troubles of Trump and his most fanatical followers, Republicans' transformation into a cult with little connection to its past grew. In imitation of Trump, a party that long associated itself with law and order had learned to hate certain police officers, like the ones who were beaten at the Capitol. They also turned those convicted and awaiting trial for January 6 crimes into political prisoners. Trump's most loyal acolytes toured the jail where six were held (including two from the violence-prone Proud Boys and Oath Keepers) and emerged to say the accused had been denied medical treatment, assaulted by other inmates, and threatened with rape.

Like most around the country, the District of Columbia jail has been subject to legitimate complaints about conditions. Fights and threats do occur in these places. Medical care is in short supply. No evidence suggests that the Trumpists were singled out for bad treatment. However, it's not uncommon for prisoners associated with violence against cops to suffer less-than-equal treatment from prison authorities.

As they turned the prisoners into political martyrs, Trumpists sought to transform Ashli Babbitt, the woman shot and killed as part of the mob trying to smash into the House Chamber, into a martyr. She was no innocent. She was a thirty-five-year-old woman with a record of road rage that included ramming another car with hers. She was so devoted to conspiracy theories that she took to the internet to post rageful threats and angry screeds. Her rants, laced with profanities, targeted immigrants, Democrats, and public-health officials who tried to contain the COVID-19 epidemic. On the day before the attack on the Capitol she posted a message on Twitter: "Nothing will stop us. They can try and try and try but the storm is here and it is descending upon DC in less than 24 hours . . . dark to light!"

The contortions required to make Babbitt a hero reflect the methods of Donald Trump, who is a bully who likes to play the victim. In his view, every person involved in investigating or prosecuting him was corrupt, deeply partisan, or both. At the annual Conservative Political Action Conference (CPAC), he said he didn't know that "they want to lynch you for doing nothing wrong." He added, "I didn't know they want to lynch you for doing a great job. I didn't know they want to put you away because your poll numbers are better than anybody's they've seen in years." This appropriation of the Black historical experience in a country where more than two thousand Black people were lynched by racists is disgraceful. Also, on January 6 it was his vice president, Mike Pence, who was the subject of chants about being hanged. It was his followers who brought symbolic gallows to the Capitol that day.

But as twisted as Trump may be, the prospect of his return to the White House, or at least the top of the 2024 ticket, is not. Today his most viable opponent for the nomination is Florida governor Ron DeSantis, who has positioned himself as a Trump Lite campaigner but whose record, which includes an ideological war with Disney World, aligns him well with the fanatical GOP base.

The fanaticism of the hard-core of the Republican Party is the most troubling shift in the party since it was founded, in 1854, as an antislavery political movement. Filled with Christian nationalists who believe God favors their rule, these folks constitute a minority of a political minority (the GOP) and are stained with traces of racism as well as utter intolerance of others' views.

At this moment, the party can count on dominance of the state legislatures that gerrymander congressional districts and on US Senate seats in sparsely populated "red" states to find some success in Congress. However, the results in presidential elections show a national weakness. One has to go back to Ronald Reagan to find a GOP candidate elected with a clear majority of the vote. (Though he was reelected with a slim popular-vote majority, George W. Bush gained the Oval Office with a minority.) Trump, despite all his bellowing about his significant 2020 vote count, always leaves out the fact that Biden beat him by 4.45 percent. With the exception of Barack Obama's sweep in 2008, no one had had a bigger win since 1996.

The problem for the country, of course, is that minority rule via the Electoral College, court packing, and Senate filibuster rules that can thwart the majority are still available to the GOP. This seems to be the most likely political course for the next six years. The tide could be turned if right-wing gerrymandering is thwarted in state legislatures, but this would be, as they say in politics, a "heavy lift." As we wait, the best thing we can do is conduct ourselves as if there were no one coming on a white horse to save us. That is necessary because it is true.

My vehicle for fighting back is the Country First organization, which I founded in the days after January 6. Formed to welcome Republicans, Democrats, and independents, we advocate civic engagement, ranked-choice voting that rewards top vote-getters, and nonpartisan primaries. All these agenda items fall under the umbrella of defending democracy. You can help us with contributions and personal activities. These will help us pursue tactics that include television advertising, direct print mailings, digital ads, deployment of campaign volunteers, and help turning out the vote in key races. In a short time, Country First has drawn a surprising number of donors who have helped us build an infrastructure, and supporters who back our belief that there is a "reasonable majority" looking for ways to help. These people get it.

We have faced lesser but nevertheless serious challenges in the past. But we must keep in mind that the people must be the first to demand change. Leaders rose in response to the call. Franklin Delano Roosevelt, Dwight Eisenhower, Ronald Reagan, and even Martin Luther King Jr. arrived when the nation was embattled and required someone who appealed to our morality and ideals.

I know that morality and ideals can feel like weak tools against men who drive around in big pickup trucks decorated with pictures of assault rifles and the words "Come and take it." The answer to this isn't more anger, but an upwelling of goodness. We must form small groups that affiliate with other small groups until they become part of a national movement that will not be ignored. This cannot be done in anger, and it cannot include a rejection of those with other views. If they don't listen to us with respect, we must nevertheless listen to them. Turning the other cheek while holding your ground is a powerful thing. Most of all, we have to love our country in a clear-eyed way.

The idea of civic compassion I suggest has emerged out of conversations I've had with many good people who have contacted me to offer their support. Evangelical theologian Russell Moore, a religious conservative who stresses Christ's own compassion, called me out of the blue. Moore is deeply worried about Christian nationalism and Evangelicals' support for a man, Trump, who is a florid liar, a consummately divisive politician, and a cruel leader. When many Christian nationalists call for shutting our borders to refugees, Moore argues for giving them shelter. He had criticized Trump for making racist and sexist remarks. He thinks Christians should have nothing to do with Confederate flags and criticized, on the basis of religious freedom, those who would shut down mosques in reaction to Islamic terrorism.

I would say that overall, Christianity has been harmed by Trump. During his presidency, the moderate and liberal Christians accelerated their move away from the church, and the image of Christianity has suffered. When Trump was elected, pollsters found that 45 percent of respondents agreed that "people with a religious faith are better citizens." Today that number is 39 percent. In the same period the percentage who said they "lose respect for people when [they] find out that they do not have a religious faith" also fell six points, to 14 percent. A different survey found that between 2015 and today, the percentage of Americans who think one must believe in God "to be a moral person" has dropped from 39 percent to 29 percent.

Moore's view of Christianity was consistent with traditional theology, which does not have a place for religious nationalism. He said that nothing in the Bible said the world would be won over by *American* Christianity and he saw no place for religious violence. (You would think the Crusades would have taught everybody that one.) Of course, people can, and Moore might say should, live according to Christian principles. You don't need to go to the mat because they say "Happy Holidays" instead of "Merry Christmas" at Target. Just as I am trying to shake up politics to save us from authoritarianism, Moore is trying to shake up the church to bolster Christianity. He urges believers to follow Christ's true example as a peacemaker who welcomed strangers, befriended criminals, and never imposed his will on others. I want our politics to serve our country. Moore wants people of faith to serve humanity. He is disturbed by how so many have lost sight of Jesus's call for us to turn the other cheek and resist judging others. But he told me he refused to give up and he thought I should hang tough. He also introduced me to N. T. Wright, a religious scholar at the University of Oxford, whose writings make him a sort of C. S. Lewis for our time.

Wright takes issue with much of conservative Christianity in America, including the widespread idea that we are living in the End Times and that before the Second Coming of Christ believers will be literally lifted into heaven in an event called the Rapture. His best-known book, *Surprised by Hope*, argues for Christians to focus not on the shedding of our suffering when we get to heaven but on the idea that we can begin to address the problems that afflict humanity right now. He is a deep thinker but also a man of deep warmth who reinforced my sense that the rage I encountered from people who claimed to be Christians represented the opposite of what's taught in the Bible and represented by Jesus.

More personal inspiration came to me from Jamie Winship, who is a former Washington, DC, police officer who had spent decades working in the Muslim world for the CIA. Along the way he had developed a faith-based philosophy that centered on rejecting all the pressure you feel to conform to society in order to recognize what God is calling you to do. He prays, tries to sense what God wants, and then acts without fear. Fear, he says, destroys authenticity and creativity. I had been living with a lot of fear. Jamie has helped me to recognize that lots of people share the same fear of confrontation, rejection, and, given how threats of political violence are routinely made against school board members as well as presidents, physical harm. But there we keep going despite the fear. This, and not some heroic act, is the definition of courage.

ACKNOWLEDGMENTS

Every author is molded by the lessons, values, examples, friendships, and love of those who nurtured, encouraged, and edu-
cated them. No one writes without them all standing in the
background offering reminders of your true self.

In the long journey from the military to Congress to sitting in
front of a keyboard, I was guided—perhaps edited?—by my parents,
Rus and Betty Jo, whose example of service, respect for others, kindness, and humility shaped the way I encounter others and consider
ideas. Humility can be a tough lesson for any politician, which means
I am grateful to my older brother and sister, Nathan and Chelise.

Many talented and caring teachers influenced me in deep ways
and helped me understand both academic subjects and the world
outside my little corner of it.

Kelly Keogh, who taught political science and international relations at my high school, had the most impact on me. He made it

exciting to study how US society, politics, and government intertwined, and how America relates to the rest of the world. He came at things from a rather liberal standpoint but welcomed what this conservative had to say. After 9/11, he developed a curriculum on terrorism that was used nationwide and brought TV news cameras to his classroom.

At Illinois State University I learned that failure wasn't the end of the world and also that big institutions can be supportive and give people second chances. As I recovered to become a good student, I discovered I was resilient in ways I never knew. College also taught me lessons in friendship, especially from my roommate Bill Heart, who remains a support to this day.

In Congress I learned the art of listening and leading from John Boehner, whose positive and open-minded approach to politics is sorely missed at every level, from local school boards to Washington, DC. Late in my House service, I found friendship and kindred spirits in Representatives Bob Dold, Tom Rooney, Martha Roby, Jaime Herrera Beutler, Kevin Yoder, and Duncan Hunter, who became real friends as we responded to the tragedy of January 6. Among the experts who confirmed what I knew about the 2020 election, Chris Krebs stands out.

A thank-you goes to every person on the House Committee to Investigate the January 6 Attack on the United States Capitol. Chairman Bennie Thompson, co-chair Liz Cheney, and members Zoe Lofgren, Adam Schiff, Pete Aguilar, Elaine Luria, Jamie Raskin, and Stephanie Murphy walked the walk of bipartisanship and showed what it's like to fight fairly and valiantly.

ACKNOWLEDGMENTS

Truly fearless, my wife, Sofia, has been a true rock amid all the crises and threats to her life as well as mine. She and our son, Christian, have kept me grounded by reminding me of what really matters in life. Sofia could never have known what she signed up for when we got married, but through it all she has generously acted as my sounding board, adviser, and ever-present backup at home.

I want to thank the team at The Open Field who took a chance on me, including publishers Maria Shriver and Brian Tart, editorial director Meg Leder, and my editor, Nina Rodríguez-Marty. Thank you also to my publicist, Lindsay Prevette, and Kate Stark in marketing, as well as Tricia Conley and Jennifer Tait in managing editorial and production editorial, and designers Jason Ramirez, who designed the cover, and Claire Vaccaro and Cassandra Mueller, who designed the interior. And finally, I am grateful to literary agents Heather Schroder and Madeleine Morel, who put our team together and stayed part of it themselves until our work was done, and to my collaborator, Michael D'Antonio.